Magnetic Reading™

GRADE 3

NOT FOR RESALE

ISBN 978-1-7280-3815-5

North Billerica, MA 01862

15 14 13 12 11 10 9 8 7 6 24 23

Curriculum Associates

BTS23

807201

Table of Contents

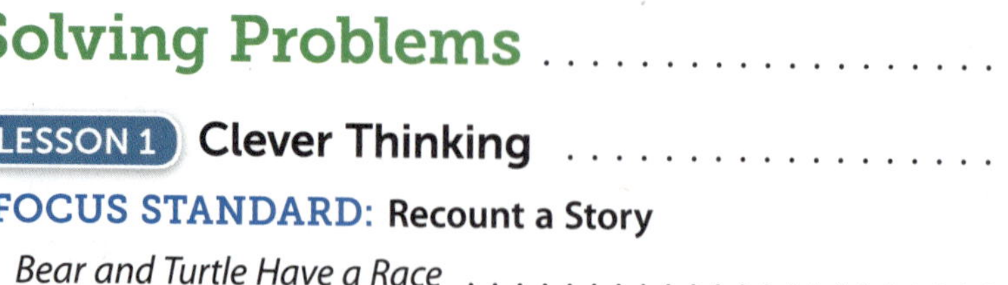

UNIT 2

Table of Contents (continued)

UNIT 4

Changes in the West 220

Table of Contents (continued)

UNIT 5

UNIT 6

Solving Problems

UNIT 1

Clever Thinking

FOCUS QUESTION

How do story characters use their wits to solve problems?

NOTICE AND WONDER

Look at the three stories you will read in this lesson. What do you notice? What do you wonder? Discuss your ideas with a partner.

USE YOUR WITS!

When do you need to "use your wits"? Circle the activities that you need to use your wits to complete. Talk with a partner about one activity you circled. Explain why you need to use your wits to do it.

solve a puzzle

run fast

play a trick

carry a heavy object

You have to use your wits to ___. I think so because ___.

You circled ___. I agree/disagree because ___.

Bear and Turtle Have a Race

retold by Pat Betteley

Howling Up the Moon

by Diana C. Conway

Ants Live Everywhere

by Pleasant DeSpain

BEAR AND TURTLE HAVE A RACE

retold by Pat Betteley

1 It was winter and the river was frozen. Bear had not yet learned that it was wiser to sleep through the White Season. As he walked through the woods, he began to brag about himself, as usual. “I am Bear the speedy. I am the fastest animal in the forest,” he said.

2 A little voice piped up. It was Turtle. “Pardon me, Bear, but I think I am faster.”

3 “Turtle? You are the slowest of all animals. If we raced, I would leave you far behind.” Perhaps Bear forgot that Turtle’s greatest speed was in his wits.

4 “Let me swim in the river while you run on land,” said Turtle. “I will make holes in the ice and peek up through the holes so you will know where I am.”

5 Bear agreed.

Stop & Discuss

Why does Bear think he can beat Turtle in a race?

Underline the sentences that show why Bear thinks he will win the race. Then discuss those sentences with a partner.

Bear calls himself "___." He thinks he is ___.

6 The next day, the woodland animals lined the riverbank to watch the race. Turtle's head appeared in a hole by the starting line. Fox gave the signal to start.

7 Turtle's head disappeared into the first hole. Bear walked at an easy **pace**.

pace = speed

8 *I will easily beat Turtle,* he thought. Ahead in the river, Bear saw Turtle's little green head poke through a hole in the ice.

9 "I am here, Bear. Catch up to me!" called Turtle.

10 *How did he get ahead of me?* Bear wondered. He began to walk **briskly**.

briskly = quickly

11 Farther ahead, Turtle's little green head popped through another hole in the ice.

12 *I cannot believe it. Turtle is beating me*, thought Bear.

13 Bear ran as fast as he could, but Turtle reached the finish line far ahead of him. Bear was so embarrassed that he dragged himself back to his den and slept through the rest of the White Season.

14 After bear had left, Turtle turned to face the river.

15 "My dear family," he began. Many little green heads popped up in holes along the riverbank. Each looked identical to Turtle. "You helped me beat Bear. Now we will not have to listen to him brag anymore. When we work together, we can accomplish things we could never do alone."

Stop & Discuss

How does Turtle beat Bear?

Find details that help you understand how Turtle tricks Bear. Discuss those details with a partner.

Recount a Story

- When you **recount** a story, you use your own words to retell events and other key details in the order in which they happen.
- **Key details** tell about the characters, settings, and events.
  - — **Characters** are the people or animals a story is mostly about.
  - — **Settings** are where and when the story takes place.
  - — **Events** are what happens in the beginning, middle, and end of a story.

Reread/Think

Reread "Bear and Turtle Have a Race." Write key details from the story in the story map below.

Setting (Where and when does the story take place?)	Characters (Who is the story mostly about?)
• winter • frozen river • woods	• Bear, who brags • Turtle, who uses his wits

Beginning	Middle	End
Bear brags about being the fastest animal, so Turtle challenges him to a race.	turtlepoed his head ih the ice.	turtles famley helped him

Talk

What happens in the beginning, middle, and end of "Bear and Turtle Have a Race"? Share the details from one part of your story map with your partners. Listen to your partners' details. Which details in your maps are the same? Which details are different?

I included the detail about ___ in the middle/end.

I did not include the detail about ___ because ___.

___ said that ___ happened in the middle/end. I agree/disagree because ___.

Write

Imagine you are writing a letter to a friend who has not read the story. Use the key details from your story map to recount "Bear and Turtle Have a Race." Include the words "beginning," "middle," and "end" in your letter.

at he beginning Bear
brags about being the
fastest animal so
turtle challenges
him to a race.
in the middle part
turtle said that he has
trick up seev and pood then
ever hole.
at the end turtles famley
helped him win the race.

WRITING CHECKLIST

- ☐ I recounted events in order.
- ☐ I told what happened in the beginning, middle, and end.
- ☐ I told about the setting.
- ☐ I told about the characters.
- ☐ I told only important details.

Howling Up the Moon

by Diana C. Conway

1 In Alaska long ago, when animals still talked to humans, Old Wolf met a girl named Nurauq at a river. She carried a bag made from a seal's stomach.

2 Old Wolf greeted her, asking, "What brings you here?"

3 "I'm taking fresh-caught eels to my grandmother," said Nurauq.

tattered = old and torn

4 Old Wolf pricked up his **tattered** ears. For months, he had eaten only scraps thrown away by the villagers. *But now,* he thought, *I will trick this girl into giving me some real food.*

5 "Dear girl, where does your grandmother live?"

6 Nurauq pointed to a cliff by the sea.

Maurluqa (mawh-LUKE-a) = Yup'ik word for "my grandmother"

7 "That's a long walk," said Old Wolf. "Allow me to carry your bag for you."

8 "Not on your life," said Nurauq. Her black eyes sparkled like wet beach stones. "My mother warned me to watch out for your tricky ways."

9 "I'll just hurry ahead and tell your grandmother you're coming," he said. "That way she can heat some water to cook those eels."

10 "No you won't!" said Nurauq. "***Maurluqa*** would NOT be happy to see a wolf at her door." She began to walk faster.

Stop & Discuss

Why does Nurauq not allow Old Wolf to carry her bag of eels?

Underline details that show what Nurauq thinks of Old Wolf.

11 On the **horizon**, the moon began to show like the edge of a white clamshell. This gave Old Wolf an idea. "Slow down," he said. "If you give me an eel, I will make the moon rise."

12 Old Wolf lifted his nose and began to howl. Because he was lonely and very hungry, his howls reached the ends of the earth. Slowly, the full moon began to rise over the tundra.

13 "How lovely!" gasped Nurauq. "But you know perfectly well the moon rises every night all by itself."

14 Old Wolf's tail drooped. Nurauq looked at his knobby ribs. "You poor thing," she said. "You really *are* hungry." She reached into her bag and tossed him a fat eel.

15 Old Wolf swallowed it in one gulp. Then he stretched out his front paws and bowed low to Nurauq. "***Quyana***."

16 "*Aa-ang*, you're welcome," she answered. 

horizon = the line where the earth and sky appear to meet

Quyana (goo-ee-YAH-nah) = Yup'ik word for "thank you"

Stop & Discuss

Why does Nurauq give Old Wolf an eel?

Circle details in the picture and underline details in the text that support your answer.

17 They finally reached the house of Nurauq's grandmother. Grandmother noticed the shiny eel oil around Old Wolf's muzzle. "Has that old thing tricked you into feeding him?" she asked.

content = happy

18 "No, Grandmother. He kept me company so no bears would bother me."

19 "I did?" said Old Wolf. "Ah, yes. I did."

20 Grandmother smiled. "Well, in that case, here's another eel."

21 That night, Nurauq and her Grandmother ate eel soup. And Old Wolf slept just outside, protected from the cold, cold wind by the mound of the underground house. The moon moved all by itself among the glimmering stars because Old Wolf was much too **content** to howl it across the sky.

Stop & Discuss

Old Wolf does not trick Nurauq, but does Nurauq trick Old Wolf?

Underline details that support your answer. Use those details to explain your thinking to a partner.

Recount a Story

- Use your own words to recount a story. Include events in order and key details about characters and settings.
- Key details and events often include a problem or problems that the characters have to solve.

Reread/Think

Reread "Howling Up the Moon." Write key details from the story in the story map. Include any problems the characters have and how they solve those problems.

Setting	Characters

Beginning	Middle	End

Talk

What happens in the beginning, middle, and end of "Howling Up the Moon"? Share the details from your story map, including any problems the characters have and how they solve those problems.

A problem in the story is ___. Another problem is ___.

A key detail in the beginning/middle/end is ___. I included this detail because ___.

Write

Use your story map to recount what happens in the beginning, middle, and end of "Howling Up the Moon." Include key details about the characters, setting, and problems. Use at least two words from the box in your writing.

setting	character	problem	event

WRITING CHECKLIST

- ☐ I described the characters and setting.
- ☐ I described the most important events in the beginning, middle, and end.
- ☐ I described problems the characters had to solve.
- ☐ I included important words in my writing.

Ants Live Everywhere

by Pleasant DeSpain

1 Lion ruled the jungle. He decided which animals could live there and which ones must leave.

2 Ant loved the jungle. It was the perfect home for his large family. One day, Ant started to crawl over a small hill, but soon he realized the hill was Lion's massive paw.

3 "How dare you walk over me, Ant? I am your king."

4 "So sorry, Elder Lion," said Ant. "But I'm in a rush and it would take me forever to walk around you. Besides, I don't weigh much. I'm sure I didn't **injure** your paw."

injure = hurt

5 "Enough," growled Lion. "I order you and your kind out of my jungle. Find somewhere else to live."

6 *This is terrible,* thought Ant. *He can't order us out of our home. Not without a fight.*

7 Ant hid under a nearby leaf until nightfall. When he heard Lion snoring, he crawled up Lion's body and into his cavernous ear. Then he scratched at the sensitive wall of the ear with his long antennae.

8 Lion mumbled in his sleep and scratched his ear. Suddenly, he heard a tiny voice from inside his head: *Ants live everywhere.*

9 Lion awoke with a start. "Who said that?"

10 Parrot squawked in the trees. Monkey screamed nearby. Lion heard the voice again: *Ants live everywhere.*

11 He shook his head and scratched his ear again. "Who's saying that?" he asked.

reply = answer

12 *You are saying it,* came the **reply** from inside his head. *Ants live everywhere.*

13 "If I'm saying it, then it must be true. I'm the king, after all." He went back to sleep.

14 As soon as Ant heard snoring, he crawled out of Lion's ear and went to sleep under a leaf.

15 The next morning, Lion roared, "Where is Ant?"

16 "I'm right here," said Ant from under the leaf.

17 "I've changed my mind. From now on, ants live everywhere. Is that understood?"

18 "Yes, and thank you, Elder Lion. You are most wise."

19 And that is why, even today, ants live everywhere in the world.

Respond to Text

Reread/Think

Reread "Ants Live Everywhere." Choose the best response to each question about the text.

1. Read this sentence from paragraph 1 of the story.

> Lion **ruled** the jungle.

What does *ruled* mean?

A. had control of

B. drew lines on

C. lived far from

D. made noise in

2. **PART A**

What is Ant's problem in the beginning of the story?

A. Lion will not move out of his way.

B. Ant is late for dinner with his family.

C. Lion will not let him stay in the jungle.

D. Ant is tired from walking so far.

PART B

Which sentence from the story **best** supports your answer in Part A?

A. "It was the perfect home for his large family." (paragraph 2)

B. "'I'm sure I didn't injure your paw.'" (paragraph 4)

C. "'I order you and your kind out of my jungle.'" (paragraph 5)

D. "Ant hid under a nearby leaf until nightfall." (paragraph 7)

Reread/Think

3. Which detail could be left out when recounting this story? *had trouble answering*

A. Lion orders Ant out of the jungle.

B. Ant crawls into Lion's ear.

C. Ant hears Lion snoring.

D. Lion decides that Ant can stay.

4. Which detail is **most** important to include when recounting this story?

A. Ant crawls over Lion's paw without hurting it.

B. Lion hears a voice that tells him ants live everywhere.

C. Ant is under a leaf when Lion calls to him the next morning.

D. Lion mumbles in his sleep and scratches his ear.

Write

Recount the story of "Ants Live Everywhere." Include one character's problem and how the character solved that problem.

in the begching ant Wanted to Live in the Junke but Lino decides to not Let Ant in. in the Midle Ant crawls on Lion paw and not hurting it. in the end Ant crawls into Lion his caverhous ear. Lion hears a voice say ant Live everywhere Lion Lets ant stay

WRITING CHECKLIST

- ☐ I recounted key details and events in order.
- ☐ I included the important events from the beginning, middle, and end of the story.
- ☐ I included the setting and characters.
- ☐ I used my own words.
- ☐ I described a problem.

Respond to the Focus Question

How do story characters use their wits to solve problems?

Reread/Think

Choose one story from the lesson to reread.

TEXT: ______________________________

What did you learn from the story about how characters use their wits to solve problems? Write an example from the story you chose.

EXAMPLE: ______________________________

____

Talk

Share what you learned from the story you reread. Use the sentence frames to get started.

The story I read is ___.

The character ___ uses wits to solve a problem when ___.

Take notes on what you learn from the other students in your group.

Name:	Name:

Write

How do story characters use their wits to solve problems? Use examples from all three texts in your response.

SESSION 1 TALK ABOUT THE TOPIC

Learning from Others

FOCUS QUESTION

How can others help us learn and grow?

NOTICE AND WONDER

Look at the three texts you will read in this lesson. What do you notice? What do you wonder? Discuss your ideas with a partner.

I notice ___. This makes me think the text is about ___.

I think something similar/different. My idea is ___.

TALK ABOUT WORDS

The words listed below connect to the idea of learning a lesson. Circle the words you already know. Pick one word and tell a partner what the word means. Explain how you think it is connected to learning a lesson.

insist	listen	stubborn
obey	change	courage

King of the Meadow

by Stephen Krensky

from ***The Turtle Ship***

by Helena Ku Rhee

The Three Wishes

by Anika Aldamuy Denise

King of the Meadow

by Stephen Krensky

1 In the middle of a sunny field grew a tall and beautiful sunflower. Because of his greatness, he was named the king of the meadow. One cold spring morning, the king stretched his petals to capture the warming sunlight for himself.

2 "Excuse me," said a daisy from below. "Could you please pull in a petal or two? You're creating a shadow."

3 The king was shocked. "How dare you make such demands?"

4 "I meant no harm," said the frightened daisy. "But I need the sunlight, too."

5 "So do we!" some violets agreed.

6 "Nonsense!" the king insisted. "However, your **sacrifice** is noted. You have my thanks."

7 The daisy could not warm himself with thanks, but fearing the king's anger, he shivered in silence.

8 As the weeks passed, the cold changed to a burning heat. During a rare shower, a geranium spoke up.

9 "Sire," he whispered hoarsely, "we are very thirsty. If you could just part your petals so the rain can reach us . . ."

10 "Silence!" shouted the king. "Your needs must wait." 

sacrifice = something important that you give up for someone else

Stop & Discuss

What do the king's words and actions show about him?

Use details from the story to support your answer.

The king shows he is ___ when he ___. He also shows it when he says ___.

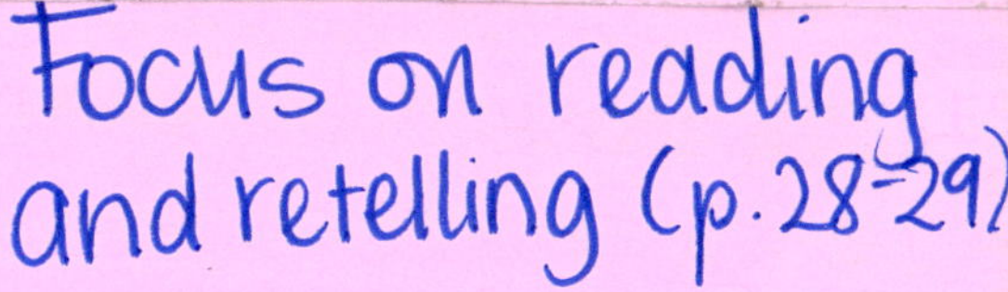

Try completing graphic organizer on page 30

11 Before long, the other flowers were too weak to speak at all. It was then that new sprouts grew quickly around them.

12 The king frowned at the new plants. "I order you to stop growing," he said sternly. "And you must obey me. I rule the flowers here."

13 "But we are weeds, not flowers," they replied. "And we will do as we please."

14 The king grew alarmed at that. He looked to the other flowers. "Don't you see what is happening? If the weeds are not stopped, we are all **doomed**."

doomed = sure to die

15 "We know," whispered the daisy. "But without sunlight and water, we lack the strength to fight back."

16 In that moment, the king realized his foolishness. There was still time to make things right.

17 That night it rained hard, and the king lifted his petals, letting the water fall on the flowers below him. When the sun returned, the king made sure its rays reached all his **subjects**. Soon, the flowers began to straighten up.

subjects = those who are ruled by someone else

18 The next day, the flowers woke up refreshed. They spread their roots and leaves, leaving no room for the weeds, and the meadow was bright with their many colors once more.

19 "That was close, Your Majesty," said the daisy.

20 "I suppose it was," said the king. "We will have to make sure it doesn't happen again."

21 And it never did.

Stop & Discuss

How does the king help the flowers?

Underline details in paragraph 17 that support your response.

Determine the Central Message

- In a story, **key details** are the most important details. Key details often show readers a lesson or central message.
- A **lesson** is something that you learn and that teaches you something new.
- The **central message** is a story's lesson about life.

Reread/Think

Reread "King of the Meadow." What is the central message of the story? Write it in the chart. Then add the key details that the author includes to help show the central message.

Central Message		
Key Details (paragraphs 1–7)	**Key Details (paragraphs 8–10)**	**Key Details (paragraphs 11–18)**

Talk

Talk about the central message with a partner. Look at your chart. Which of your key details are the same as your partner's? Which ones are different? Tell why the key details in your chart are important. Why did you choose them?

My partner chose the key detail about ___. I agree/disagree because ___.

I chose the key detail about ___ because it shows that ___.

Write

Write a paragraph explaining the central message of "King of the Meadow." Use key details from your chart that helped you figure out the central message.

WRITING CHECKLIST

- ☐ I included the central message of the story in my response.
- ☐ I included the key details that helped me figure out the central message.
- ☐ I used complete sentences.
- ☐ I used correct spelling, punctuation, and capitalization.

from
The Turtle Ship

by Helena Ku Rhee

Long ago in Korea, the king announced a contest to find the best design for a new battleship. The prize: money and a trip with the royal navy. Sun-sin had always dreamed of exploring, and he wanted to enter the contest. As the story begins, Sun-sin watches as his pet turtle, Gobugi, rides on one of his test designs, a boat made from logs and rope.

1 It wasn't long before water filled the boat and it started to sink. The ship was too heavy! Gobugi floated on the waves and made it safely to shore. That's when Sun-sin noticed that his turtle was small but mighty, slow but steady. Gobugi was an excellent swimmer and impossible to sink. Suddenly, Sun-sin had an idea for a battleship. Sun-sin begged his parents to let him enter the contest.

2 "No!" said his father. "The king will never listen to a little boy with a pet turtle."

3 "If I win," he said, "we'll have enough money to buy food for an entire year." His parents finally agreed. They traveled on foot for days through valleys and forests. They passed rivers, lakes, and streams.

4 At last, they arrived at the royal palace. It was the most **majestic** building Sun-sin had ever seen. Sun-sin and his family stood among hundreds of people who had drawings and models of battleships. Each ship was bigger and better than the next. Some people stared at Sun-sin and whispered, "Why is that child here with a turtle?"

majestic = large and very beautiful

Stop & Discuss

What makes Sun-sin realize he should enter the contest?

Underline three sentences in paragraph 1 that support your response.

5 When it was finally his turn to present to the king, Sun-sin and his parents got on their knees and bowed deeply. Sun-sin was terribly nervous. He didn't know what to say.

6 One of the king's **counselors** yelled, "Hurry up, boy!"

7 Sun-sin gathered all his courage, and with his head still bowed, he held Gobugi up to the king. In a loud voice he said, "Your Highness, my turtle is strong and steady and never sinks. A battleship designed like this turtle will protect our land from invaders."

8 The king's counselors laughed and laughed. One counselor said, "That's the **puniest** turtle I've ever seen!"

9 Another said, "A turtle is the slowest creature in the sea. A shark would eat it in two seconds!"

10 Suddenly a cat leaped through the air! It pounced onto Gobugi's back, but the turtle's slippery shell made the cat tumble to the floor. Then it bit at Gobugi, but the turtle's armor was too tough to crack. The cat swiped Gobugi with its sharp claws, but the turtle hid deep within his shell, tucking his limbs safely inside. Defeated, the cat ran away.

counselors = people who give advice

puniest = smallest

Stop & Discuss

How does the turtle win the fight?

Tell your partner the three things mentioned in paragraph 10 that help the turtle win the fight.

The three things that help the turtle win the fight with the cat are ___, ___, and ___.

vessel = ship

11 Sun-sin checked on his friend. Slowly, the turtle moved his arms and legs. He poked out his head and wiggled his tail. Gobugi was perfectly fine.

12 The king approached Sun-sin. "Your turtle is indeed strong and steady. A ship designed like this turtle will surely protect our kingdom from invaders." The king awarded Sun-sin ten bags of copper coins.

13 The king named the **vessel** *Gobukson,* which means "Turtle Ship." Just like Gobugi, the Turtle Ship was small but strong.

14 After the first Turtle Ship was built, the king remembered his promise. Sun-sin and his family were invited to travel with the royal navy to different lands.

Stop & Discuss

Why does the king decide to design a ship like Sun-sin's turtle?

Tell your partner why the king makes this decision.

The king decides to design the ship like Gobugi because ___.

I agree/disagree because the text says ___.

Determine the Central Message

- Think about the central message or lesson when you finish a story.
- Remember, a story may not directly state the central message, but you can use key details to help you figure it out.

Reread/Think

Reread the story from *The Turtle Ship*. What is the central message of the story? Write it in the chart. Then add the key details that help you figure out the central message.

Central Message		
Key Details (paragraphs 1–4)	Key Details (paragraphs 5–10)	Key Details (paragraphs 11–14)

Talk

Talk about the central message with a partner. Look at your chart. Is your central message the same as or different from your partner's? Use the key details in your chart to tell how you figured out the central message.

I think the central message is ___. I chose the key detail about ___ because it shows that ___.

My central message is ___. It is the same as/different from yours because ___.

Write

Write a paragraph explaining the central message of *The Turtle Ship*. Use key details from your chart that helped you figure out the central message.

WRITING CHECKLIST

- ☐ I included the central message of the story in my response.
- ☐ I included the key details that helped me figure out the central message.
- ☐ I used complete sentences.
- ☐ I used correct spelling, punctuation, and capitalization.

The Three Wishes

by Anika Aldamuy Denise

1 Once there were two sisters, Fidelia and Esperanza. They lived on a small farm high in the mountains, where they grew coffee and cocoa beans. Esperanza kept their ***casita*** tidy and clean. Fidelia tended the fields. Esperanza enjoyed their simple life, but Fidelia always wanted more.

2 One hot day, Fidelia was feeling grouchy. The sun had chased away the mountain's cool breezes. She would have given anything for a horse and wagon to help carry water to the crops.

3 Meanwhile, Esperanza rode Toro, their donkey, into town. There, she traded their coffee and cocoa beans for rice and pigeon peas, Fidelia's favorite foods.

4 On her way home, Esperanza met an old woman. The woman looked tired.

5 "Please," said Esperanza. "You can ride Toro and I will walk beside you."

6 When they were near the sisters' *casita*, Esperanza welcomed the woman inside. The woman rested, and Esperanza cooked ***arroz con gandules*** in a big pot.

7 "You have been so kind," the woman said. "In return, I will grant your family three wishes."

8 "But we have everything we need," Esperanza said.

9 "Surely you can think of something to wish for," said the woman, helping herself to supper.

10 "Hmm . . . I wish my sister were here to help me decide," said Esperanza.

casita = cottage

arroz con gandules = rice with pigeon peas

11 Just then—POOF! Fidelia appeared in the kitchen. When Esperanza explained what had happened, Fidelia roared, "How could you waste a wish when you have a bell to call me home? You are no smarter than Toro! I wish you had a tail and ears like his!"

12 Then—POOF! Esperanza sprouted ears and a tail.

13 Fidelia gasped. "Oh, no! I wish I had never said those angry words."

14 POOF! Esperanza's ears and tail disappeared.

15 "Your three wishes have been granted," said the old woman. "Thank you for the tasty supper." Then she left the *casita*.

16 The next morning, the sisters ate breakfast as the sun rose in the sky.

17 "You are so smart to trade our coffee and cocoa beans for delicious food," Fidelia said.

18 Esperanza sipped her coffee. "It is thanks to your hard work in the fields that we have the crops to trade." She thought for a moment. "We have some spare wood from the tree that fell. Let's use it to build a wagon. And Toro is as strong as any horse. He can help you water the fields."

19 Fidelia knew then that Esperanza was right—they had everything they needed.

Respond to Text

Reread/Think

Reread "The Three Wishes." Choose the best response to each question.

1. PART A

What is the central message of "The Three Wishes"?

A. Kindness brings rewards.

B. Hard work makes life better.

C. Be polite to those you meet.

D. Be thankful for what you have.

PART B

Which key detail from the text **best** supports the answer to Part A?

A. Esperanza keeps the *casita* tidy and clean.

B. Esperanza asks the old woman to ride Toro.

C. Fidelia knows that they have everything they need.

D. Fidelia wants a horse and wagon to help carry water.

2. Read this sentence from paragraph 1 of the story.

> Fidelia **tended** the fields.

What does the word *tended* mean?

A. found

B. served

C. cared for

D. moved toward

3. Which paragraph shows that Fidelia is sorry for saying Esperanza is "no smarter than Toro"?

A. paragraph 11

B. paragraph 13

C. paragraph 14

D. paragraph 18

Reread/Think

4. Which sentence from the text shows that Fidelia has learned to value her sister?

A. "'But we have everything we need,' Esperanza said." (paragraph 8)

B. "'How could you waste a wish when you have a bell to call me home?'" (paragraph 11)

C. "'I wish I had never said those angry words.'" (paragraph 13)

D. "'You are so smart to trade our coffee and cocoa beans for delicious food,' Fidelia said." (paragraph 17)

Write

What is a lesson that the sisters learn from the wishes they make? Include at least two key details that show the lesson that Esperanza and Fidelia learn.

WRITING CHECKLIST

- ☐ I told about a lesson the sisters learn from their wishes.
- ☐ I included at least two key details from the text that show the lesson that the sisters learn.
- ☐ I used complete sentences.
- ☐ I used correct spelling, punctuation, and capitalization.

Respond to the Focus Question

How can others help us learn and grow?

Reread/Think

Choose one story from the lesson to reread.

TEXT: ______________________________

1. What does a character learn from one or more of the other characters?

____

____

2. What lesson does that knowledge teach the character?

____

____

Talk

Share what you learned from your story with your group, using these questions:

The character ___ learns the lesson that ___. I learned a similar lesson when ___.

What do the characters in my story learn?

How do the characters change from the beginning to the end of the story?

When have I learned a similar lesson?

Listen to the other students in your group. Take notes on what they say.

____

____

Write

How can others help us learn and grow? Tell about a lesson one character learns, and describe a time when you learned a similar lesson.

SESSION 1 TALK ABOUT THE TOPIC

The Simplest Solution

FOCUS QUESTION

How can people help each other solve problems?

NOTICE AND WONDER

Look ahead at the story in this lesson. What do you notice? What do you wonder? Discuss your ideas with a partner.

WHAT IS WISDOM?

What does the word *wisdom* mean? What are some traits, or qualities, of a *wise* person? Who are some *wise* people you know? Complete the boxes below. Discuss your ideas with a partner.

Definition	Traits
Example(s):	

The Hermit's Secret, Parts 1–3

by Leslie J. Wyatt

The Hermit's Secret

Part 1 by Leslie J. Wyatt

1 Once upon a time, long before the Kingdom of Rillen became known for its silver trees, there lived a wise old hermit. He lived alone on the tallest mountain in the **kingdom**. His hut was close to a rushing river that flowed down into the sea. He passed his time quietly caring for his animals and garden. However, hardly a day went by that someone did not travel to see the humble man. Down in the village, whenever anyone was confused, worried, or sad, people would say, "Go see the wise hermit. He will help."

kingdom = a country with a powerful ruler

2 A young boy by the name of Aden lived at the foot of the mountain. He watched people start up the path to the hermit's house with troubled faces. Aden would see these people come back looking peaceful and comforted.

3 *What happened on that mountain?* Aden wondered. *Who was this man who lived alone yet seemed to have an answer to every problem?*

Stop & Discuss

What does Aden notice about the people who visit the hermit?

Underline two sentences that help you understand what Aden notices.

At first, the people look ___. After they come back, they look ___.

4 One morning, Aden decided to visit the old man.

5 "Mother," he said, as he picked up his pack, "I am going up the mountain. I will return when I know the hermit's secret."

6 The journey was not hard because the path was **well trodden**. As the sun was setting, Aden arrived at the old man's hut.

7 "Greetings, young traveler," the hermit said. His hair and beard were as white as the clouds that rested on the mountains. "What brings you here?"

8 "If you please, sir, I would like to learn the secret of how you help the travelers who **seek** your advice."

9 The man laughed. "You are not the first to want to know. I will say to you what I say to all of them—if you watch carefully, you will understand."

well trodden = walked on by many people

seek = to search for something

Stop & Discuss

What does Aden have to do to learn the hermit's secret?

Underline the answer the hermit gives. Then talk to a partner about how this will help Aden learn the hermit's secret.

Ask and Answer Questions

- After you read a paragraph or section, stop and make sure that you understand it. Ask yourself, "What happened?" If something is unclear, ask *who, what, where, when, why,* and *how* questions.
- Look for text details that help you answer your questions. Sometimes answers are right in the text.

Reread/Think

Reread Part 1 of "The Hermit's Secret." First, answer the questions using text details. Then write other questions you asked as you read the story. Use *who, what, when, where, why,* or *how* to start your questions.

Question	Answer	Text Detail
Why do people visit the hermit? (paragraphs 1–3)	because he helps people who are confused, worried, or sad	"'Go see the wise hermit. He will help.'"
Why does Aden visit the hermit? (paragraphs 4 and 5)		
What does the hermit say to Aden about his secret? (paragraphs 7–9)		
My Question:		
My Question:		

Talk

Review your chart with a partner. Discuss your questions and the answers you found in the text. Work with your partner to think of a question you cannot answer yet.

I had a similar/different answer. I thought ___ because ___.

A question I cannot answer yet is ___.

Write

Write about two questions you had about Part 1 of "The Hermit's Secret." Tell about one question you were able to answer and one question that you cannot answer yet. Use text details in your response.

WRITING CHECKLIST

- ☐ I included two questions: one I can answer, and one I cannot answer.
- ☐ I included details from the text.
- ☐ I used complete sentences.
- ☐ I used correct spelling, punctuation, and capitalization.

The Hermit's Secret

Part 2 by Leslie J. Wyatt

poorly = badly

entire = whole

1 Soon a farmer appeared, and Aden got his chance to watch how the hermit would help.

2 "Oh, kind sir!" said the farmer, shaking the hermit's hand. "You must tell me what I should do. I have the chance to buy a new field from a neighbor, but it will take every last coin I have. If my other crops do **poorly** this season, I could lose not only the new field, but my **entire** farm, too."

3 "Mmmm. Buying a new field might be a good opportunity," said the hermit.

4 "Yes. Sort of. I mean—it's my family that wants the land. They think it will make us rich." The man dug his toe into the dirt. "To be honest, I don't want any more land. I've got enough work as it is."

Stop & Discuss

Why might buying more land be a good thing? Why might it be a bad thing?

Find two reasons to buy the land and two reasons not to buy the land. Discuss them with a partner.

5 “Ah. I understand.” The wise man’s voice was **soothing**, like a drink of cool water on a hot summer day. The hermit asked Aden to fetch a honey melon from the garden. As the three ate the golden fruit and chewed the sweet red seeds, the farmer talked on. He spoke of his wish to live a simple life. Most of all, he spoke of the beautiful trees he had recently planted.

soothing = comforting

6 “You must see my trees someday, sir. Twelve of them as silver as a stack of new coins,” he said, his eyes glowing with excitement. “I spend much of my time taking care of them.”

7 Aden wondered when the hermit would give the farmer the answer to his problem. But the old man only said, “Perhaps you have a greater treasure in your silver trees than your family knows.”

Stop & Discuss

What is important to the farmer?

Underline text details that show what is important to the farmer. Tell your partner whether you think the farmer should buy the land.

8 The man **blushed**. "That I couldn't say, sir, but I do know I am happiest while looking upon their shining leaves." He sighed. "Why should I want more land and more work, which would take me away from them? Or cause me to lose them . . ." He fell silent then, his eyebrows moving up and down as he thought. All the while, the old hermit said nothing.

9 When the farmer finished his melon, he rose to go. "I think you are right," he said. "I do not need the new field, and I would be better off caring for my silver trees. I thank you very much."

10 Aden stared in surprise as the man walked away whistling a tune. *Why was he so happy?* Aden wondered. *The hermit hadn't given him any advice at all!*

11 Aden's confusion only grew with each new visitor. Though he listened and watched like a hawk, he heard the wise man give no answers. Yet most of the people who traveled up the mountain thanked the hermit for his wise words, as if he had told them exactly what to do.

12 Several months passed, but Aden felt no closer to discovering the hermit's secret.

blushed = became red in the face

Stop & Discuss

What does the farmer decide to do about his problem?

Underline the farmer's choice. Then discuss whether you think he makes the right choice.

Ask and Answer Questions

- Sometimes the answer to a question is stated directly in the text.
- When the answer is not directly stated in the text, details in the text may help you figure out the answer.
- This kind of answer is an **inference**, an idea you form using details in the text and what you already know.

Reread/Think

Reread Part 2 of "The Hermit's Secret." Write answers and text details in the chart.

Question	Answer	Text Detail
How does the farmer feel about buying the land? (paragraphs 1 and 2)		
How does the farmer feel about the silver trees? (paragraphs 5 and 6)		
What does Aden think the hermit will tell the farmer? (paragraph 7)		
Why does the farmer walk away whistling? (paragraphs 8–10)		
What does Aden think is confusing? (paragraphs 10–12)		

Talk

Discuss the ideas in your chart with a partner. Compare your answers and the text details you used to support your ideas. Why do you think Aden is confused? What text details help you form this idea?

Aden notices ___ and ___.

Aden is confused because ___.

Write

What has Aden noticed about the hermit and his visitors? Why is Aden confused? Use text details to support your response.

WRITING CHECKLIST

- ☐ I answered all parts of the question.
- ☐ I included text details to support my response.
- ☐ I used complete sentences.
- ☐ I used correct spelling, punctuation, and capitalization.

The Hermit's Secret

Part 3 by Leslie J. Wyatt

1 One morning, the old man became ill and had to stay in bed. As Aden brought him soup, there came a knock on the door.

2 "Oh, no!" exclaimed Aden. "Someone is here to see you. Shall I tell them to come back another day?"

3 The old man smiled. "No, you go."

4 With his heart in his stomach, Aden greeted the visitor at the door. "Hello," he said uncertainly.

5 "Good morning," she replied. "I am here to see the wise old man."

6 Aden bowed low. "I am truly sorry, but he is sick today. Is there anything I can do to help?"

7 The woman sighed and sank into a chair. "What answer could you give me? You are so young. You don't know how it is to have a son who wants to become a merchant and leave me and our farm behind."

8 "How difficult that must be for you," Aden said. He was sorry that he had no words of wisdom.

9 "Yes, it is difficult. I **desperately** need someone to take care of the farm. All my son wants to do is buy and sell and make money."

10 "Mmmm," murmured Aden as he handed her a cup of tea. "It's hard to know what to do, isn't it?"

desperately = very badly

certainly = surely

11 Together they sipped tea and talked about the latest news in the kingdom. After a while, the woman stood.

12 "You know, I think my son would be very happy to be a merchant. He is **certainly** very unhappy on the farm, and I do want him to be happy. Perhaps if he became a merchant, we could sell the farm, and I could go live with him in the town . . ." Her voice trailed off.

13 Aden waited, wondering what to say. He had no advice to give. What a failure he had been!

14 The woman turned to him. "Young man, thank you very much. I thought that I would receive no help without the wise old man, but I must say that he has a clever assistant." She waved farewell and started off down the mountain.

15 Carrying another cup of tea, Aden went to check on the old man.

16 "Tell me how the visit went," the hermit said. "Did you know the answers?"

17 "No. I knew no answers. I just listened."

18 "H'm . . ." the hermit said.

19 "No wise words," Aden sighed. "No great advice."

20 Then he remembered that the woman had called him clever, and he realized that he finally knew the hermit's secret. He turned to the old man and smiled.

21 "It turns out that sometimes just listening is the best answer of all."

Respond to Text

Reread/Think

Reread Part 3 of "The Hermit's Secret." Choose the best response to each question.

1. Fill in the blanks in the sentence below.

While ____________________ is in bed,

____________________ answers the door and meets

____________________ with a problem. After the two talk,

Aden learns an important lesson.

2. What does the visitor decide to do after speaking with Aden?

A. Move to another farm in a different kingdom

B. Work with her son to take care of her farm

C. Sell her farm and live in town with her son

D. Tell her son that money is of little importance

3. Why does Aden think he has failed?

A. He was too tired to listen to the visitor talk.

B. He was not able to solve the visitor's problem.

C. The visitor was not able to meet with the old man.

D. The visitor was disappointed with the advice he gave.

4. Read this sentence from paragraph 4 of the story.

> With **his heart in his stomach**, Aden greeted the visitor at the door.

What does the phrase *his heart in his stomach* tell about Aden?

A. He needs a doctor.

B. He wants a meal.

C. He feels nervous.

D. He feels sad.

Reread/Think

5. What is the hermit's secret?

A. Listening can be better than giving advice.

B. Friends can be found in surprising places.

C. Working hard leads to happiness in life.

D. People should always help family members.

Write

Explain how Aden's feelings change from the beginning of this part of the story to the end. Include at least two details from the story in your response.

WRITING CHECKLIST

- ☐ I described how Aden's feelings change through the story.
- ☐ I included at least two details from the story.
- ☐ I used complete sentences.
- ☐ I used correct spelling, punctuation, and capitalization.

Respond to the Focus Question

How can people help each other solve problems?

Reread/Think

Reread one part of "The Hermit's Secret." In the part you reread, how do people help each other solve problems? What did you learn about what happens when people ask for advice?

I reread part ______________________________

____

Talk

How can people help each other solve problems? Discuss your ideas with a partner. Tell how someone helped you solve a problem or how you helped someone else.

Someone helped me solve a problem when they ___.

I helped someone else solve a problem when I ___.

WHAT WE LEARNED

As a group, discuss how you would respond to this question.

What did you learn about how people help each other solve problems?

Take notes on what other students say.

Things I learned about how people help each other solve problems:

____

____

____

____

Write

What can you do to solve a problem you have? What can you do to help others solve their problems? Use examples from the story and ideas from your own life.

Everyone Makes Mistakes

FOCUS QUESTION

What happens when characters make mistakes?

NOTICE AND WONDER

Look ahead at the story in this lesson. What do you notice? What do you wonder? Discuss your ideas with a partner.

WHAT IS AN *ITCH?*

Read the sentences below. What phrases are related to the word *itch* in the second sentence? Circle phrases that are related.

Sasha couldn't wait to go hiking with her aunt.
She felt a powerful itch to explore the mountains.
She thought about hiking all the time.

excited to   can't stop   just okay

The phrase ___ is similar to/different from *itch*.

I think so because ___.

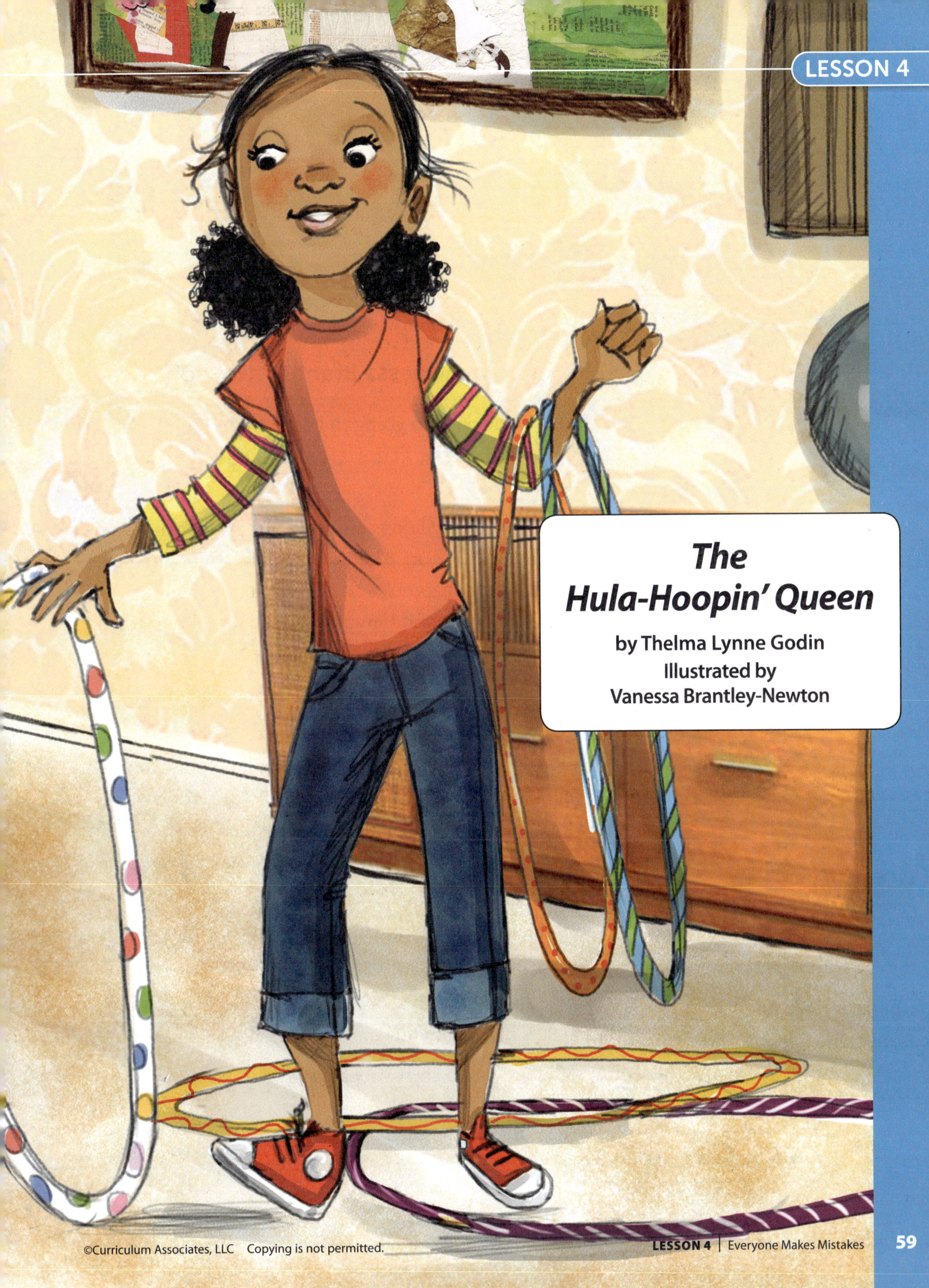

The Hula-Hoopin' Queen

by Thelma Lynne Godin
Illustrated by
Vanessa Brantley-Newton

SESSION 1 READ

The Hula-Hoopin' Queen PART 1

by Thelma Lynne Godin
Illustrated by Vanessa Brantley-Newton

1 Today is the day I'm going to beat Jamara Johnson at hooping. Then I'll be THE HULA-HOOPIN' QUEEN OF 139th STREET!

2 I sort through my hoops and pick out my favorite. And then I feel it comin' on. The itch. The Hula-Hoopin' itch. My fingers start snappin', and my feet start tappin'. My hips start swingin', and I'm just reachin' for a hoop when Mama says . . .

3 "Girl, don't you even think about it. You know today is Miz Adeline's birthday."

stamp = lift and put down very hard

4 Heat washes up over me, and I **stamp** my foot. Don't get me wrong. I love Miz Adeline. She lives right next door. Miz Adeline took care of Mama when she was little, and she took care of me too. She's like my very own grandmama.

5 "But, Mama," I burst out. "I can't help with Miz Adeline's party. I'm supposed to meet Jamara."

6 Mama stands as still as water in a puddle. She gives me her look. Then she hands me a broom.

7 I sigh loudly and start sweeping. 

Stop & Discuss

How does Kameeka feel when her mother tells her they are having a party for Miz Adeline?

Underline details in the text that show how Kameeka feels.

Kameeka feels ___. A detail that shows this is ___.

8 Mama and I dust every room and scrub down the floors. We polish each window 'til we can see clear to New Jersey. After that I peel potatoes while Mama starts mixing up her special double-fudge chocolate cake.

9 "Kameeka, set the oven to 350 **degrees**," Mama says as she empties the last of the sugar into the mixing bowl. "And add sugar to the grocery list."

degrees = a measure of how hot or cold something is

10 I push the button on the oven and look out the window. It's already getting late. I bet Jamara's telling everyone I'm too scared to hoop her.

11 While the cake bakes, we make up plates of fancy sandwiches. When the timer rings, Mama opens the oven.

mission = an important task

12 "Kameeka!" Mama yells as she checks the oven temperature. "You only set it to 250 degrees!" Miz Adeline's birthday cake looks like someone sat on it. Mama says we'll have to start over.

13 Mama sends me to the store to buy more sugar. On my way out the door, I grab a hoop like I usually do, but when I get outside, I remember that I'm on a **mission**. Miz Adeline's party will be starting in a couple of hours.

Stop & Discuss

What is Kameeka's mission at the end of Part 1?

Discuss Kameeka's mission with a partner.

Describe Characters

- You can understand and describe characters by identifying their traits, motivations, feelings, and actions.
  - — **Traits** tell what the character is like.
  - — **Motivations** tell what the character wants; this affects how the character acts, thinks, or feels.
  - — **Actions** tell what the character does.

Reread/Think

Reread Part 1 of *The Hula-Hoopin' Queen.* In the chart, write the traits, motivations, feelings, and actions that describe Kameeka. Then write where you found the evidence.

Kameeka	Description	Evidence
Traits What is the character like?		1. paragraphs ___, ___ 2. paragraphs ___, ___, ___
Motivations What does the character want?		
Feelings What does the character think or feel?		
Actions What does the character do?		

Talk

What happens when Kameeka's mother explains that Kameeka has to help with Miz Adeline's party instead of Hula-Hoopin' with her friends? Think about details that show Kameeka's traits, motivations, feelings, and actions. Share your ideas with a partner.

In the story, Kameeka ___.
This detail shows ___.

You said ___. I agree/ disagree because ___.

Write

How does Kameeka react when she cannot meet Jamara to hoop? Refer to Kameeka's traits, motivations, feelings, and actions to explain her reaction.

WRITING CHECKLIST

- ☐ I included one trait, one motivation, one feeling, and one action.
- ☐ I used complete sentences.
- ☐ I used correct punctuation, spelling, and capitalization.

The Hula-Hoopin' Queen PART 2

by Thelma Lynne Godin • Illustrated by Vanessa Brantley-Newton

1 I'm coming out of the store when I see Jamara and Portia hoopin' on the corner of 139th and Broadway.

smirk = unfriendly smile

2 "We thought you weren't coming, Kameeka," says Jamara with a **smirk**. I need to get the sugar back to Mama, but Jamara sounds so smug I can't stand it. "You ready?" she asks.

3 "I was born ready." And then I feel it comin' on. The itch. The Hula-Hoopin' itch.

4 "Whoever hoops the longest is the winner," Portia says.

5 As soon as she shouts "Go!" my fingers start snappin' and my feet start tappin'. My hips start swingin', and I just know I'm gonna beat Jamara today. *Swish, swiggle, swish.*

6 The sun moves between the buildings, and the sidewalk starts cooling down, but Jamara and me keep on hoopin'.

Stop & Discuss

What details show that Kameeka and Jamara hoop for a long time?

Underline those details and discuss with a partner.

7 "I've got doughnuts for Miz Adeline's party," Mr. John calls out as he closes up the bakery.

8 "Miz Adeline's cake!" I shout.

9 My hoop **clatters** to the sidewalk. I grab it and the sugar, and race up the block. I can hear Jamara laughing behind me.

clatters = makes a loud rattling sound from hitting a hard object

10 By the time I reach our apartment, Mama is madder than a hornet. "Kameeka Hayes!" she scolds.

11 "I'm sorry, Mama. I saw Jamara and—"

12 "Girl, I don't want to hear that Hula-Hoopin' nonsense. It's too late now. Miz Adeline's already here. You take yourself on into the living room and explain to Miz Adeline why she won't have cake for her birthday."

13 "Hi, Miz Adeline," I say. "Happy birthday."

14 "Kameeka, come here, baby. Give me a kiss."

15 I come in close and kiss Miz Adeline's soft cheek. Then I whisper in her ear, "You don't really like cake much, do you?"

16 "Baby girl, you know I sure do love cake. Chocolate cake with strawberries and real whipped cream on top." I can't tell her about the cake just yet.

Stop & Discuss

How does Kameeka feel about telling Miz Adeline that there is no cake?

Underline two details that help you understand Kameeka's feelings.

sashay = walk in a graceful and noticeable way

17 Pretty soon the neighbors start arriving. Miss Evelyn's wearing her church hat, and Mr. John's all spruced up in a pin-striped suit. Jamara and Portia **sashay** in with their parents.

18 Most of the presents are still unopened when Miz Adeline says, "Well, I do believe it's time for birthday cake."

19 I swallow hard. "Miz Adeline," I say slowly. "We made a cake, but it didn't turn out right. Then we needed more sugar to make another one, but I didn't get the sugar back to Mama in time 'cause I was hoopin'. I was trying to beat Jamara so I could be the Hula-Hoopin' Queen of 139th Street. It's my fault there isn't any cake."

20 "No cake?" says Miz Adeline, raising her eyebrows.

21 I look over at Jamara. She's spinning one of Mr. John's doughnuts round and round on her finger like it's a Hula-Hoop.

22 Suddenly that gives me an idea. "I'll be right back," I yell as I race from the room.

Stop & Discuss

What do you think Kameeka will do?

Discuss your prediction with a partner.

Describe Characters

- A character's **actions** are what the character does. A character's actions can affect what happens in a story.
- The **sequence** of events is the order in which events happen.

Kameeka's Action in Part 1	What Happens Because of the Action
cooks the cake at a too-low temperature	The cake is ruined. Kameeka and Mama have to bake another one.

Reread/Think

Reread Part 2 of *The Hula-Hoopin' Queen.* Then look at Kameeka's actions in the box below. Write each action in the chart next to the number where it belongs. Then write what happens because of the action.

Kameeka's Actions

- arrives home late
- sees Jamara spin a doughnut
- tells Miz Adeline there is no cake
- feels the Hula-Hoopin' itch

Kameeka's Actions in Part 2	What Happens Because of the Actions
1.	
2.	
3.	
4.	

Talk

Work with a partner to describe events at the beginning, middle, and end of Part 2. Use the chart to help you recount the sequence of events.

At the beginning, ___.

In the middle, ___.

At the end, ___.

Write

How do Kameeka's actions affect the party for Miz Adeline? Describe actions that Kameeka takes and what happens because of those actions.

WRITING CHECKLIST

- ☐ I described Kameeka's actions.
- ☐ I described what happened because of those actions.
- ☐ I used complete sentences.
- ☐ I used correct spelling, punctuation, and capitalization.

The Hula-Hoopin' Queen

PART 3

by Thelma Lynne Godin • Illustrated by Vanessa Brantley-Newton

1 In the kitchen I set a chocolate doughnut on a pretty plate. I add whipped cream and strawberries. As I carry the doughnut cake to Miz Adeline, Mama starts singing "Happy Birthday," and everyone joins in.

2 "Why, this is just about perfect," Miz Adeline says, taking a bite of her doughnut birthday cake. "Now, Kameeka, did you say you were hoopin'? When I was a girl, I was the best Hula-Hooper on this block."

3 "Adeline, don't you start that nonsense," Miss Evelyn says. "You know very well I was the best."

4 "Baby girl, why don't you bring some hoops on in here and let me show this old girl what she forgot."

5 My eyes find Mama's. She shakes her head. But Miz Adeline's already pushing back chairs to make room. Then she slips a hoop over her head.

6 And right then I know. Miz Adeline's just like me. She's got the itch. The Hula-Hoopin' itch. Her fingers start snappin', and her feet start tappin'. Her hips start swingin', and before we know it that hoop is swishin' right around Miz Adeline's waist. Then she's got it swingin' around her neck.

in spite of herself = even though she did not expect to

shimmies = shakes the hips

7 I glance over at Mama and see a smile pulling at her lips **in spite of herself**. Miz Adeline **shimmies** the hoop down past her knees. She spins it around her ankle as she hops on one foot, then the other. With the hoop still swishin' round and round, Miz Adeline heads for the door.

8 Miss Evelyn grabs one of my hoops, and Mr. John grabs another. Even Mama's hips are swingin' as the whole party spills out on to the street.

9 "Kameeka, this is the best birthday party I've ever had!" Miz Adeline hollers.

10 Jamara hoops on over to me. "Kameeka," she says. "I know who the real Hula-Hoopin' Queen of 139th Street is."

11 "I do too," I say.

12 Jamara settles her hoop around her waist. "You ready, Kameeka?"

13 "I was born ready," I say.

14 The sidewalk is cooler than a spring rain, and the streetlights shine like stars. *Swish, swiggle, swish. . . .*

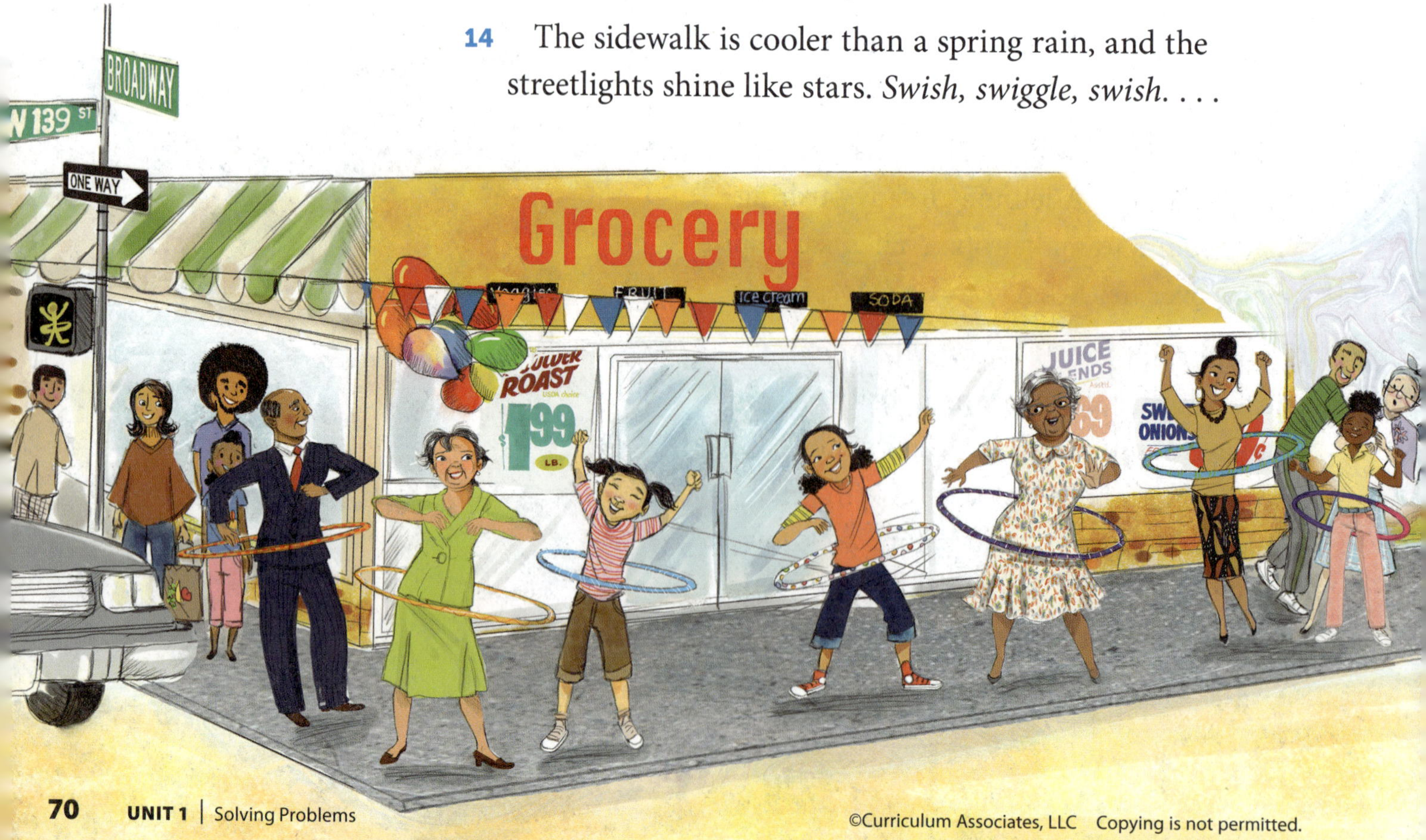

Respond to Text

Reread/Think

Reread Part 3 of *The Hula-Hoopin' Queen.* Respond to each question about the text.

1. PART A

What trait do Kameeka and Miz Adeline share?

A. They both like doughnuts more than cake.

B. They both enjoy planning birthday parties.

C. They both enjoy hooping.

D. They both like cooking.

PART B

Choose one detail from the story that **best** supports the answer to Part A.

A. "In the kitchen I set a chocolate doughnut on a pretty plate." (paragraph 1)

B. "I add whipped cream and strawberries." (paragraph 1)

C. "Miz Adeline's already pushing back chairs to make room." (paragraph 5)

D. "Miz Adeline's just like me. She's got the itch." (paragraph 6)

2. How does Kameeka finally solve the problem of having no birthday cake?

A. She asks her mom to help make a cake.

B. She uses a doughnut to make a cake.

C. She asks Mr. John to bring a cake.

D. She invites everyone to Hula-Hoop instead.

Reread/Think

3. Why does Miz Adeline *holler* in paragraph 9?

A. She is angry there was not a cake.

B. She is calling for Kameeka in the crowd.

C. She is happy about her birthday party.

D. She is telling Jamara not to hoop.

4. Who is the real Hula-Hoopin' Queen of 139th Street?

A. Kameeka

B. Jamara

C. Mr. John

D. Miz Adeline

Write

Was Miz Adeline's party a success? Why or why not? Think about Kameeka's traits, motivations, feelings, and actions. You can use evidence from all parts of the story.

WRITING CHECKLIST

- [ ] I used details from Parts 1, 2, and 3.
- [ ] I included traits, motivations, feelings, and actions to explain.
- [ ] I explained my answer with more than "yes" or "no."
- [ ] I used complete sentences.
- [ ] I used correct spelling, punctuation, and capitalization.

Respond to the Focus Question

What happens when characters make mistakes?

Reread/Think

Choose Part 1, 2, or 3 of the story to reread.

TEXT: ______________________________

Describe one mistake Kameeka makes and what happens as a result.

____

____

Talk

First, share what happens in the part of the story you reread.

One mistake Kameeka makes is ___.

What happens because of her mistake is ___.

Take notes on what other students say about the part of the story they read.

Name:	**Name:**

Write

What happens when characters make mistakes? Use what you have learned and evidence from all parts of the story in your response.

A Hero Among Us

TALK ABOUT WHAT YOU KNOW

Use the illustrations to remember the texts that you read in this unit about characters and how they solve problems. Turn and talk with a partner about what you already know about solving problems. Use the illustrations and the sentence frames to help you.

In the text ___, the character ___ solves a problem by ___.

In a different text ___, the character ___ solves a problem by ___.

LESSON 1

Clever Thinking

LESSON 2

Learning from Others

LESSON 3
The Simplest Solution

LESSON 4
Everyone Makes Mistakes

WORD SORT

Read the words below. Think about how to sort the words into pairs. Then explain your thinking to a partner.

brains | cleverness | fail

give up | mistake | muscles | problem

solution | succeed | try

HERCULES AND THE BIRDS OF DOOM

by Brooks Benjamin

1 Hercules shoved his science book into his backpack. How was he supposed to be the hero of Sylian Lake if he couldn't remember simple science concepts?

2 "Why is fifth-grade science so hard?" he **grumbled**.

3 "Whatever, dude," said his friend Philip. "You'll figure out that science stuff. You're smart."

4 "I'm smart enough to know people think the only thing I am good at doing is moving heavy things." Hercules sighed.

5 "Being strong isn't bad," Philip said, clapping his friend on the shoulder. "Did you see how far you sent that soccer ball flying today? I bet it still hasn't landed."

6 Hercules forced a smile. He loved being strong, but he wished that Philip wasn't the only person who knew he was more than his muscles.

7 They spotted a crowd of people in front of the cafe on the main street in town. "What do you think's going on?"

8 Philip shrugged. "I don't know. Let's check it out." 

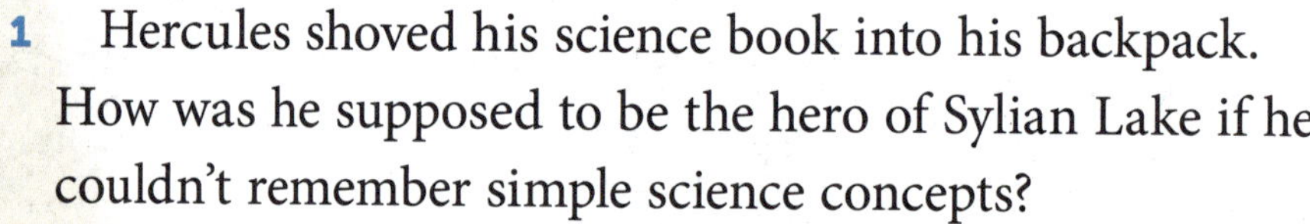

grumbled = complained in a grouchy way

Stop & Discuss

What two problems does Hercules have?

Underline the sentences that tell his problems.

One problem is ___.

Another problem is ___.

9 They approached the crowd, and the fearful voices grew louder. Everyone was looking up, and whatever they were staring at wasn't good at all.

10 "Hercules! Oh, thank goodness, you're here!" Ms. Augustus, the owner of the cafe, came bounding down the sidewalk toward Hercules. Her face was red and sweaty. "My cafe is under attack!"

11 "Attack?" Hercules froze as his eyes drifted up to the top of the building. **Perched** on the roof were three birds, each one the size of an elephant! Customers **cowered** outside as the birds snapped their enormous beaks.

perched = sitting high up on the edge of

cowered = crouched down in fear

12 "You have to do something," Ms. Augustus pleaded. "Like when you tied that giant nine-headed snake in a knot last year! Those birds are ruining my business!"

13 Science may have confused Hercules, but when monsters attacked, he knew exactly what to do. He tossed his backpack aside and nodded. "You got it, Ms. A."

Stop & Discuss

Why does Ms. Augustus ask Hercules and not someone else to help her?

Discuss your response with a partner.

14 Hercules waved everyone back. Then he climbed the neighboring building, using his strong fingers to pull himself up. He leaped toward the cafe roof, but one flap of the birds' mighty wings sent Hercules hurtling back to the ground. The crowd gasped.

15 Embarrassed but unhurt, Hercules stood and wiped the dirt from his shorts. "Well, that didn't work."

16 He looked around for another idea. Spotting a large tree nearby, he uprooted it with a single pull. Using it like a baseball bat, he tried to knock the birds off the roof. But one of them chomped through the tree's trunk with its razor-sharp beak.

17 Hercules dropped the stump he was holding. *Maybe I can scare them off,* he thought. He dashed into the forest and gathered three humongous boulders. He stacked them in front of the cafe, forming an enormous stone giant. He started to carve a scary-looking face with his fingernail. But the largest bird knocked over the boulders with its **vicious** talons.

vicious = very dangerous

18 Hercules sighed. Nothing he tried was working. He looked around, desperate for another plan. Just then, a baby in a stroller shook her rattle. At the sound, the birds clamped their wings over their ears and stuck out their tongues, as if to say, "Your taste in music is HORRIBLE!"

19 Hercules suddenly had a wild idea. He would use his smarts instead of his strength. "Everyone! Grab whatever you can—rattles, instruments, pots, pans, anything!"

Stop & Discuss

What is Hercules's new plan? How is it different from the other things he has tried to make the birds go away?

Underline details that help you answer the question and then discuss with a partner.

20 Once Hercules shared his plan, he gave the signal. The crowd **erupted** into a chorus of crashes and thumps. The birds gave up. They flew up and out of sight.

erupted = suddenly began to do something

21 The crowd burst into cheers. "How'd you think of it?" Ms. Augustus asked.

22 Hercules held up his science book. "Sound energy."

23 Philip grinned. "Right! Loud sounds cause **vibrations**..."

vibrations = quick, shaking movements

24 "...and they hurt the birds' ears!" Hercules finished.

25 "I guess it does help to have a brain along with those muscles," Philip said.

26 Hercules couldn't help but smile. Between his muscles and his brain, Hercules was the hero he always wanted to be.

Stop & Discuss

How does solving Ms. Augustus's bird problem help Hercules solve his own problems?

Discuss with a partner.

SESSION 3 PRACTICE

Respond to Text

Reread/Think

Reread "Hercules and the Birds of Doom." Choose the best response to each question.

1. How does Hercules feel at the beginning of the story?

A. upset that he is known only for his muscles

B. happy to be spending time with his friend Philip

C. proud to be called the hero of Sylian Lake

D. disappointed to see Ms. Augustus at the cafe

2. What do paragraphs 3–5 show about Philip?

A. He is a kind friend.

B. He is a skilled athlete.

C. He is interested in science.

D. He is good at lifting things.

3. How does Hercules use the boulders?

A. He uses them to help climb up the building.

B. He bangs them together to make a loud noise.

C. He stacks them together to make a stone giant.

D. He throws them at the roof to try and scare the birds.

4. Read this sentence from paragraph 16.

> Spotting a large tree nearby, he **uprooted** it with a single pull.

What is the meaning of *uprooted*?

A. noticed something on the ground

B. lifted something out of the ground

C. dug a hole in the ground

D. planted a tree in the ground

5. **PART A**

What trait **best** helps Hercules solve the problem with the birds?

A. his strength

B. his smarts

C. his speed

D. his kindness

PART B

Which detail **best** supports the answer in Part A?

A. "'You got it, Ms. A.'" (paragraph 13)

B. "Then he climbed the neighboring building, using his strong fingers to pull himself up." (paragraph 14)

C. "He dashed into the forest. . . ." (paragraph 17)

D. "Once Hercules shared his plan, he gave the signal." (paragraph 20)

6. Using the sentences provided, fill in the graphic organizer to recount the key details of the story.

Hercules tries to use a tree to stop the birds.

Ms. Augustus asks Hercules for help.

The loud noises make the birds leave.

Hercules tries to jump at the birds.

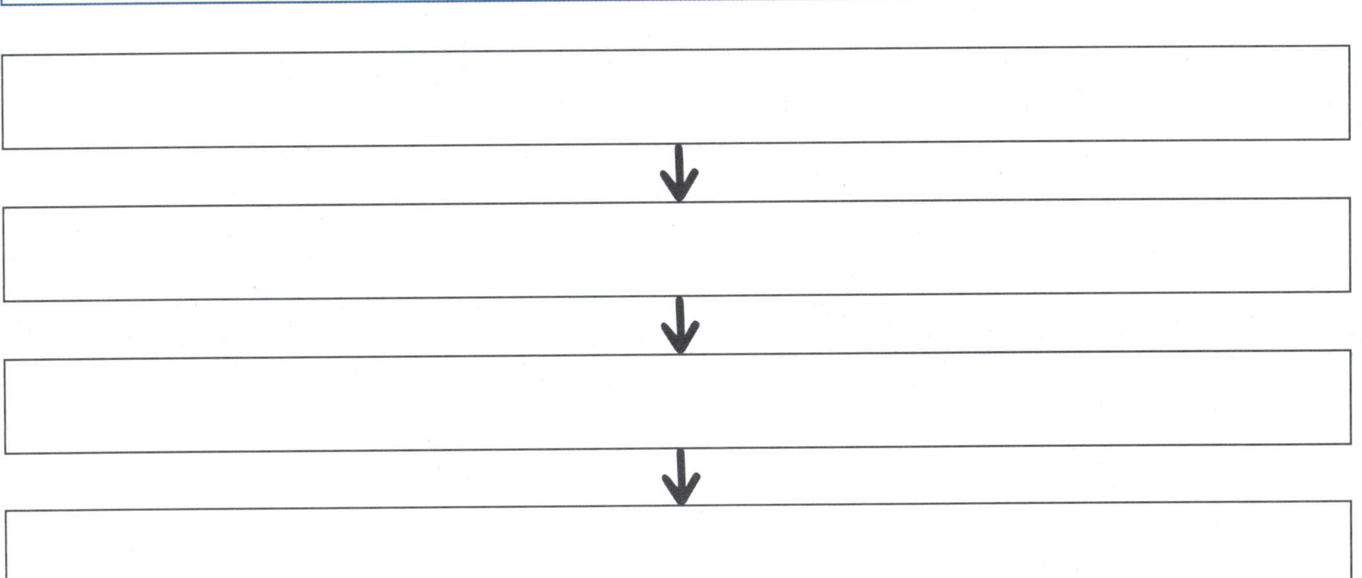

Write

What lesson does Hercules learn about solving a problem? Use evidence from the text to support your response.

WRITING CHECKLIST

- ☐ I described the lesson Hercules learned.
- ☐ I used evidence from the text.
- ☐ I used complete sentences.
- ☐ I used correct spelling, punctuation, and capitalization.

Make Connections

Reread/Think

Look back at the stories you read in this unit. Think about the different ways the characters solve their problems. Which character do you think has the best solution to a problem? Give reasons for your answer.

TEXT: ______________________________

My opinion: ______________________________

____

____

Text evidence that supports my thinking:

1. ______________________________

____

____

2. ______________________________

____

____

Talk

As a group, discuss the character you think has the best way to solve a problem and why. Use the sentence frames to get started.

I think ___ has the best way to solve a problem because ___.

Another reason that supports my thinking is ___.

I agree/disagree that ___.

I think this because ___.

Ocean Survival

LESSON 5

Habitats of the Ocean

86

LESSON 6

Survival Skills

102

UNIT 2

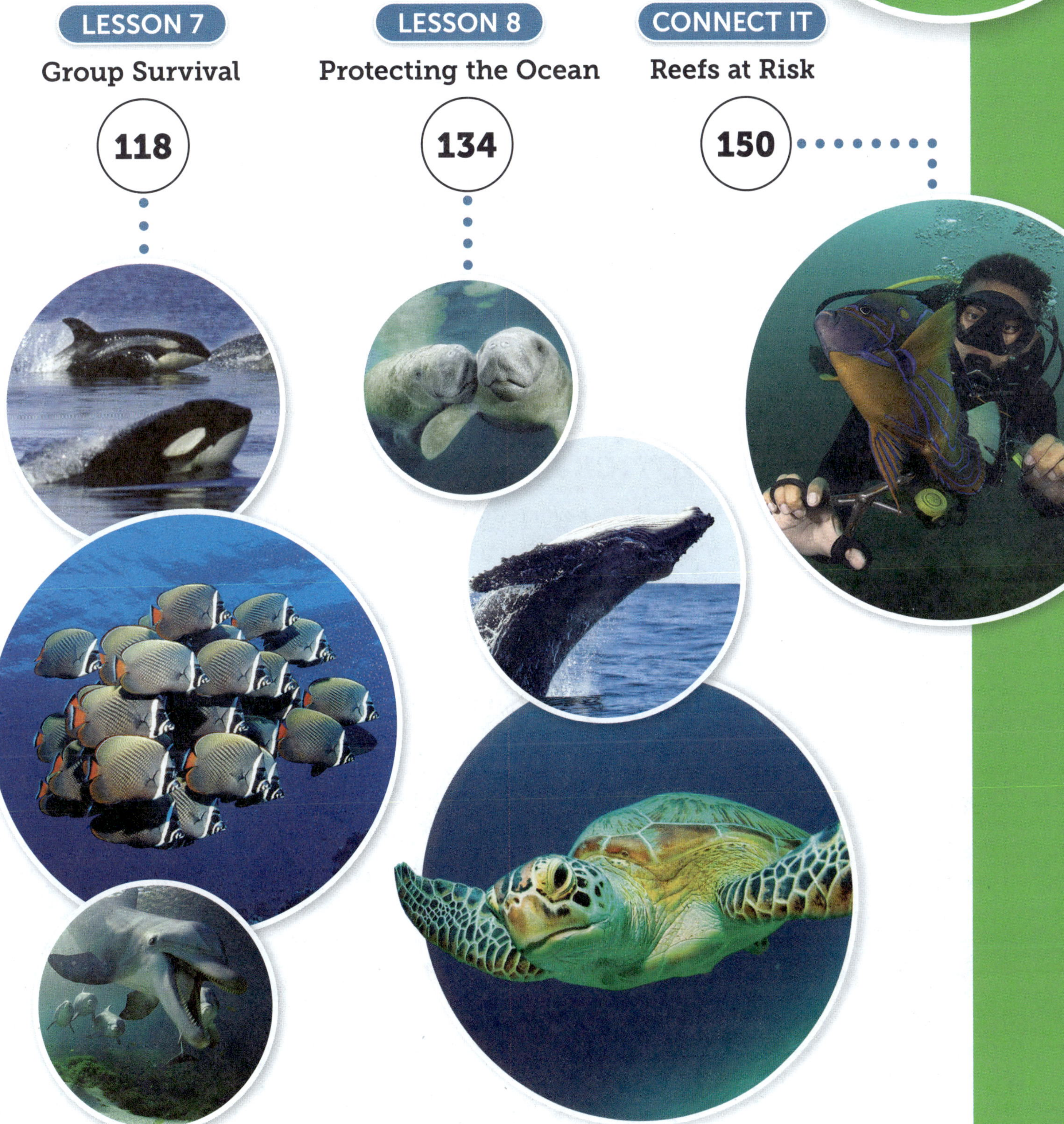

SESSION 1 TALK ABOUT THE TOPIC

Habitats of the Ocean

FOCUS QUESTION

How do sea animals survive in their habitats?

NOTICE AND WONDER

Look at the three texts you will read in this lesson. What do you notice? What do you wonder? Discuss your ideas with a partner.

WHAT DOES *SURVIVE* MEAN?

Think about what the word *survive* means. Pick a word you can relate to the word *survive*. Talk about how that word and *survive* are related.

food **home** **leafy** **darkness**

colorful **ocean** **protection** **live**

The word __ is related to *survive*.

I think this because __.

Ocean Homes
by Kathryn Hulick

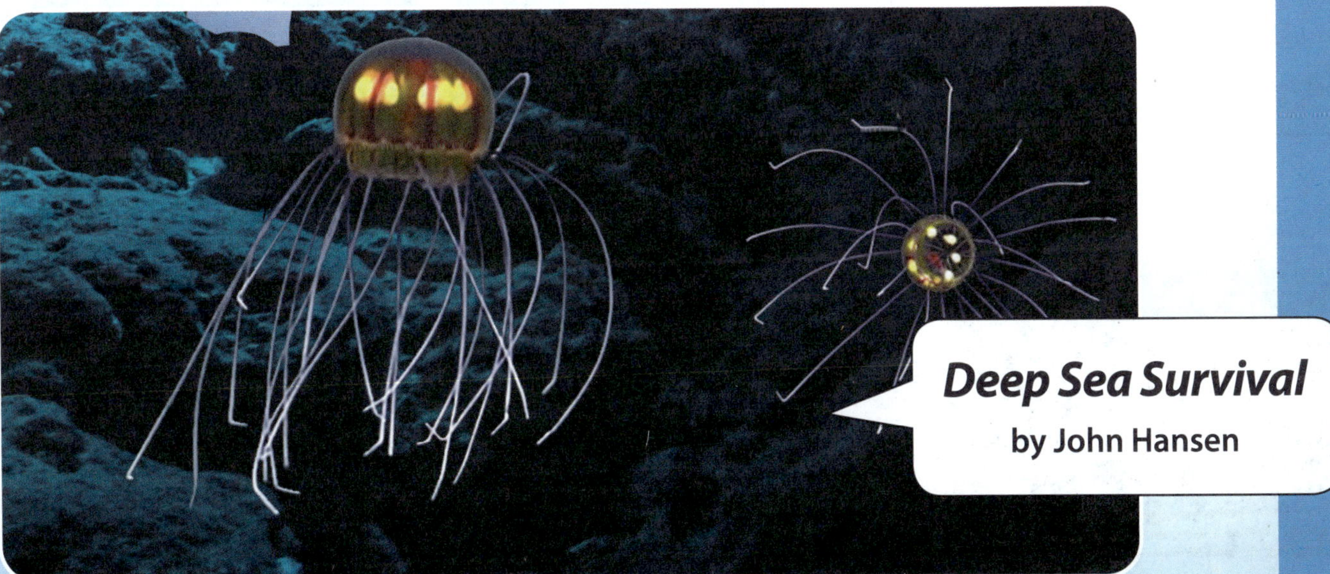
Deep Sea Survival
by John Hansen

Welcome to the Reef
by Hazel Meador

SESSION 1 READ

OCEAN HOMES

by Kathryn Hulick

1 Do you live in a city or town or out in the country? Is your home in the mountains, or is it on flat land? People live in all sorts of places, and so do animals!

2 The places where animals naturally live are called habitats. The ocean contains many habitats, and each is home to different kinds of animals. These animals **depend on** the safety and food provided by their underwater homes to survive.

depend on = need

3 Coral reefs are one type of ocean habitat. Lots of different kinds of animals, or species, live among these colorful, stony, underwater structures. These animals depend on the reef's special features, or important parts, in order to survive. For example, fish depend on the reef's many holes and caves to hide from passing predators. Without hiding places, the colorful fish would be lunch!

Seagrass beds are home to animals like crabs.

4 Seagrass beds create homes for other ocean animals. These habitats are mostly found in shallow waters. From the sandy sea floor, the long green leafy plants wave back and forth with the movement of the water. Animals depend on the leaves and sand of the seagrass beds for food and shelter. Other creatures use this habitat to hide from tiger sharks and other predators. The bobtail squid, for example, buries itself in the sand. This keeps it hidden from larger hunters. Hiding in the sand also helps the squid catch prey. When small shrimp and crabs go by, the squid jumps out and grabs them.

Stop & Discuss

Underline the names of two ocean habitats. How do animals survive in these habitats?

Discuss your ideas with a partner.

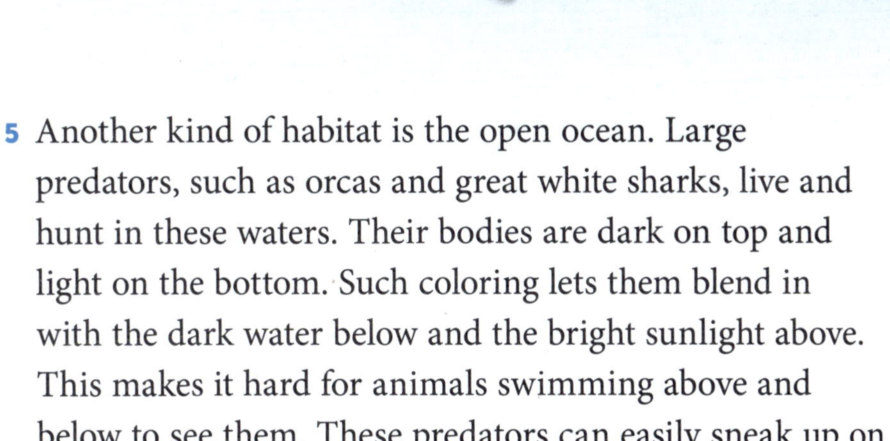

Great white sharks live in the open ocean.

Some squid that live in the deep sea make their own light.

5 Another kind of habitat is the open ocean. Large predators, such as orcas and great white sharks, live and hunt in these waters. Their bodies are dark on top and light on the bottom. Such coloring lets them blend in with the dark water below and the bright sunlight above. This makes it hard for animals swimming above and below to see them. These predators can easily sneak up on their prey.

6 No light reaches the deepest parts of the ocean. This deep sea habitat is dark and cold. No plants grow here. However, some of the world's strangest animals live here. More than half of deep-sea animals have **adapted** by making their own light. This habitat is full of glowing jellyfish, worms, squid, and larger fish. These animals use their light in different ways, such as to **attract** prey, trick predators, or communicate with one another.

7 From the colorful coral reefs to the deep, dark sea, ocean habitats are all very different. In each one, animals must find the food and shelter they need to survive.

adapted = changed over time

attract = to cause to come near

Stop & Discuss

What helps orcas and great white sharks sneak up on their prey in the open ocean?

Draw a picture to show this. Then explain your picture to a partner.

Recount Key Details

- **Details** are facts, examples, and other information in a text.
- **Key details** are the most important details in a text.
- When you **recount** key details, retell them in your own words. Recounting key details can help you understand what a text is mostly about.

Reread/Think

Reread "Ocean Homes." Look for key details about what animals do to survive in each habitat. In the chart, write the key details in your own words.

Habitat	Key Details About What Animals Do to Survive
coral reef	Fish hide from predators in holes and caves in the reef.
seagrass beds	
open ocean	
deep sea	

Talk

Talk with a partner about what animals do to survive in each ocean habitat. Use key details from the chart as you talk. What do these key details help you understand about the text?

Some of the key details tell about ___.

This helps me understand that the text is mostly about ___.

Write

Choose two ocean habitats and explain how animals survive there. Include key details from the text in your response.

WRITING CHECKLIST

- ☐ I wrote about what animals do to survive in two habitats.
- ☐ I recounted key details.
- ☐ I used complete sentences.
- ☐ I used correct spelling, punctuation, and capitalization.

Deep Sea Survival

by John Hansen

1 In deep, dark ocean waters, a strange-looking fish searches for something to eat. As it nears its prey, it turns on its "headlights." Yes, the black dragonfish has actual lights on the side of its head to help it see. It also has a wide mouth that is full of sharp teeth. Even its tongue has teeth!

2 People used to think that nothing could live on the ocean floor or in the deepest water. Wow, were they ever wrong about that! They thought it was much too dark and cold for anything to survive, but it is still filled with life. It's a habitat for thousands of kinds of animals! They have unusual features that allow them to survive in this very cold, very dark place where food can be hard to find.

3 The "deep sea" starts at 650 feet (200 meters) below the water's surface. Deeper than that, the light starts to **fade**. At 3,280 feet (1,000 meters) below the surface, there's no sunlight at all. Living in darkness would be difficult without the right tools. Yet these animals survive in the deepest waters.

fade = lose brightness

Stop & Discuss

Which statement is true?

☐ Animals cannot survive in the deep sea.

☐ Many animals live in the deep sea.

Underline the key details that support your response.

4 Making light is an important feature for survival. About nine out of ten of deep-sea animals make their own light. They use that light both to find food and to **avoid** being eaten. The anglerfish, for example, has a thin rod with a glowing tip attached to its head. The light from the glowing tip attracts prey. An animal's light can be used for protection, too. Some deep-sea squid squirt out a glowing cloud of liquid light when attacked. This confuses the predator while the squid escapes.

avoid = keep from

5 Another feature that helps survival is **adjusting** to the cold water. No sun means the water is near freezing. But this isn't a problem for deep-sea animals. Their bodies are built for living in such cold temperatures. Cold water has more oxygen in it than warm water. Oxygen is needed for most life on Earth to survive and grow. The animals don't move much because the water is very cold, so their bodies have extra oxygen. The extra oxygen makes some animals grow bigger. The deep-sea spider can grow as large as a dinner plate!

adjusting = changing

Stop & Discuss

How does making their own light help animals survive in the deep sea?

Discuss your answer with a partner.

Making their own light helps animals survive by ___.

Black dragonfish have "headlights" so they can see in the dark water.

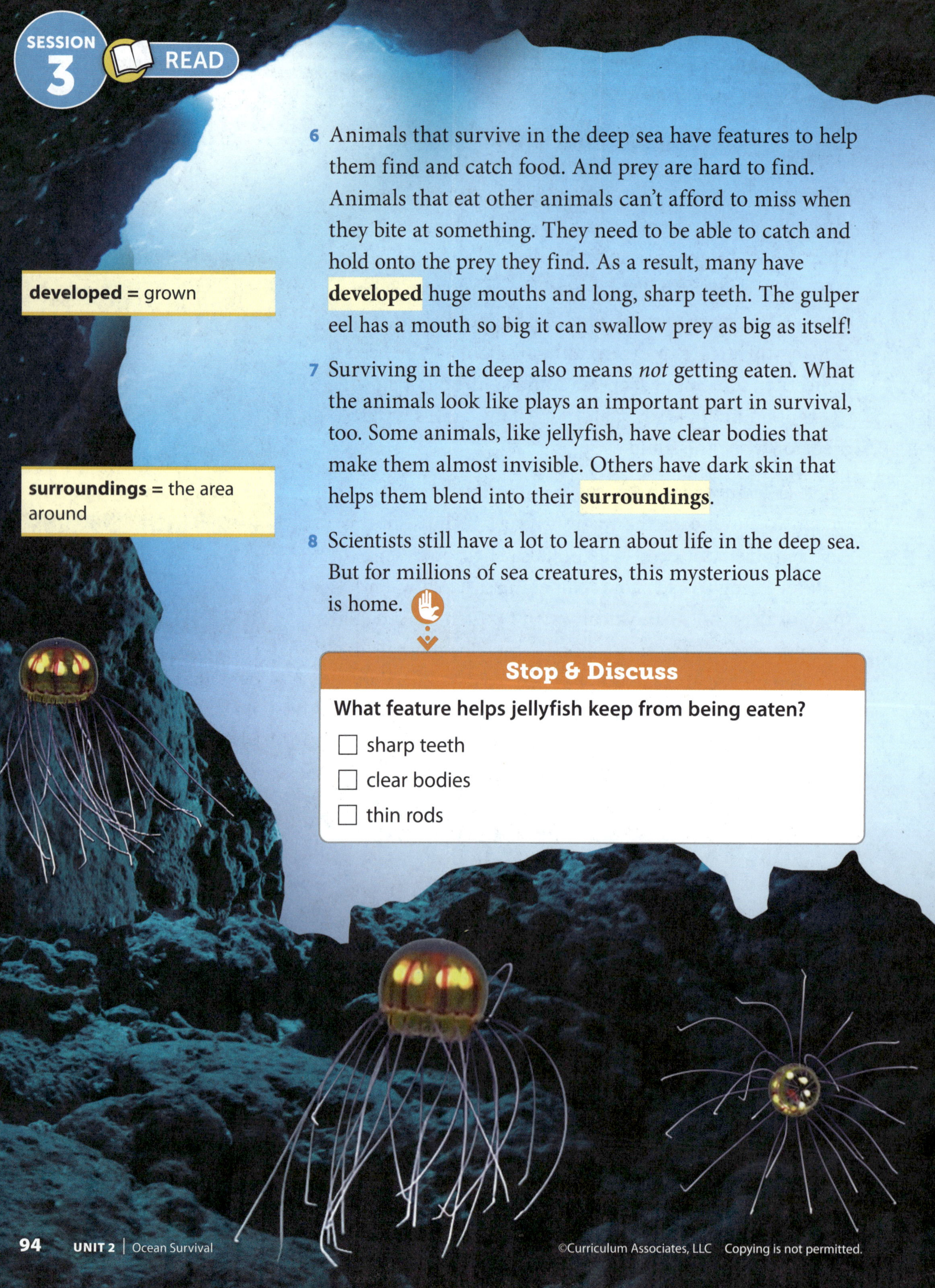

6 Animals that survive in the deep sea have features to help them find and catch food. And prey are hard to find. Animals that eat other animals can't afford to miss when they bite at something. They need to be able to catch and hold onto the prey they find. As a result, many have **developed** huge mouths and long, sharp teeth. The gulper eel has a mouth so big it can swallow prey as big as itself!

developed = grown

7 Surviving in the deep also means *not* getting eaten. What the animals look like plays an important part in survival, too. Some animals, like jellyfish, have clear bodies that make them almost invisible. Others have dark skin that helps them blend into their **surroundings**.

surroundings = the area around

8 Scientists still have a lot to learn about life in the deep sea. But for millions of sea creatures, this mysterious place is home.

Stop & Discuss

What feature helps jellyfish keep from being eaten?

- ☐ sharp teeth
- ☐ clear bodies
- ☐ thin rods

Recount Key Details

- The **main idea** is something important that the author wants readers to understand.
- Key details are important information that tell about the main idea. Recounting key details helps you understand the main idea.

Reread/Think

Reread paragraphs 4–7 in "Deep Sea Survival." Look for key details about each animal's features. Write those key details in the chart.

Animal	Key Details About the Features That Help Animals Survive
black dragonfish	The lights on its head, a wide mouth, and sharp teeth help it catch prey.
anglerfish	
deep-sea squid	
deep-sea spider	
gulper eel	
jellyfish	

Talk

Look at the chart and talk to a partner about the key details about each animal's features. Why did you include those details in your chart?

One key detail I included in my chart is ___.

The reason I included it is because ___.

Write

Recount the key details in the text and explain how they support the main idea that deep-sea animals have special features that help them survive. Begin your writing by stating the main idea and then recount the key details.

WRITING CHECKLIST

- ☐ I wrote about the main idea.
- ☐ I used key details to explain the main idea.
- ☐ I used complete sentences.
- ☐ I used correct spelling, punctuation, and capitalization.

WELCOME TO THE REEF

by Hazel Meador

1 Imagine an underwater city with colorful buildings and busy sea creatures swimming in every direction. That's one way to describe a coral reef. Millions of plants and animals live in coral reefs.

2 Coral reefs are made of millions of creatures called polyps. Polyps can be as small as the head of a pin or as big as a basketball. They have soft bodies with big mouths on top. Polyps create hard skeletons to protect their soft bodies. Their skeletons connect and form a coral reef. Polyps are slow builders. Reefs grow for thousands or even millions of years. The world's biggest reef is the Great Barrier Reef, off the coast of Australia. It has grown to be 1,600 miles (2,600 kilometers) long.

3 The reefs provide food and shelter to **organisms**. At the same time, the plants and animals protect the reefs and keep them healthy. In this way, coral reefs and the organisms that live there help each other.

organisms = living things

4 **Algae** and coral reefs could not exist without each other. Coral reefs supply a safe home for algae. Algae live and grow inside each polyp, where they are well-protected. At the same time, the algae provide food for the coral. Polyps use this food to grow. The algae are also why corals are so colorful. The bodies of polyps are clear, and their skeletons are white. The coral reef's bright colors are created by the algae living inside each polyp.

algae = plant-like living things

relationship = the way things are connected

5 Another important **relationship** is the link between the coral reefs and other animals. Tens of thousands of different animal species live in reefs around the world. Animals like shrimp, lobsters, crabs, and fish move in and out of coral's many holes and caves. These hiding spots also help sea animals keep their babies safe from predators.

6 Lots of these sea animals also help protect and clean the coral reefs they depend on. For example, certain crabs act as guards for some reefs. They scare away sea stars and sea snails, which can damage reefs. Parrotfish are also important helpers. They use their strong teeth to eat dead coral and extra algae that can be harmful to the coral. While getting a meal, parrotfish clean the reef and help it grow bigger and stronger. After eating, parrotfish poop out sand, which helps to form beaches.

providers = animals and plants that give something to the reefs

7 For millions of plants and animals, the coral reefs are perfect habitats. And the plants and animals living in the reefs are perfect **providers** and protectors. Coral reefs and the organisms that live there help each other grow and stay strong.

Respond to Text

Reread/Think

Reread "Welcome to the Reef." Choose the best response to each question.

1. Which creatures' skeletons form the coral reef?

   A. algae

   B. polyps

   C. shrimp

   D. parrotfish

2. Which detail supports the idea that coral reefs are a good place for sea creatures to live?

   A. "Polyps can be as small as the head of a pin or as big as a basketball." (paragraph 2)

   B. "At the same time, the plants and animals protect the reefs and keep them healthy." (paragraph 3)

   C. "The coral reef's bright colors are created by the algae living inside each polyp." (paragraph 4)

   D. "These hiding spots also help sea animals keep their babies safe from predators." (paragraph 5)

3. Read this sentence from paragraph 4.

   Coral reefs **supply** a safe home for algae.

   What is the meaning of the word *supply*?

   A. find

   B. give

   C. catch

   D. damage

Reread/Think

4. What is a key detail of paragraph 6?

A. Parrotfish search for food in the coral reef.

B. Crabs scare away sea stars and sea snails.

C. Sea animals protect the reef in different ways.

D. Sea animals help make sand that forms beaches.

5. Which detail does **not** support the main idea that coral reefs and the organisms that live there help each other?

A. Orcas eat the reef and the reef provides shelter to the orca.

B. Algae provide food for the coral and the coral protects the algae.

C. Crabs hide in the holes of the coral and they scare away sea stars that damage the reef.

D. Parrotfish eat dead coral, which is harmful to the reef.

Write

Describe how coral reefs help sea animals and how sea animals help coral reefs. Use at least two examples from the text in your answer.

WRITING CHECKLIST

- ☐ I described how coral reefs help animals.
- ☐ I described how animals help coral reefs.
- ☐ I used at least two examples from the text.
- ☐ I used complete sentences.
- ☐ I used correct spelling, punctuation, and capitalization.

Respond to the Focus Question

How do sea animals survive in their habitats?

Reread/Think

Choose two animals from the texts that you think have the most interesting ways to survive. Then write one key detail from the text that explains how each animal survives.

Animal	Key Detail

Talk

Discuss with a partner the sea animals that you found the most interesting and explain why.

> I think the ___ is the most interesting sea animal because ___.

As a group, discuss how you would respond to this question.

If you could have a special feature like one of the sea animals, which would it be, and why?

Take notes on how others in your group answer the question.

Name:	Name:

Write

How do sea animals survive in their habitats? Choose two animals to write about. Support your response with key details from the texts.

SESSION 1 TALK ABOUT THE TOPIC

Survival Skills

FOCUS QUESTION

How do an animal's special features help it survive?

NOTICE AND WONDER

Look at the three texts you will read in this lesson. What do you notice? What do you wonder? Discuss your ideas with a partner.

WHAT DOES IT MEAN TO DISGUISE SOMETHING?

Read the phrases. Circle the phrases that mean nearly the same thing as "to disguise."

to hide	to show	to change
to mask	to cover up	to decorate

One phrase that means nearly the same thing as to *disguise* is ___.

One way to disguise a(an) ___ is to ___.

Anglerfish: Fish That Fish

by Julie Murphy

Bobtail Squid: Masters of Disguise

by Dan Risch

Parrotfish: Slimy Snugglers

by Caryl Gobin Ulrich

Anglerfish: Fish That Fish

by Julie Murphy

1 A deep-sea anglerfish **lurks** 10,000 feet (3,000 meters) below the surface of the ocean. Floating in the dark, lonely water, it prepares to catch its dinner. Huge mouth? Check. Long, curved, needle-sharp teeth? Check. Fishing rod? Check. That's right—anglerfish are fish that go fishing! They have a sneaky way of catching their food.

lurks = waits out of sight

2 Anglerfish get their name from the word *angler*. An angler is a person who catches fish using a rod, line, and bait. Anglerfish have their own fishing rod, called an illicium. The illicium is a spine that sticks out of the anglerfish's head. They use this unusual body part to trick fish they want to eat. At the end is a globe-shaped lure called the esca. Millions of tiny **bacteria** that live within the esca create the light.

bacteria = tiny living things

3 Some ocean creatures can catch their dinner because of their size or speed. However, deep-sea anglerfish are not big or fast. They can't see in the dark very well, either. So they have to be sneaky instead. Their dark coloring helps them blend in with their environment. They sit very still, and they slowly move their illicium around so it looks like something good to eat. The glowing esca on the tip of the illicium attracts the interest of nearby animals. The soft light is easy to see in the darkness.

Stop & Discuss

How are anglerfish sneaky when they catch their food?

Underline three details that show how anglerfish trick other animals. Discuss with a partner.

4 When a curious sea creature comes closer, the anglerfish holds the esca directly in front of its own mouth. Then the **unsuspecting** prey moves even closer. Just before the prey bites the tasty-looking lure, the anglerfish opens its mouth. Water rushes into the big, gaping hole and sucks the prey in along with it. The anglerfish devours its food in one gulp. Thanks to stretchy jaws and stomachs, anglerfish are able to consume very large prey. Some anglerfish can gobble up fish twice their own size!

unsuspecting = wrongly having trust in

5 With a big meal in its belly, a deep-sea anglerfish can survive for months. The next time it's hungry, the anglerfish will get its built-in fishing rod ready and go fishing.

Stop & Discuss

How do anglerfish eat big prey?

Discuss the details in the text with a partner.

One feature that helps anglerfish eat big prey is ___.

Esca

Illicium

Mouth

Determine the Main Idea

- The **main idea** of a text is what the text is mostly about. It is the big idea that the author wants readers to understand.
- **Key details** are important facts, examples, or other pieces of information in a text that help explain the main idea.
- To figure out the main idea, think about what the text is mostly about. Then identify key details that support the main idea.

Reread/Think

Reread "Anglerfish: Fish That Fish." In the chart, write the main idea and the key details that support it.

Main Idea		
Key Details (paragraphs 1 and 2)	Key Details (paragraph 3)	Key Details (paragraphs 4 and 5)

Talk

Recount the key details in your chart. Talk about how each detail supports the main idea.

One key detail is ___.

It supports the main idea by ___.

Write

What is the main idea of "Anglerfish: Fish That Fish"? Recount two key details and explain how they support the main idea.

WRITING CHECKLIST

- ☐ I organized my writing by telling the main idea first, followed by key details.
- ☐ I included two key details that support the main idea.
- ☐ I used complete sentences.
- ☐ I used correct spelling, punctuation, and capitalization.

Bobtail Squid: Masters of Disguise

by Dan Risch

1 Hawaiian bobtail squid must taste good. During the day, big, hungry fish try to find and eat them. At night, seals try to gobble them up. So what's a little squirt like a bobtail squid to do? Become invisible! Bobtail squid have many ways of hiding from predators.

2 During the day, tiny bobtail squid hide in the sand. They snuggle into the sea floor in the waters off the coast of Hawaii. Then they use their **tentacles** to flip sand onto their backs. Their sticky skin holds the sand in place. Not even a predator like a sharp-eyed barracuda will spot a sand-covered bobtail squid.

tentacles = long, thin body parts or feelers

3 But what if a bobtail squid is **attacked** in open water, with no place to hide? When that happens, the squid disappears by tricking predators. First, the bobtail squid squirts out ink. The ink forms a cloud that is similar to the size and shape of the squid. Then the squid itself changes color and becomes almost see-through. The predator sees the ink cloud and bites the inky shape while the nearly invisible squid swims to safety.

attacked = put in danger

Stop & Discuss

What do bobtail squid do to hide from hungry fish?

Draw a picture showing one way they hide from predators. Then tell a partner what you drew and why.

A bobtail squid in the sand

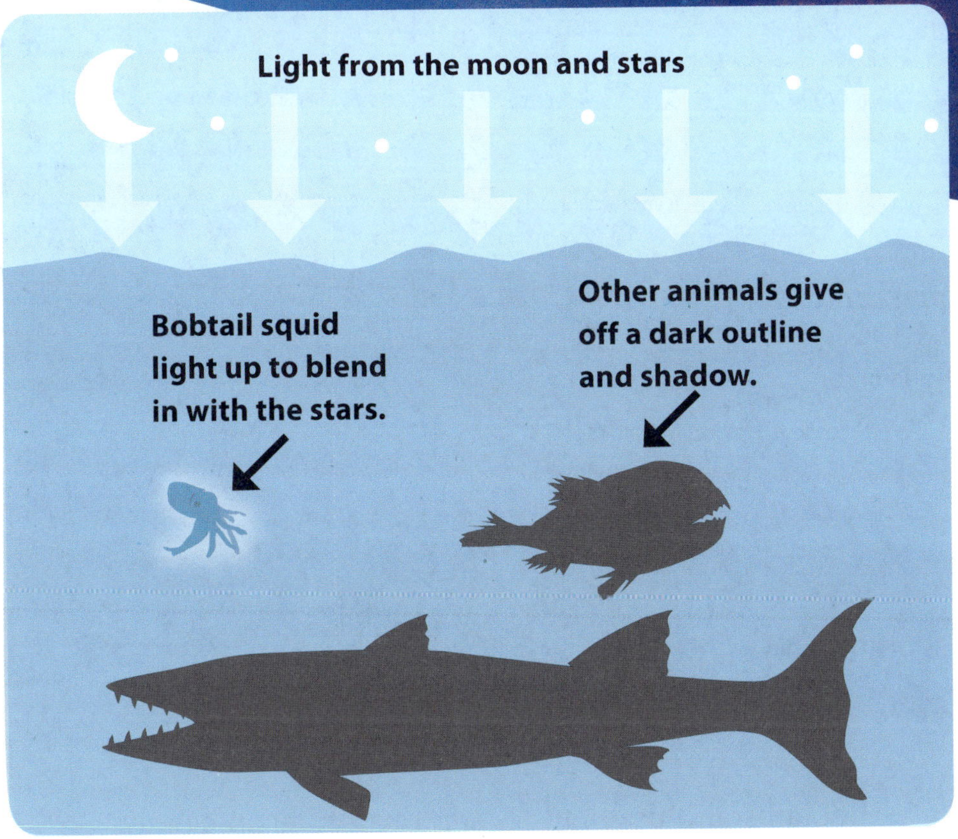

Light from the moon and stars

Bobtail squid light up to blend in with the stars.

Other animals give off a dark outline and shadow.

4 When the sun goes down, these squid's hiding skills really shine. They hide by lighting up! At night, bobtail squid swim through the water, eating worms and shrimp. The moon and stars light up the water. Predators swimming below the squid look up to **search** for the dark outlines of their prey in the starlit water. But they can't see the bobtail squid—because the squid look like stars.

search = to look for

5 Bacteria that live inside the squid's bodies "glow," or make light, much like a firefly does. The bacteria live in pockets on the bottom of the squid. With their bottom pockets shining with bacteria, the bobtail squid can swim around, safely hidden by their own starlight. Their predators don't see them. Instead, they see "stars" against the night sky!

Stop & Discuss

How do bobtail squid stay safe on starry nights?

Tell a partner what details help you to know.

Bobtail squid can turn their lights "on" when the sky is clear and "off" when it is cloudy.

6 Bobtail squid use light to help them hide on cloudy nights, as well. Scientists believe that the bobtail squid's eyes "tell" the bacteria about how much—or how little—light to **produce**. When it's cloudy out, these squid can turn off their pocket lights. By controlling how much light shines from its pockets, the squid can **match** its light to the light in the water.

produce = to make

match = to be the same as

7 With many ways to hide, the bobtail squid is perfectly suited to survive in its warm water home. Some might even call the tiny bobtail squid a master of disguise.

Stop & Discuss

How are bobtail squid able to stay safe on cloudy nights?

Underline one detail that explains how bobtail squid do this. Then discuss with a partner.

Determine the Main Idea

- The **main idea** is something important that an author wants readers to understand.
- To figure out the main idea, ask yourself questions as you read: *What does the author want me to know? What is the text mostly about?*
- Then identify the key details. Ask yourself: *Does this detail tell something important about the main idea?*

Reread/Think

Reread "Bobtail Squid: Masters of Disguise." In the chart, write the main idea and key details that support it.

Key Details (paragraph 2)	Key Details (paragraph 3)

Main Idea

Key Details (paragraphs 4 and 5)	Key Details (paragraph 6)

Talk

Recount the key details in your chart. What do all these details tell about? How does each detail support the main idea?

All of these details tell about __ so I think the main idea is __.

One supporting detail is __.

Write

What is the main idea of the text? Use two key details that support the main idea.

WRITING CHECKLIST

- ☐ I organized my writing by telling the main idea first, followed by key details.
- ☐ I included two details that support the main idea.
- ☐ I used complete sentences.
- ☐ I used correct spelling, punctuation, and capitalization.

Parrotfish: Slimy Snugglers

by Caryl Gobin Ulrich

1 When you're ready for bed, do you snuggle up in a favorite cozy quilt? Some **tropical** fish called parrotfish do—only their favorite blanket is made of slime! Why do these fish sleep in goo? Scientists have learned that the slick covering on these fish protects them from parasites and predators.

tropical = an area near the equator and very hot

2 Parrotfish live in coral reefs. Coral reefs are busy places. Thousands of kinds of fish and other sea life make their homes there. Parrotfish get their name from their bright colors and teeth that stick out like a beak. They use these chompers to munch on coral. Parrotfish eat the algae inside the coral. They crunch their food very loudly. If you are looking for parrotfish on a reef, follow your ears!

3 At sunset, parrotfish settle in to make their beds. First, they choose a sandy spot. Then they spit out slimy mucus. Again and again, the fish open their mouths. More and more mucus comes out. Finally, the fish are surrounded by balloons of spit that keep them safe. Then the parrotfish go to sleep. In the morning, they swish their tails to clear the slime away. They are ready to start a new day.

Parrotfish live in coral reefs.

parasites = living things that live on or inside other living things

slippery = wet and slimy

4 Why do parrotfish go to all of this trouble every night? Scientists were curious, so they did a test. They set up cameras to film sleeping parrotfish. Then the scientists removed the slime blankets from some of the fish. During the night, **parasites** nibbled on the fish. The fish without slimy covers got the most bites. Ouch! Some parasites carry diseases that could make parrotfish ill. Scientists discovered that the slime protects parrotfish from these underwater pests.

5 A parrotfish's **slippery** cover doesn't just protect it from small creatures. The slime also prevents large creatures from eating the parrotfish. Predators such as the moray eel search for food by smell. But the mucus coating on a parrotfish seals in its smell, like zipping stinky cheese into a plastic bag. Under its slippery blanket, the parrotfish is hidden from nosy noses! Smells can't get through the slime, and the moray eel will pass by without noticing the sleeping parrotfish.

6 Who knew that a blanket of slime was such an important tool for survival? For the parrotfish, it provides protection from big and small dangers in the coral reef. At night they can sleep in safety and comfort. Sweet, slippery dreams!

A parrotfish sleeps under a blanket of slime.

Respond to Text

Reread/Think

Reread "Parrotfish: Slimy Snugglers." Choose the best response to each question.

1. **PART A**

   What is the main idea of the text?

   A. Parrotfish live in coral reefs.

   B. A slimy blanket protects parrotfish.

   C. Smells cannot get through the slime.

   D. Parrotfish crunch their food loudly.

   PART B

   Which key detail **best** supports the answer to Part A?

   A. Parrotfish get their name from their bright colors.

   B. At sunset, parrotfish choose sandy spots to sleep.

   C. The parrotfish without slimy blankets had the most bites.

   D. Parrotfish have teeth that stick out like a beak.

2. Which detail in paragraph 3 supports the main idea?

   A. "At sunset, parrotfish settle in to make their beds."

   B. "Again and again, the fish open their mouths."

   C. "Finally, the fish are surrounded by balloons of spit that keep them safe."

   D. "They are ready to start a new day."

Reread/Think

3. Read the sentence from paragraph 4.

> Some parasites carry **diseases** that could make parrotfish ill.

What does the word *diseases* mean?

A. bugs

B. animals

C. slime

D. sicknesses

4. In paragraph 4, what happened to the fish without slimy covers?

A. They could not sleep.

B. They slept too long.

C. They got the most bites.

D. They got the least bites.

Write

What is the main idea of "Parrotfish: Slimy Snugglers"? Use two key details that support the main idea to explain your response.

WRITING CHECKLIST

- ☐ I included the main idea.
- ☐ I shared two key details that support the main idea.
- ☐ I used complete sentences.
- ☐ I used correct spelling, punctuation, and capitalization.

Respond to the Focus Question

How do an animal's special features help it survive?

Reread/Think

Choose one text from this lesson to reread. Write the title on the line below.

TEXT: ______________________________

What is one feature of the animal from your text that helps it survive?

____

____

Talk

What do you think is the most interesting feature of one animal you read about?

I think the most interesting feature is ___. I think this because ___.

WHAT WE LEARNED

As a group, discuss how you would respond to this question:

In what ways do animals disguise themselves to stay safe?

Take notes on what you learn from the other students in your group.

Name:	Name:

Write

Choose one animal you read about. Write about how that animal's special features help it survive. Add information about other animals you know about that use disguises.

Group Survival

FOCUS QUESTION

How do animals work together to survive?

NOTICE AND WONDER

Look at the three texts you will read in this lesson. What do you notice? What do you wonder? Discuss your ideas with a partner.

WHY WORK TOGETHER?

What are some of the reasons ocean animals might work together? Write your ideas in the web. Then discuss your ideas with a partner.

Working together might be good for:

One reason ocean animals might work together is so they can ___.

Another reason is so they can ___.

Orcas on the Hunt

by Alicia Z. Klepeis

Stay in School!

by Kathy Kranking

Dolphin Chatter

by Wendell Riley

Orcas on the Hunt

by Alicia Z. Klepeis

1 It is a cloudy evening off the coast of Antarctica. A freezing cold breeze blows. A pod, or group, of orcas swims just below the waves. The large dorsal fins on their backs cut through the water's surface. The orcas swim to a sheet of floating ice. They are hunting seals.

ice floe = floating ice

2 First, the orcas lift their heads out of the water. One of the pod members sees a seal lying on an **ice floe**. A female orca moves in. She is huge, a lot bigger than the seal. The other members of her pod notice the seal and come closer. The orcas must work together to catch the seal. Their survival depends upon it.

3 Next, the female orca pushes her body against the ice floe, turning it around. When the seal is in the perfect position, the orcas line up. Then they charge the ice floe, creating a big wave. Finally, they dive under the ice floe, using their tails to push water over the ice. This causes the seal to slide into the water, where the hungry orcas are waiting.

Stop & Discuss

Why do the orcas work together to get the seal off the ice?

Look for details in paragraph 3 to figure out why they hunt in a group. Discuss with a partner.

An orca begins the process of carouseling herring.

4 Orcas have been called the wolves of the sea. Like wolves, orcas live and hunt together. Pods may have just a few members or as many as fifty. They live all over the globe, from the Arctic Circle to Antarctica. Females are pod leaders. Some orcas eat fish such as salmon and herring. Others feed on marine mammals such as porpoises, seals, and sea lions. Orcas even attack whales larger than themselves.

5 Orca pods use a wide variety of hunting **techniques**, depending on their prey. One technique is called carouseling. First, the orcas swim underneath and around a school of fish. They herd the fish into a bait ball, forcing them to swim in a tight circle. Second, the orcas slap this ball with their tails. The slapping **stuns** the fish, making it easy for orcas to finally gulp them down.

techniques = ways of doing something

stuns = confuses

6 Orcas are talented hunters. They are fast and smart. Working together allows these amazing animals to survive in the wild ocean waters.

Stop & Discuss

Why do orca pods use a variety of hunting techniques?

Use details from the text to explain why pods use certain hunting techniques.

Describe Steps in a Process

- Scientific texts often describe steps in a process. The **steps in a process** tell how something works or happens. The steps are connected in a certain **sequence**, or order. If the steps are not in sequence, the process might not work.
- Signal words and phrases can help you understand the sequence. These words include *first, second, then, next, after that, when,* and *finally.*

Steps of Hunting Seals

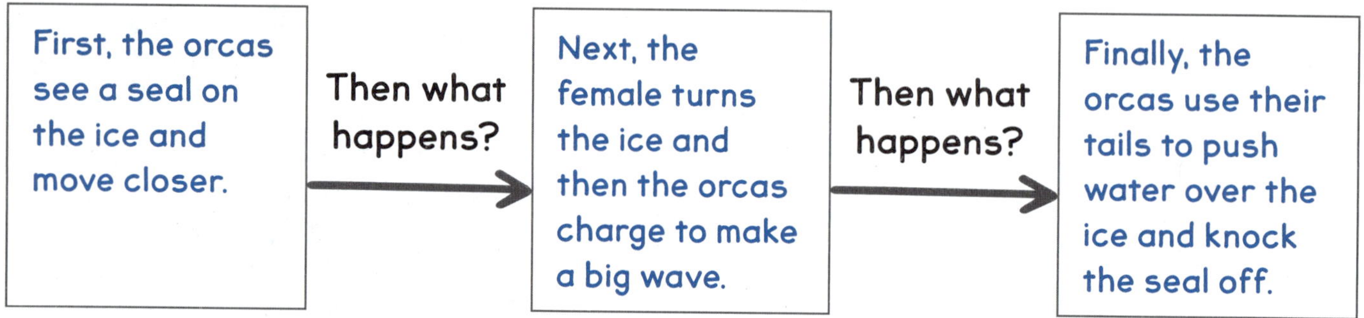

Reread/Think

Reread paragraph 5 of "Orcas on the Hunt." Complete the chart to show how the steps of carouseling are connected.

Steps of Carouseling

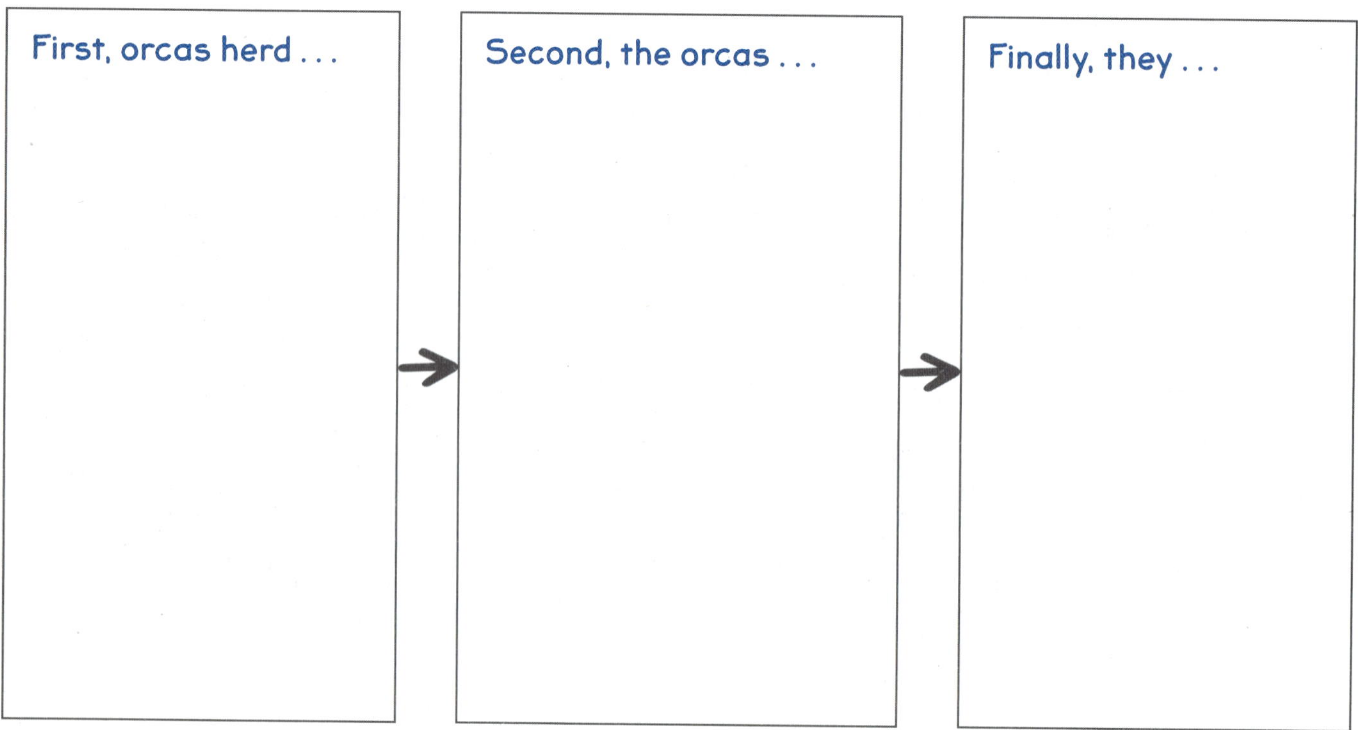

Talk

Look at the two charts to review the steps of hunting seals and carouseling. Talk about how orcas hunt for seals and fish. What might happen if the steps happened in a different sequence, or order?

___ needs to happen first so that ___.

If the second step happened first, ___.

Write

Describe one of the ways orcas work together to survive. Use sequence words and three details from the text to support your response.

WRITING CHECKLIST

- ☐ I answered the question.
- ☐ I used sequence words to show how the steps are connected.
- ☐ I included at least three details from the text for support.
- ☐ I used complete sentences.
- ☐ I used correct spelling, punctuation, and capitalization.

Stay in School!

by Kathy Kranking

1 For some fish, schooling is a smart way to survive.

translucent = letting light pass through

2 A school of golden sweepers swims along a coral reef. Because of their **translucent** bodies, the fish shimmer with each tiny movement. There are at least a thousand of them, all packed tightly together. Every time the fish in front turn, the ones in back follow. Right, left, up, down—the fish always stick together.

3 Suddenly, a hungry checkered snapper appears. The golden sweepers sense the predator, so they speed off. When the snapper gets too close, the sweepers split into two groups and swim in opposite directions. As a result, the snapper is confused. It lurches at the school, but the tricky fish dart away again. Eventually, the snapper becomes tired and swims away. At last, the sweepers are safe!

Circle Time

species = type, sort

4 Some schools of fish have millions of members. A school doesn't have to be big, though. Even a few fish can be a school. The fish in a school are all the same **species**.

5 To a predator, this shimmery ball of small fish may look like one giant fish. As a result, it can be hard to pick a single fish out of the crowd. But if a predator does attack, being in a school helps a fish's chance of survival. Because so many fish are in a school, there's a good chance "the other guy" will get caught.

Stop & Discuss

How does swimming in a school protect fish from predators?

Discuss with a partner. Use details from the text to support your answer.

A school of golden sweepers

A school of fish works together.

Quick Studies

6 Some schools of fish swim in loose groups at a relaxed pace. But others zip around, with the fish barely a fin's length apart. They change direction quickly, but they never run into each other. They can avoid each other because fishes' eyes are on the sides of their heads, which makes it easy for them to watch each other. They copy each other's movements so that they don't collide, or crash into each other.

7 Fish also use what are called lateral lines to help them stay together. These lines are rows of tiny **cells** that run along a fish's head and body. The cells let fish feel their neighbors' movements in the water. Due to this ability, the fish can move in the same way.

cells = small pieces of plant or animal life

Stop & Discuss

Why are fishes' eyes and lateral lines important?

Underline two details in paragraphs 6 and 7 that explain how eyes and lateral lines help schools of fish.

Cafeteria Line

8 Staying in a school can be a good way to get help finding food. If there are a lot of fish looking for something to eat, then the chances of finding food are better. For this reason, schools of fish use teamwork to catch food. For example, they may herd smaller fish into a group and then take turns darting in to grab a meal.

School Uniforms

9 Some schooling fish have markings that help disguise them. For example, due to the markings on butterflyfish, it is hard for a predator to tell where one fish ends and another begins. The fishes' eyes are hidden in stripes, and their body patterns blend together.

10 Each member of a school may be small, but there's a lot they can do when they stick together. Their teamwork helps them survive the biggest of predators. After all this schooling, you can see why schools rule!

Stop & Discuss

How do butterflyfish work together to protect themselves from predators?

Underline details in paragraph 9 that help you figure it out.

When butterflyfish are in a school, predators ___ because ___.

A school of butterflyfish

Connect Events

- Events in scientific texts are often connected to show causes and effects. A **cause** is the reason something happens. An **effect** is what happens because of the cause.
- Signal words and phrases can help you find causes and effects. These words and phrases include *because, so, as a result, for this reason,* and *due to.*

Reread/Think

Reread "Stay in School!" Complete the chart to provide an effect for each cause described in the text.

Cause		Effect
Paragraph 3 Sweepers sense the checkered snapper. They swim in opposite directions.	→	They speed off.
Paragraph 5 A ball of small fish looks like one giant fish.	→	
Paragraph 6 Fish have eyes on the sides of their heads.	→	
Paragraph 8 Fish use teamwork to catch food.	→	
Paragraph 9 Butterflyfish have markings.	→	

Talk

Review your chart with a partner and discuss your responses. Use text details to discuss how swimming in schools helps fish survive. You may also discuss cause-effect connections that do not appear in the chart.

> The fish in a school ___. As a result, ___.

> This helps the fish survive because ___.

> Another connection I found is ___.

Write

How does swimming in schools help fish survive? Use information in the chart and your partner discussion to help you respond. Use cause-effect signal words and text details in your response.

WRITING CHECKLIST

- ☐ I answered the question.
- ☐ I used signal words to show how causes and effects are connected.
- ☐ I included text details for support.
- ☐ I used complete sentences.
- ☐ I used correct spelling, punctuation, and capitalization.

Dolphin Chatter

by Wendell Riley

1 A huge shark glides through the ocean, hunting for food. It sees a group of dolphins swimming together. To the shark, they look like an easy—and delicious—target. But as the shark swims toward the group, the dolphins **spot** him. One whistles a loud warning. Then another whistles, and another. They are ready to fight. Working together, the dolphins attack the shark. This causes the shark to quickly give up. It swims away to find easier prey.

spot = see

2 Dolphins survive by living together in pods, which are groups of five to thirty dolphins. Dolphins work well together because they have special ways to communicate with one another. They make sounds such as whistles, squeaks, and clicks. Most of these sounds are made by air passing through special sacs located underneath the dolphins' blowholes.

3 Dolphins also communicate by moving parts of their body. They touch fins, bump heads, and slap their tails. Tail slapping can mean a dolphin is ready to attack.

4 Every dolphin has a one-of-a-kind whistle. A young dolphin will loudly repeat its "**signature** whistle" if it is scared or in trouble. Because its mother knows the sound, she will quickly swim over to help.

signature = special to someone or something

5 Whistling also helps dolphins hunt together. When a dolphin finds a school of fish, it whistles even more than usual. As a result, the rest of the pod comes to help. The pod forms a wall around the fish so they can't get away.

system = a way of doing something that follows steps

6 Dolphins also use a sound **system** called echolocation. As dolphins move through the water, they make clicking sounds that spread out like waves. When the sounds hit an object, they bounce back as echoes. As a result, dolphins can hunt prey, escape predators, and avoid anything in their way. They can also sense where fellow pod members are, which helps them work together.

7 Because of their communication skills, dolphins can even help when a member of their group gets sick or injured. In some pods, members will work together to lift a sick dolphin to the water's surface so it can breathe.

8 Scientists have been studying dolphin communication for a long time. They have learned a lot, but there is still much they don't understand. To learn more, scientists continue to listen and observe dolphin pods as they communicate with each other.

Respond to Text

Reread/Think

Reread "Dolphin Chatter." Then choose the best response to each question.

1. Fill in the blanks in the sentences below.

A dolphin will make sounds like ______________________ to prepare other dolphins to fight dangers such as ______________________. These sounds are made when ______________________ passes through sacs underneath a dolphin's ______________________.

2. Why would a young dolphin repeat its "signature whistle"?

A. to warn other dolphins of danger
B. to call its mother when it is afraid
C. to tell its pod where to find fish
D. to help find objects in the ocean

3. Read these sentences from paragraph 6.

> When the sounds hit an object, they bounce back as echoes. As a result, dolphins can hunt prey, escape predators, and avoid anything in their way.

Choose the statement that **best** describes these sentences.

A. They tell about a sequence, or order.
B. They tell about a cause and its effect.
C. They tell about a main idea and details.
D. They tell about the steps in a process.

4. How do dolphin pods help a sick dolphin?

A. They work together to find food for the sick dolphin.
B. They scare away predators from the sick dolphin.
C. They bring the sick dolphin to the surface to breathe.
D. They make sounds that help the sick dolphin feel better.

Reread/Think

5. Read this sentence from paragraph 8.

> To learn more, scientists continue to listen and **observe** dolphin pods as they communicate with each other.

What does the word *observe* mean?

A. watch

B. stop

C. hear

D. catch

Write

How do dolphins communicate? What are some reasons they communicate? Use at least two examples from the text in your response.

WRITING CHECKLIST

- ☐ I explained how dolphins communicate.
- ☐ I explained why dolphins communicate.
- ☐ I used two examples from the text.
- ☐ I used complete sentences.
- ☐ I used correct spelling, capitalization, and punctuation.

Respond to the Focus Question

How do animals work together to survive?

Reread/Think

Choose one text from the lesson to reread. Then complete the column in the chart for that text. Include one way that the group from your text works together. Then describe how that helps the group survive. Fill out the rest of the chart during the Talk activity.

Orcas on the Hunt	Stay in School!	Dolphin Chatter

Talk

With your group, discuss the effects of ocean animals working together. Use the sentence frames to get started. Add ideas from your group members to the chart above.

A group of ___ works together by ___.

Working together helps ___ survive because ___.

Write

Write a guide that tells sea animals how to live and work in a group. Explain what each group should do together and how being in a group will help each animal survive. Include information from all three texts in your guide. Add sketches to explain your ideas.

Protecting the Ocean

FOCUS QUESTION

How do people help sea animals survive?

NOTICE AND WONDER

Look at the three texts you will read in this lesson. What do you notice? What do you wonder? Discuss your ideas with a partner.

WORD SORT

Circle the words that belong in the group "Things That Help Sea Animals Survive." Draw a line through words that belong in the group "Things That Can Hurt Sea Animals." Compare and discuss your answers with a partner.

freedom
predators
boats
scientists
pollution
ocean habitats

I think ___ belongs in the group ___ because ___.

I agree/disagree because ___.

The Manatees' Heroes
by Jackie Letera

Follow Those Whales!
by Mary Lindeen

Saving Sea Turtles
by Zeke Shepherd

The Manatees' Heroes

by Jackie Letera

tragedy = very sad event

1 It is sad to see a baby manatee that is alone and hungry. This **tragedy** happens all too often. These gentle ocean animals can be injured or killed by fast-moving boats. They can also be harmed by pollution and other dangers. When adult manatees die, it is difficult for their babies to survive. Some people feel it is best to let nature take its course, but others think it is important to step in and help.

2 El Centro de Conservación de Manatíes (the Manatee Conservation Center) in Puerto Rico is a place that steps in to help. They care for sick, injured, and orphaned manatees. Staff and volunteers do everything possible to help these lovable creatures. Their goal is to return the animals to the wild. Getting the manatees ready to return to the ocean takes years of hard work.

An orphaned manatee needs around-the-clock care in order to survive.

3 Baby manatees need milk to grow and be healthy. So, the tireless team bottle-feeds orphans around the clock. As the babies grow older, they learn to eat fruits and vegetables. Because a manatee must find its own food to survive in the wild, the team members teach it how. They stick lettuce leaves into slots along a plastic pipe. Then they put the pipe in the bottom of a pool. The animal learns to find and eat the lettuce, just as it will find and eat underwater plants in the ocean.

Stop & Discuss

How does the Manatee Conservation Center help manatees? What is its goal?

Discuss the details from the text that support your answer.

Staff and volunteers help manatees by ___.

The Center's goal is to ___.

4 The Manatee Conservation Center staff knows that manatees belong in the wild. To be **released**, a manatee must be healthy and able to find its own food. It must also be big enough to protect itself from predators. Most importantly, it must be able to swim and reach the surface for air on its own.

released = set free, let go

5 Sadly, some manatees can never be released. For example, when one manatee was injured by a boat, it was hard for him to float in the water. The staff made the wise decision to keep the manatee at the center. They named him Guacara. He is now part of the team. Orphans are placed in his pool, and he shows them how to eat fruit and vegetables.

6 Tureygua was one of the babies that Guacara taught. Tureygua came to the Manatee Center as a newborn. For four years the team cared for him. Then experts decided that Tureygua was ready for release. In February 2020, he and another manatee were transported to the beach. Several volunteers carried the manatees into the water. Soon the animals swam off to live a happy life in the open water.

selfless = caring about the needs of others more than one's own needs

7 The **selfless** team at the Manatee Conservation Center truly are heroes!

Thanks to the team at the Manatee Conservation Center, manatees like Tureygua can grow from helpless orphans to healthy adults.

Stop & Discuss

How does the Manatee Conservation Center know when a manatee is ready to be released to the wild?

Underline three details in paragraph 4 that explain when a manatee can be released and discuss with a partner.

Determine Point of View

- A person's **point of view** is the way that a person looks at or thinks about something.
- An author often has a point of view about a topic. The author includes text details that support that point of view.
- You can think about a text's details to form your own point of view about the topic. Your point of view might or might not be the same as the author's.

Reread/Think

Reread "The Manatees' Heroes." Add details to the chart that are clues to the author's point of view about helping manatees survive. Then review the details and write what you think the author's point of view is on the lines above the chart.

Topic: Helping manatees survive
Author's point of view about the topic:

Details Showing the Author's Point of View	
Paragraph 1	"It is sad to see a baby manatee that is alone and hungry," "This tragedy," "These gentle ocean animals"
Paragraph 2	
Paragraph 3	
Paragraph 4	
Paragraph 5	
Paragraph 6	
Paragraph 7	

Talk

Share what you think the author's point of view is with a partner. Explain your thinking using details from the chart.

Next, share your own point of view about helping manatees survive. Is it the same as or different from the author's? Why?

My point of view is ___. I think people at conservation centers should/should not help manatees because ___.

Write

Write a paragraph describing the author's point of view about helping manatees survive. Include details from the chart and the text that show the author's point of view. End by telling whether your point of view is the same as or different from the author's.

____

____

____

____

____

____

____

____

____

____

My point of view is ________________ the author's.

I think ______________________________.

WRITING CHECKLIST

- ☐ I stated the author's point of view.
- ☐ I included details from the chart and text that show the author's point of view.
- ☐ I ended my response by telling whether my point of view is the same as or different from the author's.
- ☐ I used complete sentences.
- ☐ I used correct spelling, punctuation, and capitalization.

Follow Those Whales!

by Mary Lindeen

graceful = moving smoothly and easily

1 Whales are amazing creatures. They are beautiful and **graceful**, and they are a necessary part of the ocean's food web. Without whales, entire ocean habitats could be in trouble.

2 Scientists like Grace Russell study whales to learn how to protect them. One way to do this is to follow the whales as they move around the ocean. This is called tracking. Tracking can help scientists know what whales need to survive. It tells them where whales go to eat, escape danger, have babies, and more. Scientists can track whales from land, from the water, or from the air.

Stop & Discuss

Why is tracking helpful to scientists who study whales?

Discuss the details from the text that support your response.

Tracking helps scientists learn ___.
They use that information to ___.

3 Tracking from land is the **method** that bothers the whales the least. This is because people and machines stay far away from the whales. However, even though they are very large, whales can be hard to spot. They spend most of their time in deep water, which is impossible to see from land. That makes tracking from land less useful for researchers.

method = way

4 Using boats to follow the whales offers good views of them, but it also causes problems. Boat engines are always in the water, so the engine noise is constant. The noise drives whales away from places where they need to eat or rest. It can also **interfere** with whale communication. Whales use sounds to find and follow one another underwater, and noisy boats make that hard. Boats can also bump into the whales they're tracking. This can seriously hurt the animals.

interfere = cause a problem

5 Planes can offer good views of whales, but they also make noise. In addition, planes require a pilot and fuel, and this can be expensive.

Stop & Discuss

What are the problems with tracking whales from boats and planes?

Underline details in paragraphs 4 and 5 that explain these problems. Discuss these details with a partner.

device = a machine or an object that is made to do a certain job

6 Using airplanes is not the only way to track whales from the air. Another flying **device** scientists use is a drone. Scientists on land use remote controls to fly the drones. Cameras attached to the drones take photos and videos. Later, scientists use the pictures to measure the whales. These measurements can show if the animals are healthy. Drones can even collect germ samples by flying into the breath that whales blow in the air! The germs show if whales are getting sick.

noise pollution = loud, harmful sounds

7 Drones are safer, easier, and cheaper to use than planes. Drones can also go where planes and boats can't because they are light and small. And because there are no humans on board, drones can track whales for a long time in all kinds of weather. Drones are also much quieter than planes, so they create less **noise pollution** for whales.

8 When it comes to the important work of tracking whales, it's easy to see that the best view is from the air!

Stop & Discuss

How can the use of drones help whales?

Discuss your answer with a partner. Use details from paragraph 6 to support your answer.

One way using drones helps whales is by ___. Another way is by ___. Drones can even ___.

Drones can fly through the air that whales blow out of their blowholes and gather germ samples.

Determine Point of View

- Authors include words and details that show their point of view about a topic.
- Remember, your point of view about the topic might be different from the author's, or it might be the same.

Reread/Think

Reread "Follow Those Whales!" Look for details that are clues to the author's point of view. Then review the details and write what you think the author's point of view is on the lines above the chart.

Topic: Methods of tracking whales
Author's point of view about the topic:

Details Showing the Author's Point of View	
Paragraph 3: tracking from land	
Paragraph 4: tracking by boat	
Paragraph 5: tracking by plane	
Paragraphs 6–8: tracking by drone	

Talk

What is the author's point of view about the best method for tracking whales? Use details from your chart to discuss how you know the author's point of view.

> I think the author's point of view is ___ because ___.

Now share your point of view about the topic. Is it the same as or different from the author's point of view?

> My point of view is ___ the author's. My point of view is ___ because ___.

Write

Write a paragraph about the author's point of view about the best method for tracking whales. Include your point of view and explain how and why your point of view is the same as or different from the author's. Support your ideas with details from your chart.

____

____

____

____

____

____

____

____

____

____

____

WRITING CHECKLIST

- ☐ I included the author's point of view about the best method of tracking whales.
- ☐ I included details from the text to support my response.
- ☐ I stated my point of view and explained whether it is the same as or different from the author's.
- ☐ I used complete sentences.
- ☐ I used correct spelling, punctuation, and capitalization.

Saving Sea Turtles

by Zeke Shepherd

1 A sea turtle swims underwater. It is looking for food. Suddenly, a fishing boat passes. It is dragging a net. The people on board are fishing for shrimp, but their net accidentally captures the turtle, too. The sea turtle can't breathe underwater. It will drown if it can't get to the surface. It's a good thing the net has a turtle excluder device (TED). This **clever** piece of equipment has bars that stop the turtle from going too far inside the net. The device also has an escape hatch. The turtle finds the opening and swims to freedom.

Sea turtles have been called "the lawn mowers of the ocean."

clever = useful

2 Sea turtles play an important **role** in the ocean. Some sea turtles munch on seagrass. They keep it trimmed and healthy. Other sea turtles eat ocean animals called sponges. This prevents sponges from taking over coral reefs and forcing other creatures out. Many animals depend on seagrass and coral reef habitats. Sea turtles' actions help these animals survive.

role = job

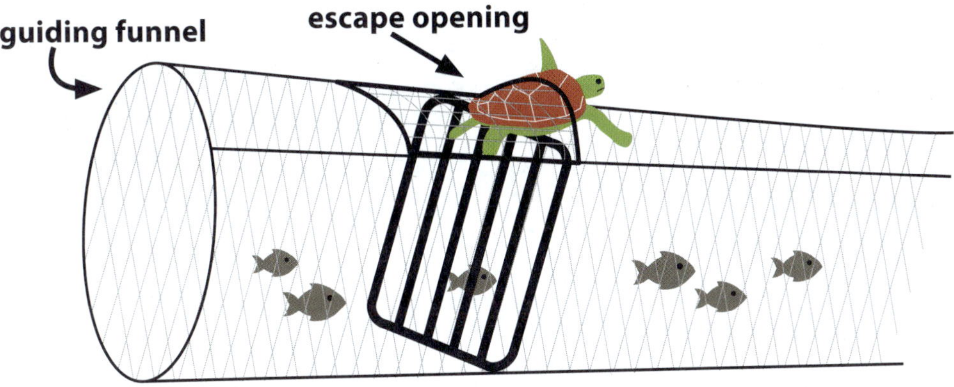

The bars in a TED stop sea turtles from going into the net and guide them to an escape opening.

A gear-monitoring team inspects a TED aboard a fishing boat.

delay = a wait

fine = money one must pay because one did something wrong

3 Sadly, sea turtles are endangered because of human activities, such as fishing with nets. Losing even one of these animals is tragic. That's why people who fish are required to place a TED inside each net. Each TED must be set up correctly. If a TED's bars bend or the net gets stretched, the device won't work properly. That's where "gear monitors" come in. Gear monitors are people who check the equipment before fishing boats leave the dock. Those who fish can call the gear-monitoring team whenever they'd like an extra check.

4 Some fishing boat captains think that having the nets checked is unnecessary and will cause a **delay**. But requesting a check is a good idea. If captains are caught fishing with a TED that doesn't work, they have to pay a big **fine**. Plus, the shrimp and fish they *want* to catch might escape because of a damaged TED. If the gear-monitoring team finds any problems, they will kindly help make repairs.

5 Experts continue to look for ways to keep sea turtles out of fishing nets. And people who fish are helping to test these new methods. When everyone works together, everyone benefits—especially the sea turtles.

Respond to Text

Reread/Think

Reread "Saving Sea Turtles." Choose the best response to each question.

1. Which **best** describes the author's point of view?

   A. Turtles are dangerous to seagrass and sponges.

   B. Sea turtles sometimes need help surviving fishing nets.

   C. Saving sea turtles is of little importance to experts.

   D. Fishing boats have created a safe place for sea creatures.

2. Use details from the text to fill in the blanks and complete the sentences.

   The turtle excluder device has ______________________ that prevent a turtle from ______________________________________ ___________. It also has an escape hatch that allows the turtle to ____.

3. Read the sentence from paragraph 2 of the text.

   > This **prevents** sponges from taking over coral reefs and forcing other creatures out.

   What is the meaning of *prevents*?

   A. helps open

   B. makes better

   C. becomes smaller

   D. keeps from happening

Reread/Think

4. Reread paragraph 3. What statement would the author **most likely** agree with?

A. Turtles can free themselves from nets without the help of a TED.

B. Checking a TED takes too much time to be useful.

C. TEDs must be checked often to make sure they work correctly.

D. TEDs are easily damaged in ocean waters.

Write

Describe the role a turtle excluder device (TED) plays in sea turtle safety. What is the author's point of view about keeping sea turtles safe? Use at least two examples from the text to support your response.

WRITING CHECKLIST

- ☐ I stated the role a TED plays in turtle safety.
- ☐ I described why it is important to keep turtles safe.
- ☐ I included at least two examples from the text to support my response.
- ☐ I used complete sentences.
- ☐ I used correct spelling, punctuation, and capitalization.

Respond to the Focus Question

How do people help sea animals survive?

Reread/Think

Choose one text from the lesson to review.

TEXT: ______________________________

Look at the classroom chart with responses to the Focus Question. Reread the responses for the text you chose. Reread parts of that text, too. What did you learn about how people help sea animals survive? Write two examples from the text.

1. ______________________________

____

2. ______________________________

____

Talk

Share with your group what you learned from the text you reread.

> One thing I learned about how people help sea animals to survive is ___. Another thing I learned is ___.

Then talk to your group about an award you would give to people who help sea animals survive. What would you call it?

> A good name for an award for people who help sea animals is ___. I think this is a good name because ___.

Write

Write about the award you would give to people who help sea animals survive. Include the award's name and how people might win it. Give examples from the texts of how people help sea animals survive. Draw a picture of the award if you wish.

SESSION 1 MAKE CONNECTIONS

Reefs at Risk

TALK ABOUT WHAT YOU KNOW

Use the photographs to remember the texts that you read in this unit. Turn and talk with a partner about what you already know about ocean survival. Use the sentence frames to help you.

Sea animals survive in their habitats by ___.

One special trait of the ___ is ___. That helps it survive by ___.

People can help sea animals survive by ___.

One way that sea animals like the ___ work together to survive is ___.

LESSON 5 **Habitats of the Ocean**

LESSON 6 **Survival Skills**

LESSON 7

Group Survival

LESSON 8

Protecting the Ocean

SEA SORT

Sort the words below into three or four groups. There are no right or wrong answers, but you must be able to explain your thinking.

ocean | seagrass bed | TEDs

orcas | disguise | coral reef | schools

dolphins | predators | fishing nets

sea turtles | pollution | pods

SESSION 2 READ

The Trouble with Ghost Gear

by Kathryn Hulick

1 Thanda Ko Gyi loves to scuba dive near her home in Myanmar, a country in Asia. "When you see a coral reef and schools of fish . . . it's just beautiful," Ko Gyi says. However, one day she went on a dive that changed her life. She and other divers were exploring the ocean when they discovered some sea creatures stuck in a fishing net. The net was a piece of ghost gear. Ghost gear is equipment that gets left behind by people who fish. Many people like Ko Gyi hate to see sea animals suffer, so they have decided to help get rid of this ocean trash.

lines = strong strings used for catching fish

dump = throw away

2 Unfortunately, ghost gear is very common. Ghost gear includes nets, traps, ropes, and **lines**. Around 640,000 tons (580,000 metric tons) of the stuff ends up as trash in the oceans each year. That's the weight of more than 3,000 blue whales. People who fish sometimes drop or lose their gear. Sometimes they **dump** equipment on purpose when it is broken or old. The gear was made to catch sea animals for people to eat. When it gets left behind, the gear keeps on doing its job.

Stop & Discuss

What is ghost gear? How does ghost gear "keep doing its job" after it has been left behind?

Use details from the text to support your response.

Trapped Animals

3 In Myanmar, Ko Gyi's group was looking for bamboo sharks in a rocky coral reef. These small sharks don't hurt people. They live under rocks or in cracks between rocks. Ko Gyi likes to watch bamboo sharks come out to hunt. But a huge net covered the reef. As a result, the sharks and other fish were trapped. They **thrashed** and struggled.

4 "It was very upsetting," says Ko Gyi. She and the other divers tried to save the animals. But they didn't have any tools to cut or move the giant net.

Sea creatures trapped in fishing lines left behind

thrashed = moved wildly

Harmed Habitats

5 Ghost gear doesn't hurt only animals. It harms habitats, too. For example, during a storm, a trap might smash into a coral reef, causing pieces of coral to break. This is bad because coral takes many years to grow back. When a net covers a seagrass bed, grasses die. Nets that drift on the open ocean also cause trouble. Large animals like whales and dolphins can get tangled in ghost gear. Some die. Others survive but drag the gear along for months.

6 If ghost gear is left in the ocean, entire habitats will be destroyed. Some animals or plants will disappear. Fish that are usually caught for food will become harder and harder to find.

Stop & Discuss

How does ghost gear harm ocean habitats and animals?

Use details from paragraphs 5 and 6 to support your response.

Ghost gear harms a coral reef by ___.

It harms a seagrass bed by ___.

It harms the animals that live in the ocean by ___.

SESSION 2 READ

impact = a strong effect

Cleaning Up

7 Ko Gyi saw the awful **impact** of ghost gear with her own eyes, so she decided to do something. She started the Myanmar Ocean Project. It is one of several organizations around the world working to solve the ghost gear problem. These groups clean up large nets and other gear in the ocean. Ko Gyi's group returned to the reef where she found that first net. They removed as much of it as they could. Now animals will slowly return to the habitat.

8 Cleaning up a place helps. But removing a net isn't always the right thing to do. Ko Gyi remembers coming across one area where "the sea floor was just nets." She couldn't even see the sandy bottom. Some of the nets had probably been in the water for several years. Plants and other creatures had made homes in and around the nets. Removing the nets would disturb this new habitat. So the team left the nets alone.

Stop & Discuss

When might Ko Gyi's team leave ghost gear where it is?

Underline two sentences that help you answer the question.

Ko Gyi carefully snips a fish out of some ghost gear.

Making Changes

9 Divers will never find every piece of ghost gear. Even if they could, the damage has already been done. The best way to deal with the problem is to stop dropping so much gear into the ocean in the first place. Organizations like Ko Gyi's are talking to fishing companies about how to make changes.

10 One change is to attach tracking devices to nets. A tracking device is an object that sends signals, letting people know where it is. If a net is lost during a storm, the tracking device can point to its location. Another change is to recycle fishing gear. Some people who fish don't have anywhere to throw away old or ruined gear, so they toss it into the ocean. In Chile and Peru, a group called Net Positiva collects old nets. They recycle the plastic in the nets to make new items like skateboards.

11 People who don't fish might think ghost gear isn't their problem. But everyone should care. When sea creatures are harmed, other animals that depend on those creatures can suffer. Thankfully, there are people like Ko Gyi who are working hard to save the ocean from ghost gear.

Stop & Discuss

What two changes are being made to help solve the problem of ghost gear? How are these changes helpful?

Use details from the text to talk about how the changes are helpful.

Respond to Text

Reread/Think

Reread "The Trouble with Ghost Gear." Choose the best response to each question.

1. PART A

What is the main idea of the text?

A. Thanda Ko Gyi likes to explore the ocean.

B. Ghost gear is a big problem for ocean life.

C. Bamboo sharks can get trapped in nets.

D. Ghost gear comes from people who fish.

PART B

Which detail from the text **best** supports the answer to Part A?

A. "Thanda Ko Gyi loves to scuba dive near her home in Myanmar, a country in Asia." (paragraph 1)

B. "People who fish sometimes drop or lose their gear." (paragraph 2)

C. "These small sharks don't hurt people." (paragraph 3)

D. "If ghost gear is left in the ocean, entire habitats will be destroyed." (paragraph 6)

2. Which sentence from the text **best** shows the author's point of view about ghost gear?

A. "The net was a piece of ghost gear." (paragraph 1)

B. "Ghost gear is equipment that gets left behind by people who fish." (paragraph 1)

C. "Unfortunately, ghost gear is very common." (paragraph 2)

D. "Ghost gear includes nets, traps, ropes, and lines." (paragraph 2)

3. Fill in the blanks to complete a summary of the text.

Thanda Ko Gyi saw nets left in the ocean near her home in ______________________. Garbage like the nets is called ______________________, and it is harmful to ocean animals and habitats. Ko Gyi started an organization called ______________________ to help remove the trash.

4. What is a result of Ko Gyi's effort to help the ocean?

A. There are fewer nets in the water.

B. Coral reefs are growing back quickly.

C. Chile and other countries have stopped using nets.

D. People have stopped placing traps in the water.

5. Read this sentence from paragraph 9 of the text.

> Even if they could, the **damage** has already been done.

What does the word *damage* mean in this sentence?

A. cost

B. harm

C. work

D. trash

Write

Explain the effect that ghost gear had on Thanda Ko Gyi. When did she first learn about ghost gear, and what has she done about it? Include signal words such as *because*. Use details from the text to support your response.

WRITING CHECKLIST

- ☐ I explained the problem that Thanda Ko Gyi saw.
- ☐ I described what Ko Gyi did to solve the problem.
- ☐ I explained how Ko Gyi affected ocean habitats.
- ☐ I used complete sentences.
- ☐ I used correct spelling, punctuation, and capitalization.

Make Connections

Reread/Think

In this unit, you have learned about ocean survival. You have read texts about the challenges to ocean animals and their habitats and the different ways that they survive these challenges.

Review "The Trouble with Ghost Gear," "Ocean Homes," "Deep Sea Survival," "Welcome to the Reef," and "Bobtail Squid: Masters of Disguise." What are some of the challenges for ocean habitats and the animals that live in them? Which ocean habitat do you think is the hardest to live in? Which is the easiest? Write details from the texts that explain why.

	The hardest habitat to live in:	The easiest habitat to live in:
The reasons I think so and the text details that support my thinking:		

Talk

Meet with your small group to discuss the ocean habitats you chose and why. Use the sentence frames to get started.

I think ___ is the hardest/easiest habitat to live in because ___.

I agree because ___.

I disagree because ___.

Another detail that supports my thinking is ___.

Making a Difference

LESSON 9

Young Voices

162

LESSON 10

Books Change the World

178

UNIT 3

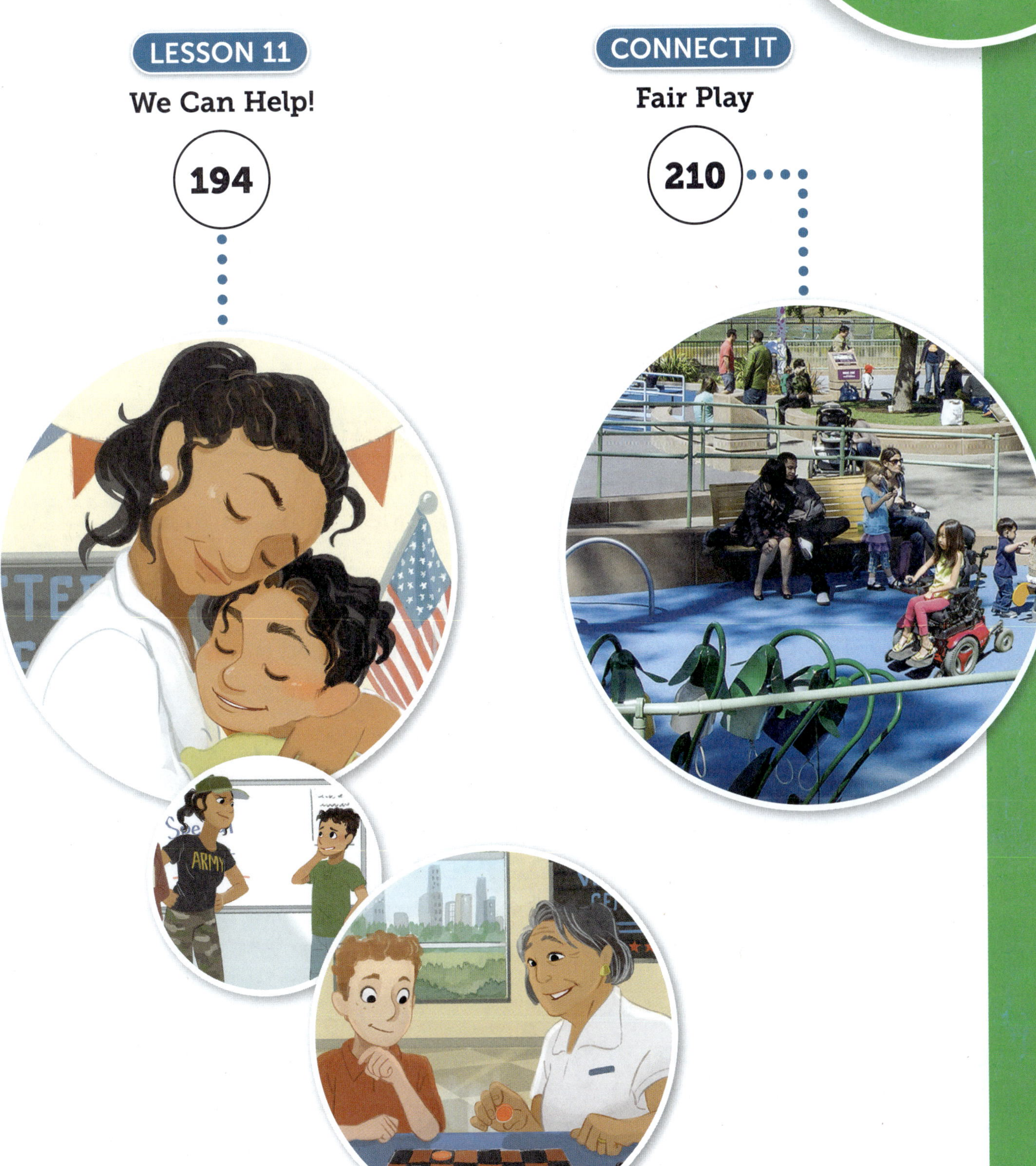

SESSION 1 TALK ABOUT THE TOPIC

Young Voices

FOCUS QUESTION

How do young people make a difference in their communities?

NOTICE AND WONDER

Look at the three texts you will read in this lesson. What do you notice? What do you wonder? Discuss your ideas with a partner.

WHAT IS A COMMUNITY?

The word *community* can mean different things. Read the words below. Underline the words that are examples of community and circle those that tell about communities.

sports teams | proud | volunteering
friendship | neighborhood | town

Calling All Volunteers

by Jacqueline Adams

Citizen Connection

by Theresa Liberatore

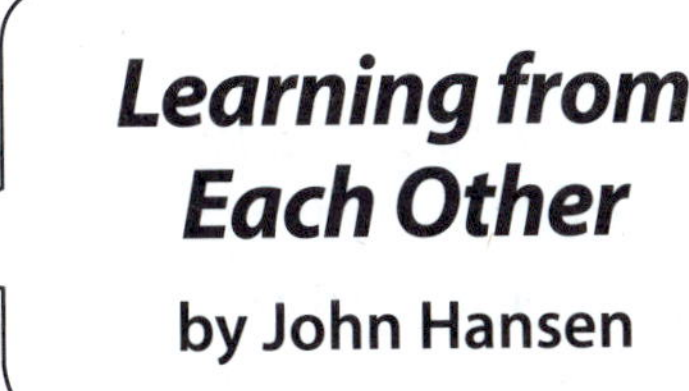

Learning from Each Other

by John Hansen

CALLING ALL VOLUNTEERS

by Jacqueline Adams

Cleaning the beach helps protect ocean life.

leisure = free time

citizen = a person who lives in a town or city

Stop & Discuss

How do the students make their community better?

Underline details that explain what the students do.

1 One spring day, 1,300 students met at a beach in California. They had come from 15 different elementary schools. They didn't arrive in swimsuits, ready for a day of **leisure**, however. Instead, they pulled on rubber gloves and got ready to collect trash.

2 These kids had learned that trash is a huge problem for oceans. Fish and other animals can swallow the trash and get sick. Plus, a beach full of garbage is no fun for the people of the community. So, the students offered to help by volunteering to clean up the beach. They worked hard for hours, picking up large items like plastic bottles. They also searched through the sand for bottle caps, straws, and other tiny pieces of litter.

3 Like the students at the beach, many people want to find solutions to problems they see in their community. When people work on a problem together, they can make a big impact. The beach volunteers filled 23 garbage bags in just that one day! That's part of being a good **citizen**—helping to make your community a better place.

4 Good citizens care about the place where they live and the people who live there. When people help make their community a better place, they show respect for others and their community. For example, they don't toss trash on a beach.

5 But you don't have to wait for a big project to volunteer. Any time you notice a problem in your community, you can step up to help. Some families spend time with residents of nursing homes who get few visitors. Other people clean up after animals at the **local** shelter.

local = nearby

6 You don't even have to leave home to volunteer. Some children write thank-you cards to first responders, such as medical workers, police officers, and firefighters. The important thing is that when you see a community need, you act on it. That's what volunteers do.

7 Although volunteers help others, they also get many benefits. When volunteers work together, they often make new friends. By learning new skills, they gain confidence and believe in themselves. They also feel the happiness that comes from knowing they've helped to make their community a better place. If you want to make a difference, just take a look around. Do you see a problem that you could do something about? Then it's time to volunteer!

Stop & Discuss

What are other ways people can help their community?

Find two examples in the text and discuss them with a partner.

People can help their community by ___.

Determine Word Meanings

- One way to determine the meaning of an unfamiliar word is to look around the word for clues to the word's meaning.
- **Context clues** are words or phrases in a text that help you figure out the meaning of an unknown word.
- Context clues can appear before or after the unknown word.

Word	Context Clues in the Text	What I Think the Word Means
volunteering	"offered to help," "clean up the beach"	helping to do something

Reread/Think

Reread paragraphs 3–7 in "Calling All Volunteers." In the chart, write down context clues that help you figure out the meaning of each word. Then write what you think the word means.

Word	Context Clues in the Text	What I Think the Word Means
solutions (paragraph 3)		
impact (paragraph 3)		
respect (paragraph 4)		
confidence (paragraph 7)		

Talk

Look back at the chart. Choose one word and discuss with your partner how the word is connected to volunteering.

The word ___ is connected to *volunteering* because volunteers ___.

Write

What do volunteers do? Why is their work important? Use two words from the chart in your response.

WRITING CHECKLIST

- ☐ I included details to support my response.
- ☐ I used two words from the chart.
- ☐ I used complete sentences.
- ☐ I used correct spelling, punctuation, and capitalization.

Citizen Connection

by Theresa Liberatore

accustomed = used to

public = for all people

1 Tate Coleman was new to Great Barrington, a small town in Massachusetts. His family relocated from New York City. It was a big change. At 13, Tate was **accustomed** to tall buildings, busy streets, and **public** transportation. He had always taken the subway to get around New York.

2 Great Barrington had houses and lots of grass and trees, but no subways. Most people got around by car. Tate didn't even see any signs for bus stops. The town did have buses, but few people used public transportation. Tate thought that one reason people were not taking the bus was because it was hard to find the facts. "If you wanted to catch a bus, you never knew how," Tate said. "I had to do a lot of research to find out about it."

3 Tate wanted to help his new community by improving the bus system. So, he wrote letters to several local newspapers to call attention to the problem. In his letters, Tate said that more people would ride the buses if they knew where the bus stops were. Some of the town's government leaders, who were in charge of making changes, took notice. They met with Tate and listened to his ideas. And because of Tate's efforts, the town put up signs at 24 bus stops in Great Barrington.

Stop & Discuss

How did Tate share his ideas about improving the bus system?

Underline two ways he shared his ideas.

4 That was just the beginning. Tate wanted to help more people get around without a car. He also wanted to help the **environment**. With fewer cars on the road causing pollution, the air would be cleaner. "This felt like somewhere I could make a difference," he said.

environment = the natural world

intern = someone learning about a job, often as a volunteer

5 So, Tate became an **intern** for the local government. He spent a summer researching by riding buses and collecting facts and information. He counted how many people rode the bus each day. He asked questions. How often did people ride the bus? What did they like about it? What didn't they like? The information helped him come up with ways to improve the bus system so people would use it more.

Stop & Discuss

Why did Tate collect information about local buses?

Talk with your partner about why Tate did this.

Tate Coleman improved the bus system in Great Barrington, MA.

6 Tate worked with the local government to create a plan that was based on his research. One of his ideas was to add more buses at night. This would help people who worked late. Another idea was to add a bus that would take people to many of the town's stores. This would make it easy to shop without a car. A third idea was to add a bus that would travel directly to the nearest big town. This express bus would skip stops, saving travel time.

experience = something a person has done

7 The town and its residents liked many of Tate's ideas. Some parts of his plan have been used to improve the bus system. Tate gained a lot from his **experience**. He learned that any citizen—even a teenager—can make an impact in the community.

Stop & Discuss

Which statement would Tate most likely agree with?

- ☐ The town needs fewer buses at night.
- ☐ The town needs an express bus.

Talk with a partner about why you chose this statement.

> Tate would agree with the statement that ___.

> Tate would disagree with the statement that ___.

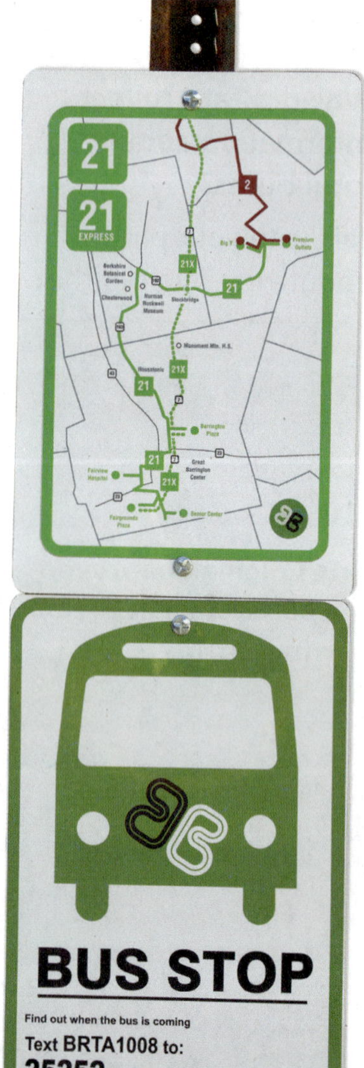

The new bus route has local stops and express stops.

Determine Word Meanings

- When you read a word you don't know, look inside the word for parts of the word that you do know.
- **Prefixes** are word parts that come at the beginning of a word and change the word's meaning.
- **Suffixes** are word parts that come at the end of a word and change its meaning.

Reread/Think

Look at the chart below. Think about how word parts and context clues help you figure out the meaning of the words. Write the meaning in the last column.

Word	Word Parts	Context Clues	Meaning
relocated	• re = again • locate = to put in a certain place • ed = in the past	• "was new to Great Barrington" • "from New York"	moved to a new place
transportation	• trans = across • port = carry • ation = the act of doing something	"He had always taken the subway to get around New York."	
subway	• sub = below • way = street	"to get around New York"	
government	• govern = rule or lead • ment = the result of an action	"who were in charge of making changes"	
pollution	• pollute = make dirty • tion = the act of doing something	"With fewer cars, the air would be cleaner"	

Talk

Look at the chart and think about the words *transportation* and *subway*. How do the prefixes of those words help you understand their meaning?

Choose one of the words to talk about with your partner.

The prefix ___ means ___.

This helps me know that the word ___ means ___.

Write

What did Tate do to help solve a problem in his community? Include two words from the chart in your response.

WRITING CHECKLIST

- ☐ I used details from the text in my response.
- ☐ I used two words from the chart.
- ☐ I used complete sentences.
- ☐ I used correct spelling, punctuation, and capitalization.

Learning from Each Other

by John Hansen

1 It's a Saturday morning in Connecticut. Inside a school gym, both elementary school kids and teen mentors are laughing. They are moving to the fast beat of the music. The elementary kids are helping teach teens how to dance the salsa. These young people are part of a **program** where teen mentors teach elementary school kids English. At the same time, everyone shares their culture, such as music and dance from their homeland.

program = a planned set of activities

2 Teenager Gabriela Garcia-Perez leads the program. She got the idea after helping at an event for families who recently moved to Connecticut from Puerto Rico after Hurricane Maria. The destructive storm caused many people to leave their homes on the island. At the event, Gabriela led activities for the younger kids. The kids all spoke their native language, Spanish. They were new to Connecticut *and* to speaking English. "At the event, the idea of students coming in and not being able to speak the language really hit me at that moment," says Gabriela.

3 Gabriela herself is bilingual. Her parents immigrated to the United States from Colombia and Ecuador. Her family speaks both Spanish and English at home. Gabriela felt a connection to the kids. She wanted to help them feel welcome.

Gabriela started the program where teen mentors work with elementary school kids.

officials = people in charge of a place

4 Gabriela talked to local school **officials** about her idea. She and other teens could share what it's like to live in Connecticut. At the same time, the younger students would learn English. One school principal agreed to try the program.

5 Teen mentors volunteer to work with elementary students to help them practice English. They also do activities together in the gym. The mix of learning and play builds friendships between the students and mentors.

6 The mentors might have thought they would be doing all the instruction. It turns out they have also learned a lot from the students. One important thing they have learned is how to be good listeners. Listening helps them understand the challenges people face when they come to a new place. Another important thing they learned is to respect each other's cultures. Gabriela says one of the best things about the program is how mentors and students are "developing love for each other and for each other's cultures and backgrounds." Together, they are making an impact on their community.

Respond to Text

Reread/Think

Reread "Learning from Each Other." Choose the best response to each question.

1. Which clue in paragraph 1 **best** explains the word *culture?*

A. "part of a program where teens"

B. "mentor elementary students"

C. "at the same time, everyone shares"

D. "music and dance from their homeland"

2. **PART A**

What is the meaning of *immigrated* as it used in paragraph 3?

A. traveled to a different city within the same country

B. went on a vacation in another country from where the person lives

C. moved to a different country from where the person was born

D. moved across the country to a different state

PART B

Which clue in paragraph 3 **best** explains the word *immigrated*?

A. "Colombia and Ecuador"

B. "connection"

C. "She wanted to help"

D. "welcome"

Reread/Think

3. When did Gabriela get the idea for the mentor program?

A. after talking to the school principal

B. after going on a trip to Puerto Rico

C. after helping kids at a special event

D. after learning about Hurricane Maria

4. The text states that Gabriela is bilingual. The prefix *bi-* means "two." The middle part, *lingua*, means "language." What does the word *bilingual* mean?

A. repeating the same word

B. eager to say a word twice

C. meeting two new people

D. able to speak two languages

5. What does Gabriela think is one of the best things about the program?

A. how everyone gets to learn many kinds of dances

B. how everyone learns to love each other's cultures

C. how the program takes place inside the gym

D. how the program uses a mix of learning and play

Write

How do the teen mentors and the new elementary students help each other? Reread the text for context clues if you need to better understand the word *mentor*.

____

____

____

____

____

____

WRITING CHECKLIST

☐ I used details from the text in my response.

☐ I used correct capitalization and punctuation.

☐ I checked the spelling of my words.

Respond to the Focus Question

How do young people make a difference in their communities?

Reread/Think

Choose one text from this lesson to reread.

TEXT: ______________________________

Write two details about how young people make a difference in their communities.

1. ______________________________

2. ______________________________

Talk

Describe one way that you could make a difference in your community.

One way that I could make a difference in my community is by ___.

WHAT WE LEARNED

As a group, discuss how you would respond to this question.

In what ways do young people make a difference in their communities?

Take notes on what you learn from the other students in your group.

Name:	**Name:**

Write

How can young people make a difference in their communities? Use examples from all three texts in your response.

SESSION 1 TALK ABOUT THE TOPIC

Books Change the World

FOCUS QUESTION

How can people use books to make a community stronger?

NOTICE AND WONDER

Look at the three texts you will read in this lesson. What do you notice? What do you wonder? Discuss your ideas with a partner.

TALK ABOUT WORDS

You will read the following words in this lesson. Circle the words you already know. Pick two words that you think are connected in some way. Talk to a partner about how the words are related to each other.

public	community	storytelling
culture	library	free

I think ___ and ___ are related because ___.

Little Free Libraries

by Jacqueline Adams

Storyteller Pura Belpré

by Anika Aldamuy Denise

Marley Dias: Changing the World Through Books

by Alice Cary

Lili Negron

Little Free Libraries

by Jacqueline Adams

1 When Lili Negron was 12 years old, she built a library in a local park. If you are imagining a big brick building, think smaller. Lili's library was a Little Free Library.

2 A Little Free Library is a waterproof box full of books. People have built them in their yards, in public parks, and on city streets. Anyone is welcome to take some books. You can bring the books back later or replace them with different ones. The **motto** of Little Free Libraries is "Take a book, leave a book." A volunteer called a **steward** takes care of the library.

motto = a short sentence that tells an idea about how to live or act

steward = a person who takes care of something

3 Lili was the steward of her Little Free Library. She created it because books were very important to her. Lili's brain was injured before she was born from the way her skull formed. Because of this, she had memory problems that made it difficult for her to learn to read. But Lili got help, and as she got better at reading, she discovered she loved it. "I want to share the benefits of reading with everyone in the community," she said.

4 The first Little Free Library appeared in 2009, when a man in Wisconsin built a box shaped like a little schoolhouse. People were so excited about the idea that they wanted to build their own. Within 10 years, more than 100,000 Little Free Libraries had popped up in 108 countries.

Stop & Discuss

Why did Lili build a Little Free Library?

Underline three details in paragraph 3 that explain Lili's reasons.

5 What makes these little book boxes so popular? One reason is that they help people connect with each other. When people visit Little Free Libraries, they meet neighbors they didn't know before. They might run into someone adding books to the box and start a **conversation**. Another reason is that some Little Free Libraries are closer than the nearest public library. And like a library, anyone can stop by and pick up something to read for free.

conversation = a talk

6 The fun comes not only from books but also from other treasures you may find. One day, Lili opened the door of her library and found a batch of homemade, googly-eyed bookmarks. In New Orleans, a steward discovered a thank-you note in her library. It was from a neighbor who couldn't visit the public library because it was too far away. You never know what you'll find in a Little Free Library!

7 Is there a book that made a difference for you? Why not leave a copy of it in a Little Free Library? Someone else in your community might enjoy it as much as you did!

Stop & Discuss

Why do people like Little Free Libraries?

Discuss your answer with a partner. Use details from the text to support your answer.

People like Little Free Libraries because ___.
I know this because the text states that ___.

Ask and Answer Questions

- After reading part of a text, stop and make sure you understand what it says. To better understand the text, ask a question about it that begins with *who, what, where, when, why,* or *how.*
- To answer a question, look for **text evidence**, or details in the text. Sometimes the answers are stated in the text.

Reread/Think

Reread "Little Free Libraries." Answer questions 1–4 using details from the text. You will complete item 5 later.

Questions	Answers
1. What is a Little Free Library?	Paragraph 2:
2. Where do people build Little Free Libraries?	Paragraph 2:
3. Who can borrow a book from a Little Free Library?	Paragraphs 2 and 5:
4. What are the benefits of Little Free Libraries?	Paragraphs 5 and 6:
5.	Paragraph: ______

Talk

Review your chart with a partner. Compare and contrast the details you each collected. Then talk with your partner about a question you each still have about the text. Write your question in the bottom row of the chart.

After reading, I am still not sure about ___. My question is ___.

Now discuss how to answer your questions. Talk about where you find details to answer them.

We can each answer our question by ___.

One detail that helps answer my question is in paragraph ___. The text says ___.

Write

Use the plan you discussed with your partner to answer the question you wrote in the chart. Explain how and where you found the answer to the question and what the answer is.

WRITING CHECKLIST

- ☐ I asked a question in my writing.
- ☐ I explained where I found the answer to my question.
- ☐ I used text details to answer my question.
- ☐ I used complete sentences.
- ☐ I used correct spelling, punctuation, and capitalization.

Pura Belpré

Storyteller Pura Belpré

by Anika Aldamuy Denise

boroughs = parts of a large city

mission = a purpose, or reason, for doing something

At the New York Public Library, story time begins with a special tradition—the librarian lights a wishing candle. Let's imagine it together. The swish of a match against a matchbox. A candle's flame sparking to life.

And now, our story begins.

1 In 1921, New York City was growing and changing fast. Trolley cars buzzed down crowded streets. Trains rumbled through newly built subway tunnels. Buildings stood taller than ever before. And every day, people from all over the world came to live and work in the busy **boroughs** of New York City.

2 Public libraries were changing, too. They had a **mission**: to welcome immigrant families. Libraries hired bilingual assistants. Because they spoke more than one language, the assistants could help draw new families to the library.

3 In the neighborhood of Harlem, librarians searched for an assistant who spoke Spanish. At last, they found the perfect person: a young woman from Puerto Rico named Pura Belpré.

Stop & Discuss

What can you tell about Pura Belpré even though it is not stated in the text?

Check the detail about Belpré that answers the question. Underline details in paragraphs 2 and 3 that support your response.

- ☐ Belpré was bilingual.
- ☐ Belpré was friendly.
- ☐ Belpré was busy.

4 Belpré had a talent for storytelling. She grew up in a family where someone shared a silly story or tall tale each night. When she began working in the library's children's room, she looked for her favorite folktales from Puerto Rico. But to her surprise, the library didn't have them.

5 Still, she wanted to share these special stories with children, especially children who had come from Puerto Rico, like her. She knew that hearing familiar tales in their own language would make them feel at home. If she couldn't read the stories from a book, she would tell them from memory. This was how family members had told her the stories when she was a child.

patrons = people who come to a place because of what it offers

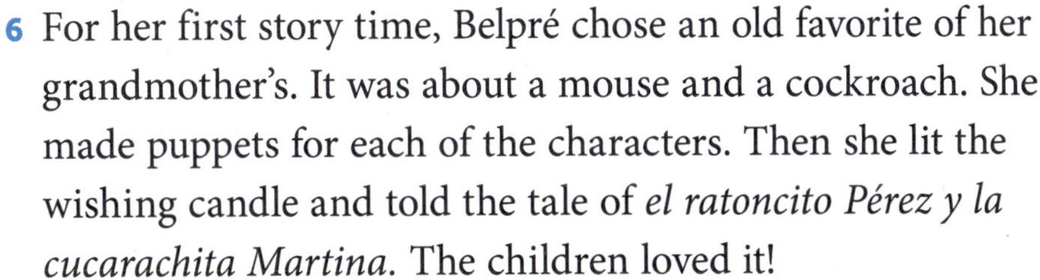

6 For her first story time, Belpré chose an old favorite of her grandmother's. It was about a mouse and a cockroach. She made puppets for each of the characters. Then she lit the wishing candle and told the tale of *el ratoncito Pérez y la cucarachita Martina*. The children loved it!

7 News of the librarian and puppeteer who spoke Spanish traveled throughout Harlem. Belpré found books of fables and fairy tales translated into Spanish and added them to the library shelves. The library began to fill up with Spanish-speaking **patrons**. Belpré invited them to get library cards and return often.

Stop & Discuss

What did Pura Belpré do to bring more Spanish-speaking people to the library?

Use details from paragraphs 6 and 7 to support your response as you discuss with a partner.

Spanish-speaking families came to the library because ___.

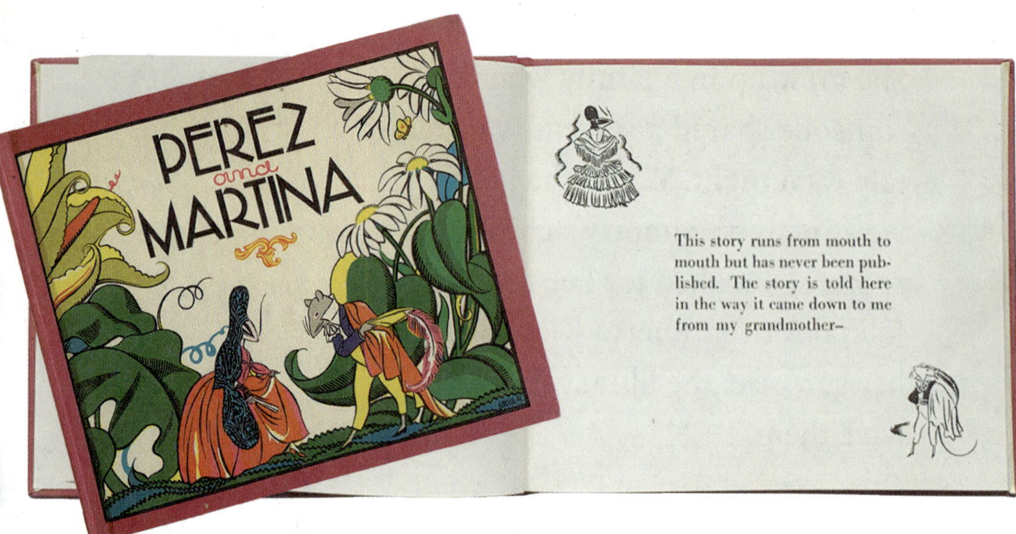

8 Meanwhile, Belpré wrote down the story of the little mouse and cockroach. In 1932, *Pérez and Martina* became the first Latino storybook published in the United States.

9 Pura Belpré was a talented librarian, writer, storyteller, and puppeteer. But her greatest gift was bringing people together in the library. She sparked a love of reading in bilingual children. Because of her, children could find books with characters who shared their language and culture. Through the power of stories, Belpré made the library a welcoming place for Spanish-speaking families.

Colorín-colorado, our story is done. Blow out the candle and make a wish!

Stop & Discuss

How did Pura Belpré use her gifts, or talents, to bring people together at the library?

Underline details in paragraph 9 that tell about how Belpré brought people together. Discuss your response with a partner.

Ask and Answer Questions

- To better understand what you read, ask questions about *who, what, where, when, why,* and *how*. Then use text evidence to answer your questions.
- Sometimes the answers are stated right in the text. Sometimes you need to use text evidence as clues to figure out the answers.

Reread/Think

Reread "Storyteller Pura Belpré." Answer questions 1–3 using text evidence. Include the paragraph number where you find text evidence. You will complete items 4 and 5 later.

Questions	Answers
1. Why did librarians in Harlem need an assistant who spoke Spanish?	Paragraph(s): 2 and 3
2. How did Belpré choose which stories to tell at the library?	Paragraph(s): ______
3. What made Spanish speakers begin to use the library?	Paragraph(s): ______
4.	Paragraph(s): ______
5.	Paragraph(s): ______

Talk

Review your chart with a partner. Compare and contrast the details you each collected. Then talk with your partner about two questions you each still have about the text. Write your questions in the last two rows of the chart.

After reading, I am still not sure about ___. My questions are ___ and ___.

That's an interesting question. My questions are ___ and ___.

Now look for details in the text that help you answer your questions and discuss them with your partner. Talk about what you can do if the answers are not directly stated in the text.

If the answer is not directly stated, I can ___.

Write

Use the plan you discussed with your partner to answer one of the questions you wrote in the chart. Explain how and where you found the answer to the question and what the answer is.

WRITING CHECKLIST

- ☐ I asked a question in my writing.
- ☐ I explained where I found the answer to my question.
- ☐ I used text details to answer my question.
- ☐ I used complete sentences.
- ☐ I used correct spelling, punctuation, and capitalization.

Marley Dias: Changing the World Through Books

by Alice Cary

Marley Dias

1 "If you could change one thing in the new year, what would it be?"

2 Marley Dias's mother asked her daughter that question near the end of 2015. Marley thought for a moment. She was unhappy with the books that were assigned in school. Not one was about a Black girl like her. At home she had read books about Black girls like the ones written by her favorite author, Jacqueline Woodson. But these books were not used in school. "I'm tired of us not being included, of our stories not being told," she said. She wanted that to change.

3 So Marley's mother **urged** her to do something about it. Soon, Marley came up with a plan called #1000BlackGirlBooks. Her plan was to collect 1,000 books about Black girls. Then she would share them with schools.

urged = suggested strongly

4 To get started, she asked for help from adults. They wrote about Marley's project on **social media**, and the idea took off like a rocket. Bookstores, publishers, authors, and readers sent her books. Donations came from all over the world. And lots of people cheered her on, including Woodson.

social media = ways to share messages and news using electronics, such as computers and phones

5 By February 2016, Marley had collected 1,000 books. As she delivered them to schools, more and more donations arrived. In March, Marley brought some of her favorites to her **former** elementary school. Two of the books' authors went with her: Rita Williams-Garcia and Jacqueline Woodson!

former = old

6 Since then, Marley has sent more than 12,000 books to schools all over the world. One reader from Chicago got the chance to meet Marley. She agrees with Marley's mission and says, "I really enjoy books more when I can connect to the characters and what they're doing."

7 Marley agrees with the idea that good books can be like mirrors or windows. You can see yourself in "mirror" books. The characters may look like you, have a family like yours, or enjoy activities you like. "Window" books let you peek into other people's lives. The characters might look different from you, live in another country, or **face** problems that are different from yours. Both kinds of books are important. Encouraging people to read books with Black characters is just one part of Marley's plan. She also hopes people will join book clubs to talk about what they are reading.

face = try to solve

8 Someday, Marley hopes to have donated a million books. Until then, she continues to build a community of readers, one book at a time.

Respond to Text

Reread/Think

Reread "Marley Dias: Changing the World Through Books." Choose the best response to each question.

1. Which question can be answered by reading paragraph 2?
   - **A.** What was Marley's favorite subject in school?
   - **B.** Who helped Marley collect books for school?
   - **C.** Which authors visited Marley's middle school?
   - **D.** What did Marley want to change about school?

2. Read this sentence from paragraph 4.

   > They wrote about Marley's **project** on social media, and the idea took off like a rocket.

   What is the meaning of the word *project*?
   - **A.** show
   - **B.** plan
   - **C.** dream
   - **D.** house

3. Reread paragraphs 5 and 6. How many books did Marley send to schools around the world?
   - **A.** about 1,000
   - **B.** 2,015
   - **C.** 2,016
   - **D.** more than 12,000

4. Based on paragraph 7, what kinds of books does Marley want people to read?
   - **A.** books about important ideas
   - **B.** books about faraway countries
   - **C.** books about windows
   - **D.** books about Black characters

Reread/Think

5. What does Marley hope to do someday?

A. donate a million books

B. visit her former school

C. meet her favorite author

D. talk to thousands of readers

Write

According to the text and Marley Dias, why is it important to read "mirror books" and "window books"? Include at least two pieces of text evidence to support your response.

WRITING CHECKLIST

- ☐ I answered the question in my response.
- ☐ I included an introduction.
- ☐ I included at least two examples of text evidence to support my response.
- ☐ I ended with a concluding sentence.
- ☐ I used complete sentences.
- ☐ I used correct spelling, punctuation, and capitalization.

Respond to the Focus Question

How can people use books to make a community stronger?

Reread/Think

Reread the responses to the Focus Question you and your classmates shared earlier in the lesson. Then review and recount each text with a partner.

Talk

Talk with your partner about the different ways that the people you read about used books to make a community stronger. Share your own experiences with Little Free Libraries, public libraries, and mirror books and window books.

One person who used books to make a community stronger is ___. The way she did it was to ___.

As a group, discuss how you would respond to these questions:

What is the most important thing that you learned about how books can make a difference? How have books made a difference to you?

Take notes on what you learned from other students.

Name:	**Name:**

Write

How can people make a community stronger through books? Use text evidence from all three texts in the lesson to support your response.

SESSION 1 TALK ABOUT THE TOPIC

We Can Help!

FOCUS QUESTION

What does it take to become a young leader?

NOTICE AND WONDER

Look ahead at the text in this lesson. What do you notice? What do you wonder? Discuss ideas with a partner.

WHAT IS A VETERAN?

Think about what the word *veteran* means. Circle the words that are related to *veteran*.

soldier protect teacher

uniform flagpole service

I think the word __ is related to *veteran*.

The reason I think this is __.

Rafael's Plan, Parts 1–3

by Cindy L. Rodriguez

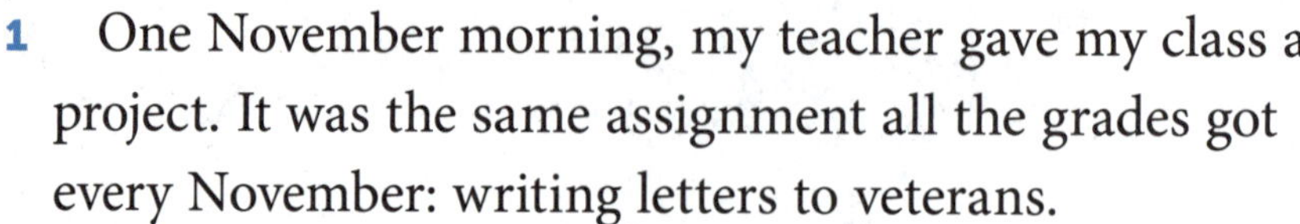

Rafael's Plan

Part 1 by Cindy L. Rodriguez

1 One November morning, my teacher gave my class a project. It was the same assignment all the grades got every November: writing letters to veterans.

2 "If you know someone who has served in the military, you can write to that person," said Ms. Ortíz. "If not, your note will go to one of the veterans at the local veterans center. I will mail them all in time for Veterans Day. Whether you write a short note or a long letter, please write something from your heart. Make it feel personal."

3 I wanted to get my ideas down as quickly as possible, so I grabbed a pencil and my thoughts poured out in a letter to my aunt Aída. She was in the Army about ten years ago, before she became a **lawyer**.

lawyer = a person whose job is to know about the law

4 *Dear tía Aída,*

5 *Hi! It's Rafael. Please don't tell my other aunts and uncles, but you're my favorite! You are strong and smart. You tell good stories about being in the Army. You always make me feel better when I'm sad. It's so cool that you can belly crawl across the floor in the blink of an eye. I've been practicing so that I can be as quick as you. Let's have a crawling race soon!*

6 *Love, Rafael*

Stop & Discuss

How does Rafael feel about his aunt?

Underline two details that tell how he feels about his tía.

7 I peeked at my friend Danny's note. It said, "*Thank you for your service.*"

8 "Are you going to write more?" I asked.

9 "No, this is what I write every year," Danny said with a **shrug**.

shrug = when you raise your shoulders to show you do not care

10 "Do you know any veterans?"

11 Danny shook his head.

12 I was glad I could write something special to my aunt. I felt bad for the people who would be getting dull, emotionless notes like Danny's, from kids they didn't know. I wished Danny could meet tía Aída and some of her friends.

disrespectful = not polite

13 Suddenly, I had an idea. I jumped up out of my chair, but then quickly sat back down. I didn't want to be **disrespectful** or make Ms. Ortíz think her assignment was bad. At the same time, my idea was too good not to share. I calmed myself down and pulled it together. I raised my hand and took a deep breath.

14 "I think writing notes is great," I said. "But maybe we could do something different this year."

Stop & Discuss

What does Rafael hope would happen if Danny could meet tía Aída and her friends?

Discuss your response and a detail that helps you understand what Rafael hopes would happen.

Determine Word Meanings

- **Context clues** are words, phrases, or sentences that can help you understand the meaning of new or hard words in the text.
- **Literal** words and phrases use their dictionary definitions.
- **Nonliteral** words and phrases can be hard to understand because they mean something other than their dictionary definitions.
- You can use literal words and phrases as context clues to figure out the meaning of nonliteral words and phrases.

Reread/Think

Reread "Rafael's Plan, Part 1." Write each nonliteral phrase from the story. Then write the clues you use to figure it out and its meaning.

Nonliteral Phrase	Context Clues	Meaning
Paragraph 2 • "from your heart"	Paragraph 2 • feel personal	• show your true feelings
Paragraph 3		
Paragraph 5		

Talk

How do your meanings for nonliteral phrases compare to those of your group members? Talk about the clues you used and how they helped you figure out the meanings.

> The context clues I found are ___.
>
> I think the phrase ___ means ___.

Now talk briefly about the nonliteral phrase "pulled it together" in paragraph 13. What do you think it means?

Write

Use your group discussion to write about the meaning of "pulled it together." Remember to look around the phrase for clues to determine its meaning. Include those clues in your writing. What does the phrase help you understand about Rafael?

____

____

____

____

____

____

____

____

____

____

____

____

WRITING CHECKLIST

- ☐ I explained the meaning of the nonliteral phrase.
- ☐ I included the clues I used from the text.
- ☐ I told what the phrase tells me about Rafael.
- ☐ I used complete sentences.
- ☐ I used correct spelling, punctuation, and capitalization.

Rafael's Plan

Part 2

by Cindy L. Rodriguez

1 The next day, I was a human jack-in-the-box. I kept popping out of my seat because I was eager to share my new plan for Veterans Day. Finally, after the spelling quiz, Ms. Ortíz nodded at me. It was her signal for me to talk.

2 I stood up excitedly and faced my classmates. My heart started pounding like a drum. "You know the Veterans Center that Ms. Ortíz was talking about yesterday? We're going to take a field trip there next week. And we're going to deliver our letters in person!"

settle = calm or quiet

3 Kids peppered me with questions nonstop, like when we were going and how long we'd be there. Before I could answer them, Ms. Ortíz clapped her hands to **settle** everyone down.

4 "You'll get all the details once Rafael has made the plans," she said. "Right now, though, he has another surprise."

5 "Yesterday, Danny said he didn't know any veterans," I said. "That's a reason why I want to do the field trip. I also thought you could meet an awesome veteran before the field trip. It's my tía Aída!"

Stop & Discuss

What is Rafael's plan? How is it different from what the class usually does?

Use details from the text to tell about the plan and how it is different than usual.

6 My tía Aída jogged into the classroom as if she were warming up for a race. She waved her arms, smiled, and said hello. I wasn't even embarrassed when she hugged me in front of everyone.

7 At lunchtime, when everyone else left for the cafeteria, I stayed behind with tía Aída and Ms. Ortíz to plan the field trip.

8 "I'll hand out the **permission slips**," said Ms. Ortíz. "Rafael, can you call the Veterans Center to match each student with a veteran?"

permission slips = notes that must be signed to allow students to do something

9 Before I could answer, tía Aída added, "Some students might not know what to talk about with the veterans, so you should create a list of conversation starters."

10 "Yesterday, you said you wanted to make a video during the field trip," Ms. Ortíz reminded me. "You'll need to borrow a tablet from the media center."

11 Suddenly I felt very warm.

12 "What's wrong, Rafael?" asked tía Aída. "You look worried."

13 "There is so much to do! Phone calls and conversation starters? It's a lot."

Stop & Discuss

What does Rafael need to do to plan the field trip?

Underline the three tasks that Rafael is responsible for.

Rafael's tasks are to ___, ___, and ___.

leading = being in charge of something

14 My tía put her arm around me. "Yup, **leading** is hard work. But here's a word to the wise. A good leader does three things: delegate, delegate, delegate."

15 "Nice advice, but isn't that just one thing, tía Aída?" I grinned.

16 Ms. Ortíz and tía Aída both gave me a look that meant I shouldn't argue.

17 "Sorry, thank you," I quickly added.

18 They were right. Even the best leader can't do everything. I would ask some classmates to help me. But what if they didn't want to?

Stop & Discuss

What is Aída's advice?

Talk to a partner about what Rafael realizes he needs to do as a leader.

Determine Word Meanings

- Use context clues and what you already know to figure out the meaning of words and phrases in a text.
- Sometimes there are no context clues. When that happens, think about what a nonliteral phrase helps you picture in your mind. You can use that picture as a clue.

Reread/Think

Reread "Rafael's Plan, Part 2." Write the nonliteral phrases from paragraphs 1–3. Then write or draw the clues you use to figure out each phrase. In the last column, write the meaning.

Nonliteral Phrase	Clues/What I Know/ What I Picture	Meaning
Paragraph 1		
Paragraph 2		
Paragraph 3		

Talk

Choose a nonliteral phrase from the chart. Talk with a partner. Have you ever heard the phrase? What does it make you think of?

The nonliteral phrase ___ reminds me of a time when ___.

Write

Write about the nonliteral phrase you or your partner talked about. How does that phrase help you understand the story, characters, or events?

WRITING CHECKLIST

- ☐ I wrote about a nonliteral phrase.
- ☐ I explained how the nonliteral phrase helps me understand the story.
- ☐ I used complete sentences.
- ☐ I used correct spelling, punctuation, and capitalization.

Rafael's Plan

Part 3 by Cindy L. Rodriguez

1 On the day of the field trip, I had butterflies in my stomach. But my nerves settled when I saw how excited my classmates looked. I'd already gotten some help with planning, and other people had volunteered to be assistants at the Veterans Center.

2 When we arrived, my team got to work. A couple of students helped make name tags. Then a few others helped match up the partners from the list I had written.

3 When everyone was settled, I walked around making a video with the tablet. Borrowing it from school was easy, and learning how to use it wasn't **stressful** either. Making a video was a piece of cake.

stressful = causing worry

4 Danny was playing checkers with a woman named María. He was asking her what it was like to be an Army nurse. I found another classmate, Gianna, outside playing basketball with her partner, Jeremy. He used to be in the Marines, and now he was going to college. In the kitchen, my friend José was helping Santiago, a former Navy chef, cook his famous grilled cheese sandwiches.

5 After capturing everyone on video, I plopped into a chair next to tía Aída and breathed a huge sigh of relief.

6 "What a great day! I'm so pleased with you," she said, bursting with pride.

edit = to get a video ready to show people by taking out parts that you do not want

7 "It turned out nice," I said, blushing. "Will you help me **edit** the video? I want to give copies to everyone."

8 "Of course!" she agreed. "May I offer one more piece of advice? A good leader thanks people."

9 I leapt forward and bear-hugged her. "Thanks for all your help!" Then I stood up tall and did the hand-clapping thing Ms. Ortíz usually did to get attention. When everyone was quiet, I was surprised that I wasn't nervous anymore.

10 "I want to thank everyone for helping me with this field trip. It was a lot of hard work, and I couldn't have done it alone."

11 "Thank *you*," said María, the Army nurse. "I enjoyed sharing stories about my time in the service."

12 "Yeah, this was cool," said Danny. "We're gonna do it again next year, right?"

13 At that moment, I was so happy I felt like I could float all the way back to school.

Respond to Text

Reread/Think

Reread "Rafael's Plan, Part 3." Then answer the questions that follow.

1. PART A

In paragraph 3, what does Rafael mean when he says that "making a video was a piece of cake"?

A. Making a video was like baking.

B. Making a video was easy to do.

C. Making a video made him hungry.

D. Making a video felt like a party.

PART B

Which clue from the text helps support your response to Part A?

A. "my team got to work" (paragraph 2)

B. "from the list I had written" (paragraph 2)

C. "When everyone was settled" (paragraph 3)

D. "it wasn't stressful either" (paragraph 3)

2. Complete the chart. Use context clues from the story to figure out the literal meaning of the nonliteral phrases.

Nonliteral Phrase	Clues	Meaning
Paragraph 1 • "butterflies in my stomach"		
Paragraph 6 • "bursting with pride"		

Reread/Think

3. Which detail from the text **best** helps you understand that Rafael has become a leader?

A. "I plopped into a chair next to tía Aída and breathed" (paragraph 5)

B. "'It turned out nice,' I said, blushing." (paragraph 7)

C. "I stood up tall and did the hand-clapping thing" (paragraph 9)

D. "'Yeah, this was cool,' said Danny." (paragraph 12)

4. Which phrase from the text supports the idea that Rafael feels better at the end of the field trip than he does at the beginning?

A. "huge sigh of relief" (paragraph 5)

B. "'so pleased with you'" (paragraph 6)

C. "bear-hugged her" (paragraph 9)

D. "'a lot of hard work'" (paragraph 10)

Write

In paragraph 13, Rafael feels like he could "float all the way back to school." Write three reasons why Rafael feels this way. Make sure to include how Rafael literally feels.

WRITING CHECKLIST

- ☐ I included three reasons from the text to explain the nonliteral phrase.
- ☐ I wrote about how Rafael literally feels.
- ☐ I used correct spelling, punctuation, and capitalization.

Respond to the Focus Question

What does it take to become a young leader?

Reread/Think

Reread the responses to the Focus Question you and your classmates shared after reading each part of the story. Then review and retell all three parts of "Rafael's Plan" with your group.

Talk

Talk with your group about how Rafael becomes a young leader. What happens that makes him want to become a leader? What are some of the things he has to do as a leader? What does he learn about being a leader from his tía?

Rafael begins to become a leader when he ___.

As a leader, Rafael has to ___.

His tía teaches him that a leader must ___.

Take notes as you discuss each question above.

Notes

Talk briefly with your group about your own experiences with being a leader, or about your dreams of one day becoming a leader.

Write

What does it take to become a young leader? Use Rafael's example to write your response.

SESSION 1 MAKE CONNECTIONS

Fair Play

TALK ABOUT WHAT YOU KNOW

Talk with a partner about ways people help their communities. Look at the pictures and use the sentence frames to get you started.

People help their communities by ___.

One example is ___.

This person made a difference by ___.

LESSON 9

Young Voices

LESSON 10
Books Change the World

LESSON 11
We Can Help!

TALK ABOUT WORDS

Read the words below and think about how they connect to a playground. Then tell a partner about a playground you like using these words.

features	design	build
enjoy	equipment	community

Fun for Everyone

by Theresa Liberatore

1 Ava Villarreal happily skips around her favorite playground in Palo Alto, California. She dashes from one play area to another. She swings in the swing zone. She climbs in the climbing zone. She slides in the sliding zone. She spins in—you guessed it!—the spinning zone.

balance = being steady when standing up

2 Before this place was built, playgrounds were not a lot of fun for Ava. She was born with a disability that affects her strength and **balance**. At many playgrounds, Ava couldn't grip the chains on the swings. Plus, it was hard for her to walk on sand and wood chips. So instead of playing, she would sit and watch.

3 Ava's mother, Olenka Villarreal, dreamed of building a different kind of playground. People of all ages, whether or not they had a disability, could use the equipment. They could get around safely, play together, and have fun. Many cities around the country had playgrounds like this.

Stop & Discuss

Why did Ava's mother want to help build a different kind of playground?

Underline the sentences that show what playing on the playground was like for Ava.

One reason Ava's mom wanted a different kind of playground is ___.

4 So Olenka talked to officials in her city. She shared her ideas with them, and they offered her a deal. If she could get the money to build the playground, the city would provide thc land.

5 Olenka worked on the project for seven years. She got help from people in the community. They learned about designing playgrounds that could be used by all people. They met with **experts** who create play equipment. Meanwhile, the community helped to raise money. Some kids even set up lemonade stands. They sold cups of lemonade to neighbors and **donated** the money to the playground.

experts = people who know a lot about a topic

donated = gave something to help people or a group

6 Finally, the Magical Bridge playground opened in Palo Alto. It became one of the most popular playgrounds in the city. Kids with disabilities, including Ava, could feel the thrill of soaring higher and higher on the swings. They could share the fun of zooming down the slide. And they could feel the *whoosh* of the wind on a spinning merry-go-round. Best of all, whole families could enjoy it together.

7 "We wanted to show you can create a park where everyone will come out and play," says Olenka.

Stop & Discuss

How did people in the community help Olenka with the playground?

Talk with a partner about two ways Olenka worked with others.

People in the community helped Olenka by ___.

8 Eight-year-old Sophie Kim, who uses a wheelchair, is one of the park's visitors. "I feel kind of left out at other parks," she says. "But now it's really, really, really exciting." For the first time in her life, she can play with her two best friends at the same playground, side by side.

9 The unique design of Magical Bridge includes special features that make that possible. All areas of the playground are connected by wide ramps. The ramps slope like gentle hills. In a wheelchair, you can glide easily from one play zone to another. There is even a ramp leading to the top of a two-story treehouse!

mound = a small hill

10 Another ramp leads to the top of a tall slide. The slide runs down a grass-covered **mound**. There are also other ways to get to the top: by walking up a staircase or by climbing up the mound. Curved bars all over the mound help people who need to grab onto something while climbing. The slide ends at a small bench. The bench is important for people who would have trouble getting up off the ground. It's also a good place to rest.

Stop & Discuss

What features make this playground good for children with disabilities?

Underline three features of this playground and then discuss with a partner.

The bench at the end of this slide helps kids land safely.

11 The playground has other helpful features, too. All of the swings have bucket seats with high backs and **harnesses** in the front. This design protects anyone who needs support to sit upright. For people who want some quiet time alone, there are cozy bubble-like tubes to hide in.

harnesses = straps to hold someone in place

12 To make Magical Bridge extra special, teenagers volunteer there as Kindness **Ambassadors**. "We greet visitors, make them feel welcome, hand out stickers, and host fun activities," says Colin Wilfrid, a volunteer. Activities include musical concerts, puppet shows, and other performances on the Magical Bridge stage.

ambassadors = people who speak for a group

13 It's no wonder that about 25,000 people visit the playground every month. It's so popular that there are plans to build more Magical Bridge playgrounds. And other groups of people are creating playgrounds similar to Magical Bridge. They will all be welcoming places for everyone to play.

Stop & Discuss

What makes the playground popular for people both with and without disabilities?

Talk with a partner about something that makes this playground popular.

This playground is popular because ___.

The cozy tubes are a great place to take a break.

All kids can play together!

Respond to Text

Reread/Think

Choose the best response to each question.

1. Fill in the blanks to describe why most playgrounds were challenging for Ava.

Ava was unable to ______________________________

__________. Also, she had difficulty ______________________

______________________. She found herself ______________

______________________________ instead of playing.

2. **PART A**

What does the word *equipment* mean in paragraph 3?

A. the items people use on a playground

B. a building for people of all ages

C. people who play on a playground

D. a safety feature for people of all ages

PART B

Which detail from the text **best** explains the meaning of *equipment*?

A. "She dashes from one play area to another." (paragraph 1)

B. "Before this place was built, playgrounds were not a lot of fun for Ava." (paragraph 2)

C. "At many playgrounds, Ava couldn't grip the chains on the swings." (paragraph 2)

D. "They could get around safely, play together, and have fun." (paragraph 3)

3. What challenge did Olenka face with the new playground?

A. Few people were interested in helping.

B. She needed to raise money.

C. Too many children wanted to use it.

D. She had to find a large space.

4. Which detail **best** supports the idea that the new playground is made to help children in wheelchairs?

A. It has bubble-like tubes to hide in.

B. It has stairs instead of ramps for the slides.

C. It has a two-story treehouse and benches.

D. It has wide ramps to connect different areas.

5. What does *soaring* mean in paragraph 6?

A. falling suddenly

B. holding tightly

C. yelling loudly

D. flying upward

Write

Choose one of the young leaders you have read about in this unit. Write about how this person makes a difference in their community. Give examples from the text about how they make their community better.

WRITING CHECKLIST

- ☐ I used details from the text to show how a person made a difference.
- ☐ I used complete sentences.
- ☐ I used correct spelling, punctuation, and capitalization.

Make Connections

Reread/Think

In this unit, you learned about ways to make the world a better place. "Young Voices," "Books Change the World," and "We Can Help!" all contain texts about people who made a difference in their community. If you could help one of these people or groups, which one would you help? Why? Use text evidence to support your response.

I think: ____________________

____

____

____

Text evidence that supports my thinking:

1. ____________________

____

____

2. ____________________

____

____

Talk

Meet with your small group to discuss your response. Use the sentence frames to get started.

I would help ___.

This work is important because ___.

Another reason is ___.

I agree/disagree because ___.

Changes in the West

LESSON 12

On the Move

222

LESSON 13

Travel Before and After Trains

240

UNIT 4

LESSON 14

Crossing Paths in the Changing West

The Ways of the West

SESSION 1 TALK ABOUT THE TOPIC

On the Move

FOCUS QUESTION

What was travel like for early Americans?

NOTICE AND WONDER

Look at the four texts you will read in this lesson. What do you notice? What do you wonder? Discuss your ideas with a partner.

PICTURE THIS!

These sentences are from the texts you will read. Picture in your mind what is happening as you read each sentence. Then choose one sentence and draw a picture to go with it.

- A huge cloud of dust was coming toward them.
- He held a squirming fish in both hands.
- The prairie grasses ripple like waves.

I drew a picture of __ to go with the sentence __.

I chose this sentence to draw because __.

Kindness on the Trail
by C. J. Castaneda

An Adventure on Deck
by C. J. Castaneda

A Storm on the Horizon
by Odia Wood-Krueger

An Uncertain Future
by Odia Wood-Krueger

Kindness on the Trail

by C. J. Castaneda

journal = a record of a person's daily events

caravan = a group that travels together

1 Abigail Miller sat on the dry grass in the shade of her family's wagon. She had eaten her lunch quickly so she'd have time to write in the family travel **journal**. She was glad her parents trusted her to keep a record of their journey to Oregon. But it was hard to find the time.

2 On June 12, 1849, she wrote: *Our* ***caravan*** *of 50 wagons is still in Nebraska crossing the hot, dusty prairie. Our old life in Missouri seems far away. But we are excited to start farming in Oregon. We left home 45 days ago. It might take five more months to reach Oregon. Yesterday started the same as usual. At dawn we ate beans for breakfast. Then we packed up our tent in the wagon. With the wagon full, Father drove while the rest of us walked. Ahead of us, the wheel on the Scott family's wagon broke. For an hour, we stopped and helped them fix it. Their daughter Jane is my age.*

3 *RUMBLE!* What was that sound? She stopped writing to listen. It couldn't be thunder—the sky was cloudless. Someone shouted, "It's hundreds of bison! They're coming this way!"

4 Her heart pounding, Abigail jumped to her feet. A huge cloud of dust was coming toward them. The ground shook. Abigail squeezed into the wagon with her mother and three sisters. They hugged each other while her father stood by the oxen to keep them calm. For five minutes, a long line of bison galloped by, snorting and grunting.

Stop & Discuss

What happens when the bison herd comes toward Abigail and her family?

Discuss with a partner.

5 Finally the dust settled, and the caravan continued on its way. Abigail relaxed. Even though she had been scared, she would finally have something exciting to write about in the journal.

6 The journal! She had left it behind! The spot where they'd stopped for lunch was far behind them. It was too late to turn back. How would she ever tell her parents?

7 That night, she was too nervous to eat supper. She watched the campfire crackle as she gathered the **courage** to **admit** her mistake. Then she felt a tug at her sleeve. It was Jane Scott, from the family with the broken wagon wheel. She was holding a book.

courage = bravery
admit = tell the truth about

8 "The journal!" Abigail cried, relief washing over her. "How did you know it belonged to me?"

9 "You wrote your name in it," Jane said, smiling. "Your family helped us, so I wanted to help you."

10 "Thank you!" Abigail hugged the journal. She couldn't wait to write about her latest adventure and its happy ending.

Stop & Discuss

Why does Jane return the journal?

Underline the sentence that explains her reason. Then discuss her reason with a partner.

Analyze Story Elements

- When you notice details about the characters, setting, plot, and theme of a story, you can have a deeper understanding of the text.
- The **characters** are the people in the story.
- The **setting** is when and where the story takes place.
- The **plot** is the events that take place in the story. You can divide the plot into the beginning, middle, and end.
- The **theme** is the message or lesson of the story.

Reread/Think

Reread paragraphs 3–10 of "Kindness on the Trail." Review the details in the story map below and complete the details about the plot. Then write what you think the theme of the story is.

Characters: Who is the story mostly about? Abigail and Jane, young people traveling to the West with their families
Setting: When and where does the story take place? 1849, in a wagon caravan crossing a prairie in Nebraska
Plot: What happens in the beginning? (paragraphs 1 and 2)
Plot: What happens in the middle? (paragraphs 3–6)
Plot: What happens at the end? (paragraphs 7–10)
Theme: What lesson do the characters learn?

Talk

Share with a partner the theme you wrote in your story map to see if your partner wrote the same theme. Explain your theme using evidence from the text. Change the theme in your story map if you need to after talking with your partner.

I think the theme is ___ because ___.

My partner thinks the theme is ___.

Together we decided the theme is ___ because ___.

Write

What is the theme of the story? Include details about the characters, setting, and plot that help show the theme.

WRITING CHECKLIST

- ☐ I identified the theme of the story.
- ☐ I included details about the characters, setting, and plot that help show the theme.
- ☐ I used complete sentences.
- ☐ I used correct spelling, punctuation, and capitalization.

An Adventure on Deck

by C. J. Castaneda

desperate = having a great need

cramped = crowded

1 Winnie Hall and her brothers, Tom and Oliver, scampered up the ladder to the main deck of the ship. After many stormy days, the ocean was finally calmer. The children were **desperate** for sunshine and fresh air. The wind was icy, but Winnie didn't mind. Being cold was better than being stuck in the dark, **cramped** cabin. Winnie felt bad for her parents. They were in bed, still feeling seasick.

2 The deck was busy. Crew members climbed one of the tall masts. The captain shouted orders at them. Some passengers talked with each other while wrapped in thick blankets. Others stood at the railing. And the chickens squawked in their coop at the ship's stern.

3 Winnie led her brothers to the railing around the open deck. The salty sea air reminded her of the beach she went to with her grandparents, back home in New York. The last time she saw them, they had been waving goodbye from the dock as Winnie's ship set sail. That was four months ago, on January 17, 1849. Would they ever see each other again?

Stop & Discuss

What is life like for Winnie and her family aboard the ship?

Discuss with a partner what life is like for Winnie, her parents, and her brothers.

Winnie's parents are in bed because they ___.

Because of stormy days, Winnie and her brothers had to ___.

4 "Can we explore?" Tom asked.

5 "No, stay with me," Winnie said firmly. "Let's look for land. We'll be rounding Cape Horn soon. We're at the tip of South America. Imagine that!"

6 "All I see is blue water," Oliver said. "And look—jumping fish!"

7 Winnie's stomach rumbled. "I wish we could catch one." For weeks, all they had eaten were eggs, salted meat, and **hardtack**. Mother said the ship might reach California in another four months. She promised the food would be better there. They could even pick fruit off the trees. Maybe California would be all right. Especially if Father found lots of gold! He was going to work for a mining company.

8 A sudden gust of wind sent Winnie's bonnet flying. She ran after it, catching it before it dropped into the sea forever. When she turned back to her brothers, they were gone. Her heart beat wildly. If anything happened to them, Mother and Father would be so upset. The ship rocked. Winnie stumbled down the deck, calling her brothers' names. The whistling wind drowned out her voice.

9 A woman touched Winnie's arm. "Do you need help?"

10 Winnie nodded and explained her problem. Together they checked every nook and cranny. Word got around, and soon a small search party was looking for the boys.

hardtack = cracker or hard bread

The journey west started in the Atlantic Ocean, went around Cape Horn in South America, and then ended in the Pacific Ocean.

Stop & Discuss

What happens to Winnie's brothers? What does Winnie do about it?

Use details from paragraphs 8–10 in your response. Discuss those details with a partner.

ruckus = a loud fuss

sprawled = lying with arms and legs spread out

11 Suddenly, Winnie heard a **ruckus**. Someone was yelling. If there was one thing her brothers did a lot of, it was yelling. Winnie and the others followed the noise. Finally, they found Oliver and Tom **sprawled** on the deck.

12 "Look, Winnie!" Oliver yelled. He held a squirming fish in both hands. "It flew over me and I caught it!"

13 Winnie laughed and cried at the same time. "Don't run away like that again, OK?"

14 The boys nodded. "We didn't mean to scare you. You do so much for us. We wanted to catch a fish for you," said Oliver.

15 "At least you didn't fall in." Winnie ruffled his hair.

16 The sky had turned dark. Most passengers were heading back down to the cabins. Winnie thanked everyone who had searched with her.

17 "Come on," she said to her brothers. "Let's ask Mother and Father if we can cook the fish for supper!"

Stop & Discuss

Why do Oliver and Tom run off?

Discuss your response with a partner.

Compare Stories

- You can compare and contrast stories by the same author to learn more about a topic the author often writes about.
- When you **compare**, you look at how the stories are alike. When you **contrast**, you look at how the stories are different.

Reread/Think

Reread "An Adventure on Deck." Work with a partner to fill out the story map.

Characters: Who is the story mostly about?
Setting: Where and when does the story take place?
Plot: What happens in the beginning?
Plot: What happens in the middle?
Plot: What happens at the end?
Theme: What lesson do the characters learn?

Circle the best ending to each sentence to compare and contrast the stories.

- The main character in both stories (travels to the West / writes in a travel journal).
- Only one story happens (in the 1800s / on a ship).
- Both main characters (want to eat fish / lose something important).
- Only one story shows that (helping others is important / travel by wagon was hard).

SESSION 4 PRACTICE

Talk

Look back at both story maps. In addition to the similarities and differences you noted by completing the sentences on page 231, talk with a partner about what else is the same and what is different in the stories. How do these similarities and differences help you understand the themes of the stories?

In both stories, ___.

One way the stories are different is ___.

Comparing and contrasting the stories helps me understand that the themes are ___.

Write

Think about the setting, characters, plot, and theme of "Kindness on the Trail" and "An Adventure on Deck." How are the stories similar and different? Use details from the story maps and your completed sentences to help you compare and contrast the stories.

WRITING CHECKLIST

- ☐ I told how the stories are the same.
- ☐ I told how the stories are different.
- ☐ I used complete sentences.
- ☐ I used correct spelling, punctuation, and capitalization.

A Storm on the Horizon

by Odia Wood-Krueger

1 I follow Lala up the steep path. I try to step where he does, watching the way the dust puffs up around our moccasins. At almost nine winters old, I spend much of my time following my grandfather, listening to his stories. "*Takojá*," says Lala, "we're here." He reaches back to take my hand.

Takojá = grandchild

bluff = a hill with sharp slope

2 The path takes us to the top of the **bluff**. We look out at the beautiful world below. The prairie grasses ripple like waves. On the horizon, we can see the dark shapes of the bison our people rely on. This bluff has been used to scout game for as long as we have called this place home.

3 Lala rests his hand on my shoulder. "Have you ever seen bison in a storm?" he asks. I shake my head. "Most animals run away from a storm, but not bison. They are brave and run toward it, facing it head on."

4 I wait for Lala to continue, but he doesn't. I wonder if he is telling me to be brave, like the bison. I can see the cuts left in the earth from the White settlers' wagons crossing the prairie. I don't know what will happen in the future, but I can feel change coming.

5 Later that night, I hear talk of an important gathering between our people and the White men. They say there will be a **treaty**, and I hope it will bring peace. Even though I am too young to take part, I want to find out why the settlers keep coming, scaring off the animals and changing the land with their roads.

treaty = an official agreement between two groups

6 The next day, I watch the Lakota men get their horses ready for the long journey. When my eyes meet Lala's, he gives me a quick nod before throwing his leg over his horse, Taté. I feel uneasy as I watch them gallop away.

An Uncertain Future

by Odia Wood-Krueger

1 It has been many winters since my grandfather brought me up this bluff. My son, Canté Wasté, hums behind me. I reach for his hand, like Lala did for me.

2 "What is this place, ***Até***?" he asks.

3 "It was once our home," I answer.

4 We step to the edge of the bluff and I am sad at what I see. Everything is different now. The waving grasses and bison have been replaced by straight fences and wagon trails. On the horizon is a military post. The United States government has broken the treaty. The Lakota are no longer welcome.

Até = father

5 I am reminded of Lala's teaching about bison. They do not run away from storms. They stay and face them, bravely. Since the White settlers arrived we have had to be brave, too. The railroad made it easy for settlers to come here and push us from our homeland. They brought their guns and shot animals for sport instead of food. Our beloved relatives, the bison, are gone. With no animals to hunt, our survival now depends on the United States government.

6 I hear the crack of a rifle. We have been spotted from below by two soldiers! They are riding quickly to get around the edge of the bluff. I know we will be faster on our footpath.

switch = a thin stick

7 I carefully break a **switch** off a tree and drag it over the ground behind us. The dust puffs and makes our footsteps disappear. We will find a place to hide. This is the land of our ancestors. Our feet know it well, even if our minds do not remember every twist and turn. At the bottom of the bluff, we find a spot among the trees where we won't be seen. The soldiers race past and we are safe . . . for now.

Respond to Text

Reread/Think

Reread "A Storm on the Horizon" and "An Uncertain Future." Choose the best response to each question.

1. Mark an X in the chart to show if the detail describes the narrator from "A Storm on the Horizon" or "An Uncertain Future."

	A Storm on the Horizon	An Uncertain Future
takes his son's hand		
hides from soldiers		
sees many bison		

2. What is one way "A Storm on the Horizon" is like "An Uncertain Future"?
   - **A.** They both show an adult talking with a child.
   - **B.** They both explain why railroads are useful.
   - **C.** They both take place on a military post.
   - **D.** They both take place during a storm.

3. What has changed from the time when "A Storm on the Horizon" takes place and the time when "An Uncertain Future" takes place?
   - **A.** The Lakota have followed the bison to a new prairie.
   - **B.** The narrator has forgotten the way up and down the bluff.
   - **C.** The settlers have made changes to the prairie with their wagons.
   - **D.** There are no animals left for the Lakota to hunt.

Reread/Think

4. What is one way these stories are different?

A. In "A Storm on the Horizon," the narrator is on a bluff. In "An Uncertain Future," the narrator is in a prairie.

B. In "A Storm on the Horizon," the narrator sees a prairie. In "An Uncertain Future," the narrator sees a military post.

C. In "A Storm on the Horizon," the narrator is on a horse. In "An Uncertain Future," the narrator is on foot.

D. In "A Storm on the Horizon," the narrator attends a gathering. In "An Uncertain Future," the narrator talks to a soldier.

5. What is the **best** meaning for *sport* in paragraph 5 of "An Uncertain Future?"

A. race

B. pet

C. fun

D. food

Write

Compare and contrast "A Storm on the Horizon" and "An Uncertain Future." Use details from the texts in your response.

WRITING CHECKLIST

- ☐ I explained how the stories are alike and different.
- ☐ I used details from the stories.
- ☐ I used complete sentences.
- ☐ I used correct spelling, punctuation, and capitalization.

Respond to the Focus Question

What was travel like for early Americans?

Reread/Think

Choose a story to reread. Look for information that helps you understand what travel was like in early America.

TEXT: ______________________________

How do the characters travel? What was it like?

____

____

____

Talk

Talk with your group about the texts. If you were going on a long trip, would you want to travel by foot, wagon, ship, or horse? Use details from the texts to explain why.

I would want to travel by ___ because ___.

Take notes on what you learn from the other students in your group about one good thing about their choice of travel.

Way of Traveling:	Way of Traveling:

Write

What was travel like for early Americans? Use details from all of the texts to explain your response. Add your thoughts about how you would like to travel as well.

SESSION 1 TALK ABOUT THE TOPIC

Travel Before and After Trains

FOCUS QUESTION

How did changes in travel in the 1800s affect people's lives in America?

NOTICE AND WONDER

Look at the three texts you will read in this lesson. What do you notice? What do you wonder? Discuss your ideas with a partner.

TRAVEL LONG AGO

How did people travel long ago? Add your ideas to the chart. Then share your ideas with a partner.

travel long ago

Into the West
by Alice Cary

Chin Lin Sou
Builder of the Transcontinental Railroad
by Mary Lindeen

All Aboard!
by Bray Summers

Into the West

by Alice Cary

1 When people from the East first began moving westward, there were not yet any planes, trains, or automobiles. Travel was slow and difficult.

2 In the late 1700s, people heading west rode horses. Most of these travelers were hunters and traders. At that time, Native Americans in the West had been riding horses to hunt bison for about a hundred years. They had discovered the best routes across the land and created horse paths. So, newer travelers also used those paths. On horseback, a person could cover 30 miles (50 kilometers) per day.

3 By the 1830s, large numbers of settlers made the journey west. The West offered land and a better life. So, families loaded up covered wagons with their belongings and left their old homes behind. Packhorses could carry only about 200 pounds (90 kilograms), but a team of oxen could pull 2,000 pounds (900 kilograms). So, the settlers often used oxen to pull their wagons. But even with the oxen's help, the heavy wagons moved very slowly. They might travel only 10 to 20 miles (15 to 30 kilometers) a day.

4 Groups of settlers usually traveled together in long wagon trains so they could help one another during the difficult journey. Many of the horse paths first used by Native Americans became part of the wagon trails.

Stop & Discuss

Why did many settlers use oxen instead of packhorses to pull their wagons?

Underline the sentence in paragraph 3 that helps you answer the question. Use the sentence frame to tell why people often used oxen to move.

Oxen were better for pulling wagons because ___.

5 Covered wagons weren't the only four-wheeled vehicles going west at that time. Some people also traveled by stagecoach. Tickets were expensive, however. For this reason, not everyone was able to travel this way. Also, stagecoaches were small. Any baggage had to fit on passengers' laps or in a small area on the roof.

6 In 1861, a stagecoach passenger wrote about his journey from Missouri to Nevada. The stagecoach was crowded, and the ride was rough. As a result, he and the other passengers constantly bumped into one another. It was a **miserable** trip. Still, it was short compared to other ways of traveling. The 1,500-mile (2,400-kilometer) journey took just 21 days in a stagecoach instead of the many months it took in a covered wagon.

miserable = unpleasant, hard

7 Before long, the number of travelers going west would grow even greater. The transcontinental railroad would soon make going there faster and safer. Trains would cross the country from coast to coast in less than a week.

8 The movement into the West would provide many people with new opportunities.

Stop & Discuss

How was the stagecoach better than other ways to travel west? How would the railroad be even better than that?

Discuss your answer with a partner. Use details from paragraphs 6 and 7 to support your response.

SESSION 2 PRACTICE

Describe Connections in Texts

- A **cause** is the reason something happens.
- An **effect** is what happens because of the cause.
- Signal words such as *because, so, for this reason,* and *as a result* often connect causes and effects in a text.
- Authors make connections between causes and effects to explain what happened and why it happened.
- To find causes and effects in texts, ask yourself, "What happened?" and "Why did it happen?"

Reread/Think

Reread paragraphs 3 through 6 from "Into the West." In each paragraph, identify a cause and its effect. Then write the cause and effect in the table. Remember to look for signal words to help find the cause-effect connections in the text.

Cause, or Why Something Happened	Effect, or What Happened
Native Americans discovered the best routes for travel by horse.	Travelers going west used those paths.

Talk

Talk with your group about each cause and effect you listed in your chart. How did you find each cause? How did you find each effect? What signal words helped you, and how did they help?

One cause in the text is ___. The effect of that is ___.

The signal word ___ helps me know that ___.

Write

Write a paragraph that tells about an important cause and effect in "Into the West." Include details from your group discussion, such as the signal words you noticed. Explain how this cause and effect helped you understand more about travel in the 1800s.

WRITING CHECKLIST

- ☐ I explained what I learned about a cause and an effect.
- ☐ I used complete sentences.
- ☐ I used correct spelling, punctuation, and capitalization.

Chin Lin Sou Builder of the Transcontinental Railroad

by Mary Lindeen

spikes = large nails

1 The sound of hammers striking metal **spikes** echoed off the mountains. In the distance, an explosion of dynamite boomed. The hot sun blazed overhead. Men in wide-brimmed hats wiped their brows and kept on working. Chin Lin Sou, a recent immigrant from China, watched over the work. They were building the transcontinental railroad.

Chin Lin Sou in the 1880s

valuable = very useful

2 Chin got the job as a supervisor because he was bilingual. He spoke both Chinese and English. His skill with languages was **valuable** because he could easily talk with his English-speaking bosses and the Chinese workers.

3 Work on the railroad began in 1863 and involved thousands of workers. Two companies raced to see who could lay the most track in the shortest amount of time. The Union Pacific Railroad started in Nebraska and laid tracks going west. At the same time, the Central Pacific Railroad began in California and laid tracks going east. Later, when the two sides met, the tracks would be joined. Before the railroad, it took months to travel from Nebraska to California. Afterward, the trip took about one week.

Stop & Discuss

What was Chin's job, and why did he have it?

Use details from paragraph 2 to support your answer.

Chin had a job as a ___ because he was ___.

His skill was valuable because he was able to ___.

4 Building the railroad was difficult and dangerous. In California, workers had to build tunnels so the trains could pass through mountains. First, they placed explosives that would blast through the thick rock. Sometimes workers hung over the edges of cliffs on ropes in order to place the dynamite. Next, workers had to clear heavy boulders that broke off during the explosion. Then they repeated these steps until the tunnel was complete.

Chinese workers on the Central Pacific Railroad

5 Few American workers wanted to do these dangerous jobs. So, the railroad companies hired immigrants. They were among the only ones willing to do the work. Thousands of these men were immigrants from China, including Chin.

6 Working on the railroad was hard for Chin and the other Chinese workers. All workers had to deal with bad weather, **landslides**, accidents, injuries, and illness. Immigrants were often given the most dangerous jobs. Few jobs were open to Chinese workers. Railroad company officials knew this, and they offered Chinese workers lower rates of pay than other workers. But Chinese workers helped each other. They shared food, cooked together, and took care of those who got sick or hurt.

landslides = lots of earth and rocks falling or sliding down a mountain

Stop & Discuss

How were Chinese workers treated differently from other workers?

Underline text details in paragraph 6 that tell how Chinese workers were treated.

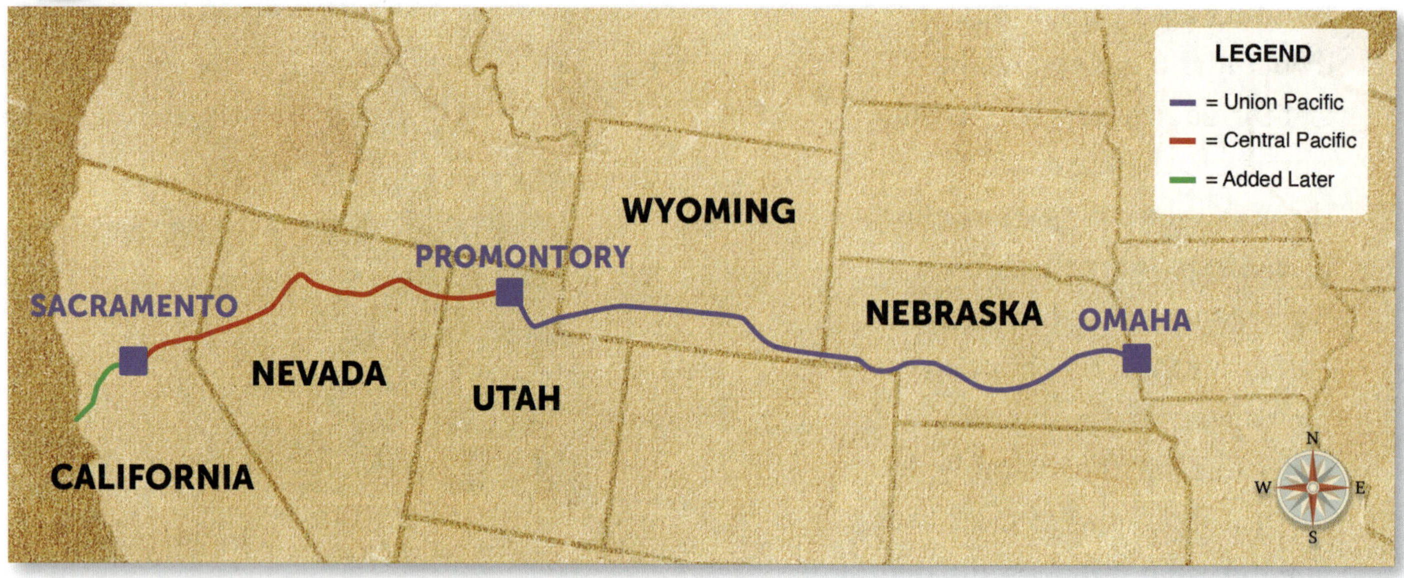

Transcontinental railroad tracks in 1869

7 After six years and almost 2,000 miles (3,200 km) of new track, the railroad was completed. The two tracks were joined together in Utah on May 10, 1869. A big celebration was held. **Officials** from both railroads were there, as well as some of the workers. But after the celebration, almost all of the workers, including the Chinese workers, lost their jobs. There was no more track to build.

officials = people who have important jobs in a business

stained-glass portrait = a picture of a person, made from colorful pieces of glass

8 Chin found work in the gold mines in Colorado. At first he was a supervisor, as he had been for the railroad. Later, Chin became the owner of two mines that gave jobs to Chinese workers. When he sold the mines, he became very rich. In Denver, Chin later became known as the "Mayor of Chinatown." After his death, he was honored with a **stained-glass portrait** in the Colorado State Capitol.

9 Chin Lin Sou and his fellow immigrant workers played an important part in the history of the United States. They faced enormous dangers and unfair treatment. And yet, without them, the railroad that connected the nation could not have been built.

Stop & Discuss

What did Chin and his fellow immigrant workers do that was important for the United States?

Reread paragraph 9. Underline the sentence that helps you figure out what important thing they did.

Describe Connections in Texts

- **Sequence** is the order in which things happen.
- Signal words about time such as *first, second, third, next, last, later, before,* and *then* all show sequence. Numbers and dates also show sequence.
- Authors use sequence when the order of events matters.
- Ask yourself, "What happened first?" and "What happened next?" to understand the sequence in a text.

Reread/Think

Reread "Chin Lin Sou: Builder of the Transcontinental Railroad." Complete the chart to tell about the important events in Chin's life in sequence.

1863	
1869	
Then	
Later	
A few years later	
Last	

Talk

Talk with your group about the sequence of events you listed in your chart. How did noticing dates and signal words help you understand the sequence of events in Chin's life?

The dates and signal words helped me know ___.

Now talk with your group about how the events in Chin's life made him an important part of United States history.

The events in Chin's life helped to ___.

Write

Write a paragraph that tells what happened in Chin's life and how those events changed the United States. Explain how the dates and signal words help you understand Chin's life over time.

WRITING CHECKLIST

- ☐ I described the sequence of events in Chin's life.
- ☐ I explained what the sequence of events helped me to understand.
- ☐ I used complete sentences.
- ☐ I used correct spelling, punctuation, and capitalization.

ALL ABOARD!

by Bray Summers

1 One day in 1875, William Smith stepped off a train in San Francisco, California. He had come from Illinois on the transcontinental railroad. "Just think of it," he later wrote excitedly to his sister, "we traveled nearly 2,000 miles [3,200 kilometers] in five days."

2 But Smith wasn't the only person amazed by the transcontinental railroad. Construction on the tracks had been a huge project. It had started in 1863 and had taken six long years. At last, on May 10, 1869, the final spike connected the eastern and western rail lines. Right away, **telegraph** messages with the exciting news were sent out across the nation. People stopped whatever they were doing to celebrate. They rang bells, blew whistles, and cheered.

telegraph = a way of sending messages over wires, often to places that are far away

3 Why all the excitement? Well, finally there was a much faster way to reach the West. Trains could cross the United States in less than a week while other types of travel took months. Because travel was now much easier, more people would choose to move. And once they did move, they could still visit family and friends if they wished.

4 The railroad helped more than travelers. Factories could now ship goods almost anywhere by train. Therefore, items like food, clothing, and tools became easier to get.

5 But the railroad also caused much pain and destruction. While it was being built, the United States government took land from Native Americans and gave it to railroad companies. As a result, many Native people were forced to leave the very land they depended upon and loved.

6 The trouble didn't end there. Many Native peoples hunted bison, which they needed for food, shelter, and clothing. As a Northwestern Shoshone chief explained, "The railroads pass through my country and have scared the game all away." And there was another problem. White hunters riding the trains shot millions of bison from the train cars. As a result, Native Americans in those areas lost their main source of survival.

bustling = lively, busy

7 The railroads brought suffering to the Native people. Too often, railroad owners chose making money over respecting the rights of Native Americans. By 1893, four additional transcontinental rail lines were built. About 7,000 train stations and water stops grew into **bustling** towns and cities. The changes would destroy the way of life that Native Americans had known for centuries.

Cheyenne, Wyoming

Respond to Text

Reread/Think

Reread "All Aboard!" Choose the best response to each question.

1. Which sentence from the text shows a cause-effect connection?

A. "One day in 1875, William Smith stepped off a train in San Francisco, California." (paragraph 1)

B. "Because travel was now easier, more people would choose to move." (paragraph 3)

C. "Many Native peoples hunted bison, which they needed for food, shelter, and clothing." (paragraph 6)

D. "By 1893, four additional transcontinental rail lines were built." (paragraph 7)

2. What happened because of faster, easier train travel?

A. Factories could send goods almost anywhere in the country.

B. Towns and cities could bring in water from faraway lakes.

C. Native Americans had better access to shelter.

D. Railroad track cost less to build.

3. Read this sentence from paragraph 7 of the text.

The railroads brought **suffering** to the Native people.

What does the word *suffering* mean?

A. food and supplies

B. a new way to travel

C. noise and dirt

D. a time of difficulty

Reread/Think

4. What problem did the transcontinental railroad cause?

A. It became harder for people to move to new cities.

B. The government was unable to buy more tracks.

C. Native Americans were forced to leave their land.

D. The noise from the trains scared passengers.

5. What is the main idea of the text?

A. The construction of the transcontinental railroad created a large number of jobs.

B. The noise from the transcontinental railroad led to the disappearance of the bison.

C. The transcontinental railroad caused many people to move away from large cities.

D. The transcontinental railroad made life easier for some but more difficult for others.

Write

Write about the transcontinental railroad. How did it affect life when it was complete? What were some good and bad things that happened because of it? Use at least two examples from the text.

____

____

____

____

____

____

____

WRITING CHECKLIST

- ☐ I wrote about the railroad.
- ☐ I explained the good and bad effects of it.
- ☐ I used examples from the text.
- ☐ I used complete sentences.
- ☐ I used correct spelling, punctuation, and capitalization.

Respond to the Focus Question

How did changes in travel in the 1800s affect people's lives in America?

Reread/Think

Choose one text from the lesson to review.

TEXT: ______________________________

Reread the responses to the Focus Question for the text you chose. Write two things you learned about how changes in travel in the 1800s affected people's lives in America.

1. ______________________________

____

____

2. ______________________________

____

____

Talk

Share with your group what you learned from your text. Listen as your classmates share what they learned.

Then discuss with your group how changes in travel both helped and hurt people.

Changes in travel helped people by ___.

Changes in travel hurt people by ___.

Write

How did changes in travel in the 1800s affect people's lives in America? Write about the helpful and harmful effects, using details from all three texts.

SESSION 1 TALK ABOUT THE TOPIC

Crossing Paths in the Changing West

FOCUS QUESTION

What is it like to journey to a new place and meet new people?

NOTICE AND WONDER

Look at the illustrations in this lesson. They are all part of one story you will read. What do you notice? What do you wonder? Discuss your ideas with a partner.

WORD PAIRS

Draw lines to match each word on the left with a word on the right that is a close match to its meaning. Compare and discuss your answers with a partner.

travel	grassland
prairie	live
settle	journey

I think ___ is close to the meaning of ___ because ___.

I agree/disagree because ___.

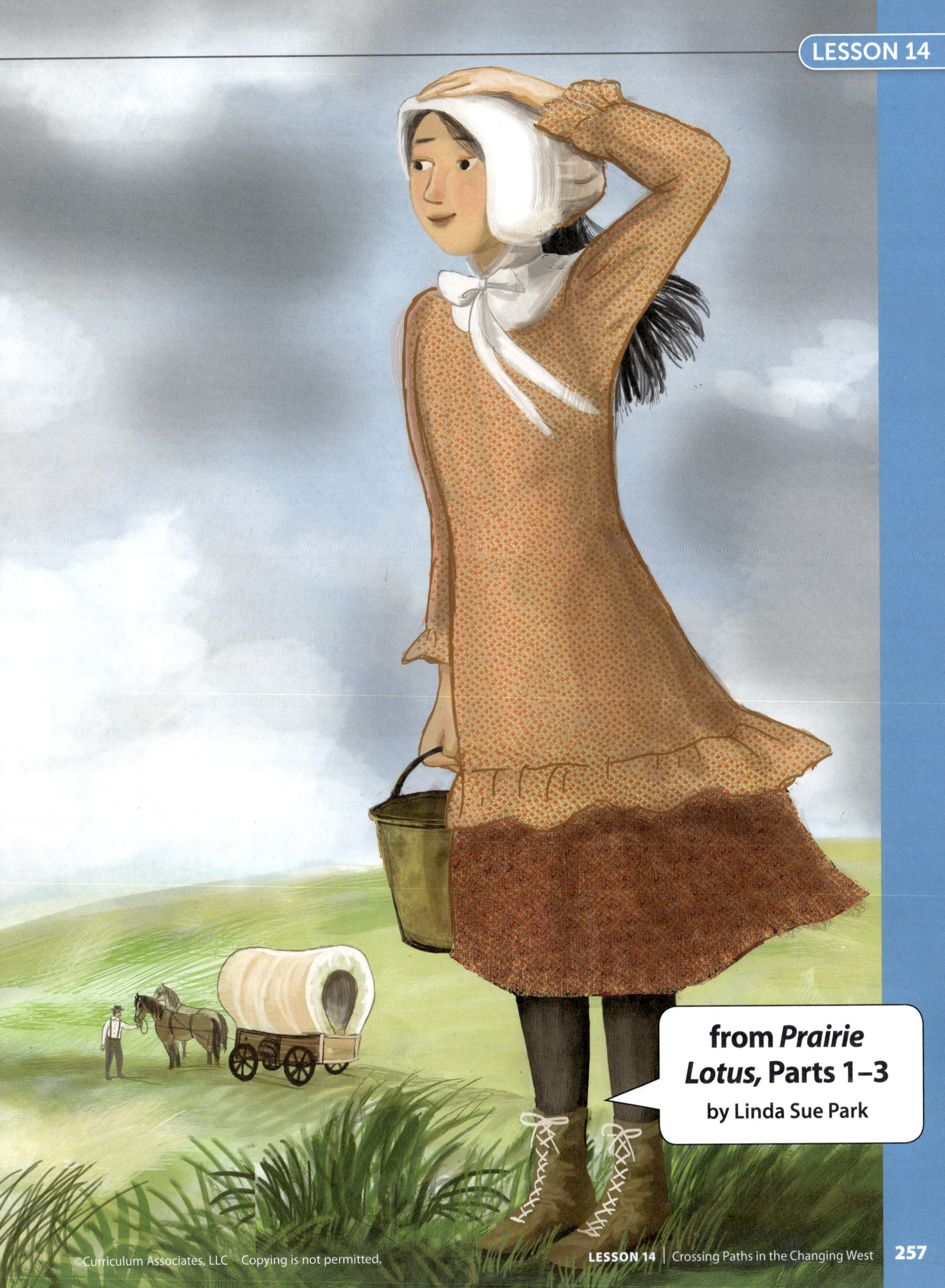

from *Prairie Lotus*, Parts 1–3

by Linda Sue Park

from *Prairie Lotus*

Part 1

by Linda Sue Park

It is 1880. Hanna and her father have left their home in California. They are looking for somewhere to settle in the western territories of the United States. Hanna is half-Chinese and half-White. She hopes to find a home where she can go to school and her father can open a shop.

1 "Should be our last day," Papa said when they stopped to make camp. He unhitched the tired horses from the wagon, then led them down a little draw to water, while Hanna began clearing the ground for a fire.

2 They had journeyed for almost a month since leaving Cheyenne, their most recent stretch in near three years of travel. Three years without a real home. Tomorrow they would reach their **destination**: LaForge, a railroad town in Dakota Territory.

destination = end of a journey

picket lines = ropes to tie horses to, so the horses can't run away

3 Hanna was looking forward to cooking supper. They had been able to buy groceries in North Platte, but since then, it had rained for almost a solid week. They'd had to make do with meal after meal of stale biscuit and cold beans.

4 She had put dried codfish to soak the night before. *Soup,* she thought. *With onions and potatoes.*

5 Papa returned with the horses and a bucket of water. He fastened the horses to their **picket lines**, then left again to gather some brushwood.

Stop & Discuss

What has the journey been like for Hanna and Papa?

Underline details in paragraphs 2 and 3 that help you figure out what the journey has been like.

6 "I'm going to make soup," she told him when he returned to start the fire.

7 "About time we had a hot meal," he said.

8 Hanna **bristled** at the note of **petulance** in his voice; the dreary weather of the past week was hardly her fault. But she said nothing, not wanting to start a row.

bristled = became angry

petulance = childish anger

9 "Sky's clearing," he said. "Maybe it'll be easier to scare up a rabbit or something." He went off.

10 Hanna watched him until he vanished behind a low rise. The endless prairie looked flat at first glance, but the land was never completely level. Rain had rinsed the gray and beige plains, leaving behind a translucence of green that was growing denser every day.

11 She lifted the three-legged cast-iron spider from its hook on one of the wagon bows; it was deep enough to make soup for two people. Spider in hand, she jumped to the ground, took a few steps, and stopped in mid-stride.

12 A group of Indians stood in a loose semicircle between the wagon and the fire.

Stop & Discuss

What do you think Hanna is thinking when she stops in mid-stride?

Discuss your response with a partner. Explain why you think as you do.

Connect Words and Pictures

- Words and **illustrations**, or pictures, work together to help you understand how characters look, feel, and act. **Characters** are the animals or people a story is about.
- Words and illustrations also work together to help you understand what the setting looks like. The **setting** is when and where a story takes place.

Reread/Think

Reread Part 1 of *Prairie Lotus* and look at the illustration. Circle details in the illustration below that help you understand more about the setting and characters. Then write what you know about the setting and characters on the chart.

Setting	Characters

Talk

Talk to a partner about the details you circled and wrote about in the chart. How do these details help you understand the setting and characters?

In this part of the illustration, I see ___. This helps me understand ___ about the setting.

In this part of the illustration, I see ___. This helps me understand ___ about the characters.

The illustration gives me more information about the part of the text that says ___.

Write

Think about the details you circled on the illustration and the discussion you had with a partner. Write about how the illustration supports what is happening in the story.

____

____

____

____

____

____

____

____

____

____

____

WRITING CHECKLIST

- ☐ I used details I circled and my partner talk to respond to the writing prompt.
- ☐ I used complete sentences.
- ☐ I used correct spelling, punctuation, and capitalization.

from *Prairie Lotus* Part 2

by Linda Sue Park

1 Hanna had seen Indians from the wagon several times, but always at a distance. At such moments, Papa seemed watchful but not particularly worried. He told her that the government had forced the Indians in this region, most of them members of the Sioux tribe, off the wide-open prairie and onto **tracts** of land reserved for them. They were not allowed to leave that land without special permission from the reservation's Indian agent.

tracts = large areas of land

2 Hanna looked over the group quickly. Three women, the eldest with gray-streaked hair. A girl a few years younger than Hanna, and two little girls. The women were wearing faded blankets or shawls. They carried cloth sacks or bundles; one had a baby tied to her back.

conjure = make something, almost out of nothing

3 Mothers and daughters. Hanna thought at once of Mama. *What would she say or do if she were here?*

4 "Hello," she said. "I was just going to make soup. Would you like some?"

5 Mama had been a great believer in soup. She could **conjure** delicious soups from nothing but scraps and bones, and she had taught Hanna the secret: One strongly flavored ingredient could make the whole pot of leftovers tasty, and you didn't need much of it. Dried mushrooms, cabbage, and garlic were all good. So was dried fish.

Stop & Discuss

How do Hanna's memories of her mother help her know what to do when she meets the new people?

Share your answer with a partner. Use details from the text to support your answer.

6 Hanna used the big pot instead of the spider. She cut up the potatoes smaller than usual, so they would cook more quickly. The Indians sat on the ground near the fire. Hanna was anxious to serve them, but she forced herself to wait until the potatoes were properly cooked through.

pursed = pressed together

7 Hanna had enough spoons for her guests, but only four bowls. The oldest of the Sioux women seemed to be the group's leader, so Hanna served her first. She glanced down at the soup in her bowl, then looked up, **pursed** her lips, and motioned with her chin toward Hanna.

8 Hanna understood at once. *She wants to be sure that I eat too.*

9 She filled two more bowls and handed them out for the rest of the group to share. The fourth bowl was for herself. She sat on the wagon steps to eat, near the group but not with them.

Stop & Discuss

How do Hanna and the women act toward one another?

Underline details that tell about their thoughts and feelings. Share your answer with a partner.

10 The women talked quietly among themselves.

11 —Oyu'l waste

12 —Sku'ya sni

13 —Nina ota mnisku'ya kte hchin

14 Hanna wondered what they were saying, but at least she could tell that they were enjoying the soup. After the oldest woman tasted it, she said something to the others. Then another woman had a bite and said something else. They each took a second taste and had further conversation. It was just like Mama's friends in Chinatown, or the lady visitors at Miss Lorna's boardinghouse: They were talking about the soup—the ingredients, the flavors.

15 By the end of the meal, the two little girls had grown brave enough to draw closer to Hanna. When she smiled at them, they shrieked in delight and ran back to the others.

Stop & Discuss

What does Hanna learn, or realize, about the women?

Use details from the text to discuss your answer with a partner.

Hanna learns that ___.

Hanna could tell ___ because ___.

Connect Words and Pictures

You know the text, or the story, and illustrations work together to tell about characters and settings. They also work together to create mood. The **mood** of a story is the feeling the story gives you, such as scary, funny, happy, or sad.

Reread/Think

Reread Part 2 of *Prairie Lotus* and look at the illustrations from the story below. Circle details in the illustrations that create the mood. Then write what you think the mood is on the lines.

The mood is cautious but friendly. ______________________

____

____

The mood is ______________________

____

____

Talk

Talk to a partner about the details you circled. How do the details help you understand the mood?

> In this part of the illustration, I see ___.
> This makes me think the mood is ___.

Now talk about the text. What details in the text also help you understand this mood?

> In this part, the text says ___.

Write

Think about the illustration details and the discussion you had with a partner. Select one of the illustrations you discussed and write about how the text and the illustration work together to create a mood in the story.

WRITING CHECKLIST

- ☐ I used the circled details and my partner talk to write my response.
- ☐ I used complete sentences.
- ☐ I used correct spelling, punctuation, and capitalization.

____

____

____

____

____

____

____

____

____

____

____

from *Prairie Lotus*

Part 3 by Linda Sue Park

> **exchange** = talk
>
> **hesitantly** = slowly and shyly

1 The women rose to leave.

2 *Mama always gave guests food to take home.* She [Hanna] turned and hurried to the wagon, found an empty flour sack, and put in a few fistfuls of dried beans, then returned to her guests. She handed the sack to the gray-haired elder.

3 The old woman turned and had a brief **exchange** with her companions. One of them reached into her bundle, pulled something out, and passed it to the leader.

4 It looked like a string of small white onions, or perhaps bulbs of garlic, braided together by their stems.

5 The old woman nodded at Hanna, then said something that sounded like "timp-sina." She gave the braid a little shake.

6 "Timp-sina?" Hanna repeated **hesitantly**.

7 The little girls giggled, and the women smiled.

8 "Timpsina," Hanna said again, this time with more certainty.

9 The old woman gave the braid to Hanna, who examined it with interest.

10 The woman pursed her lips again; this time she jerked her chin toward the kettle on the fire.

11 *It's as if she's pointing with her lips,* Hanna thought. "I cook them in water?" she asked. She pointed at the kettle.

12 Shaking her head, the woman motioned toward the kettle again, and then toward the sky, tracing the path of the sun from east to west. She held up three fingers.

13 "Oh! I should soak them for three days, before I cook them?" She made appropriate gestures as she spoke.

14 The old woman smiled and nodded. Then she waved toward one of the empty soup bowls.

murmurs = whispers

curiosity = wanting to know or learn

15 "Soak for three days and then use them in soup?"

16 At that, the other women broke into **murmurs** of agreement, and the leader nodded again approvingly.

17 "Thank you," Hanna said. "Thank you for the—the timpsina."

18 As the Indians departed, one of the little girls turned her head to stare at Hanna. Her eyes were very dark, almost black, and at the same time, bright with **curiosity**.

19 Hanna and the girl looked at each other for a long time, until the Indians disappeared beyond a rise in the prairie.

Respond to Text

Reread/Think

Reread Part 3 of *Prairie Lotus*. Choose the best response to each question.

1. PART A

Based on the illustration on page 267, what is the mood of this first part of the story?

A. angry

B. happy

C. lonely

D. funny

PART B

Which detail from the text **best** supports your answer in Part A?

A. "She . . . returned to her guests." (paragraph 2)

B. "One of them reached into her bundle. . . ." (paragraph 3)

C. "The old woman nodded. . . ." (paragraph 5)

D. ". . . the women smiled." (paragraph 7)

2. What does the word *examined* mean in paragraph 9?

A. cooked

B. enjoyed

C. looked at

D. gave back

3. What does the illustration on page 268 help you understand about the prairie setting?

A. It is a beach near the ocean.

B. It is flat land and rolling hills.

C. It has lush trees and plant life.

D. It has dry, desert-like land.

Reread/Think

4. What do the details in the illustration on page 268 help you understand about the end of the story?

A. Hanna is afraid to be by herself.

B. Hanna is upset the soup is gone.

C. Hanna is thankful for the experience.

D. Hanna is mad her guests are leaving.

Write

How do both the illustrations and the text help you understand how Hanna's feelings change during the story? Support your response with at least two details from the text and illustrations.

WRITING CHECKLIST

- ☐ I answered the question.
- ☐ I included a topic sentence.
- ☐ I included at least two details to support my response.
- ☐ I used complete sentences.
- ☐ I used correct spelling, punctuation, and capitalization.

Respond to the Focus Question

What is it like to journey to a new place and meet new people?

Reread/Think

Reread one part of *Prairie Lotus* and complete the question below for your part of the text. Review the classroom chart with answers to the Focus Question to support your thinking. Then share your answers for your part of the text with your group.

PART NUMBER: from *Prairie Lotus*, Part ______________________

In this part of the story, what is it like for Hanna to journey to a new place and meet new people? Write two examples from the text.

1. ____

____

2. ____

____

Talk

Work in a group to share what you learned about Hanna's journey to a new place. Use the sentence frames to start your discussion.

One thing I learned about Hanna's journey is ___.

Another thing I learned from the story is that ___.

Write

With your group, write questions to ask Hanna about her journey. Then work together to write the answer to each question.

Pick one group member to role-play being Hanna. The rest of the group will act like reporters and ask "Hanna" questions. Use the questions and answers your group wrote to find out from Hanna what it is like to journey to a new place and meet new people.

SESSION 1 MAKE CONNECTIONS

The Ways of the West

TALK ABOUT WHAT YOU KNOW

Turn and talk with a partner about what you know about changes in the West in the 1800s. Use the pictures and the sentence frames to help you.

Before settlers came to the West, Native Americans ___.

One change that took place was ___.
One effect of the change was ___.
Another effect was ___.

LESSON 12
On the Move

LESSON 13

Travel Before and After Trains

LESSON 14

Crossing Paths in the Changing West

WEST WORDS

Use the words below in complete sentences to write about what you learned in this unit. Challenge yourself to use as many words as you can in one sentence. Use this sentence starter if you like.

In the 1800s, ___.

wagon | transcontinental railroad | bison | prairie

travel | settlers | Native Americans | Chinese immigrants

SESSION 2 READ

Winter in the Rockies

by Janet Costa Bates

It is 1826. George Jennings, a free Black man and expert mountain man, leads a group of fur trappers east across the Rocky Mountains. Like other traders and trappers, they are widening paths created by the Crow people.

1 George was worried. He was watching Sam struggle to load supplies onto a **pack mule**. Traveling through the Rocky Mountains in the winter would be hard. They were also on Crow land, and there could be trouble. Sam was only fifteen. Was it wise to let him come along?

pack mule = animal that is part horse, part donkey and carries heavy things

2 "I expect you to work hard and talk little," George warned Sam. "The route ahead isn't clear. We must pay attention to our surroundings at all times."

3 Sam nodded. "Yes, sir." Sam trusted George to help him learn the fur trade. And he felt strong enough to brave whatever the journey would bring.

4 One of the men, Jeb Clark, **smirked** at Sam. "You're just a boy. You won't be much help."

smirked = smiled in a mean way

5 The other men laughed. Sam lowered his head. 

Stop & Discuss

What dangers do George and the others face?

Underline details in paragraphs 1 and 2 that help you answer the question.

6 "This way," George said, as he led the men along the snow-covered trail on their horses. After a while, Sam stopped and got down to check the last beaver trap. He crouched and leaned over the riverbank.

7 "You best watch your footing, Sam," George called out. But it was too late. Sam slipped, and the fast-moving water pulled him away.

8 "Mr. Jennings!" Sam yelled.

9 Sam reached up and grabbed a branch to keep his head above water. George threw off his coat and boots, and dove in. No one else dared to enter the icy river. He expected the boy to panic. Instead, Sam calmly grabbed George's shoulders, and George pulled him to shore.

10 *This boy's braver than most of these men,* thought George.

11 Out of the water, they dried themselves quickly. George covered Sam with a blanket and rubbed the boy's hands to warm them.

12 "Thank you for saving me," Sam said. He smiled broadly at George.

13 "It was your calm head and strong arms that saved you," said George. He smiled back.

Stop & Discuss

How are George and Sam alike?

Use details from paragraphs 9 and 10 to support your answer.

Summer on the Plains

by Janet Costa Bates

It has taken George Jennings and his team four months to travel east across the Rocky Mountains. They have now reached the plains and are hunting bison for dinner.

1 George took a deep breath of fresh air. Bluebirds chirped. Purple wildflowers dotted the grassy plain. But as peaceful as this scene was, George could not relax. He had joined the mountain men to put distance between himself and Alabama, where he'd been enslaved. His enslaver had set him free, but freedom for a Black man was never a sure thing. The worry was always there.

2 Suddenly, George's thoughts were interrupted.

3 "Bison!" Sam shouted. He pointed at a bison that was separated from its herd.

4 "Get back, Sam," George cautioned.

5 George waited for the perfect moment to take his shot. But before he had a chance—BOOM! Jeb Clark had fired. He missed the bison but came close enough to startle it. It stomped and raised its tail, and then galloped toward the men. Only George stood steady as it came closer and closer. When the time was right, George aimed and **felled** the animal.

felled = killed

Stop & Discuss

How do George and Jeb each hunt the bison? What does this tell you about each man?

Use details from paragraph 5 to support your answer.

When George hunts, he ___. This shows he is ___. When Jeb hunts, he ___. This shows he is ___.

6 That night another group of men joined George's party. They ate, laughed, and told stories.

7 "Mr. Jennings," Sam said. "Tell them how you shot the charging bison."

8 "Tell us!" the men shouted, eager for entertainment.

9 George stood and opened his mouth to speak. Then one of the men from his group rose to his feet.

10 "It was Jeb Clark who felled the bison," he said loudly. "Why, everyone knows what a good shot Jeb is."

11 George said nothing. "It was Mr. Jennings!" Sam **blurted**. He nudged George. "Tell them!"

blurted = said suddenly

12 "Remember as you will," George said, walking away.

13 Sam ran after him. "Why won't you tell them, sir?"

14 "I don't want to argue and make Jeb mad," George explained. "He knows slave catchers. They will pay him a lot of money if he decides to turn me in."

15 "But you're a free man," said Sam.

16 "And I'd like to keep my freedom."

17 Sam kicked at the dirt. "It's not fair. They should know the truth."

18 George put his arm around Sam's shoulders. "They are wrong, but you and I know what really happened. And nothing, *nothing*, can ever change the truth."

Stop & Discuss

Why does Sam want George to tell the men who shot the bison? Why does George not want to say anything?

Use details from paragraphs 13 through 17 to support your answer.

SESSION 3 PRACTICE

Respond to Text

Reread/Think

Reread "Winter in the Rockies" and "Summer on the Plains." Choose the best response to each question.

1. Why is George worried in paragraph 1 of "Winter in the Rockies?"

A. He thinks Jeb Clark is dangerous.

B. He thinks Sam is too young to travel.

C. He thinks the weather is getting too cold.

D. He thinks Sam is carrying too many supplies.

2. Which sentence from "Winter in the Rockies" **best** describes what is happening in the picture on pages 274 and 275?

A. "Traveling through the Rocky Mountains in the winter would be hard." (paragraph 1)

B. "After a while, Sam stopped and got down to check the last beaver trap." (paragraph 6)

C. "Sam reached up and grabbed a branch to keep his head above water." (paragraph 9)

D. "Out of the water, they dried themselves quickly." (paragraph 11)

3. Read this sentence from paragraph 5 of "Summer on the Plains."

> He missed the bison but came close enough to **startle** it.

What is the meaning of *startle* as it is used in the sentence?

A. scare

B. hurt

C. touch

D. hear

4. What does the picture on page 276 of "Summer on the Plains" help the reader better understand?

A. how Sam helps

B. where bison sleep

C. how tall the prairie grasses are

D. why bison sometimes separate from the herd

5. Read the details below. Think about whether each detail describes "Winter in the Rockies" or "Summer on the Plains." Write each detail in the chart to show which story it describes. If a detail does not describe either story, do not write it in the chart.

George helps herd bison.

An image shows Sam feeling upset.

George rides a horse on a snow-covered trail.

George helps Sam out of the water.

George chooses not to argue.

George protects Sam from a bison.

Winter in the Rockies	Summer on the Plains

6. What is one way "Winter in the Rockies" is the same as "Summer on the Plains"?

A. In both stories, the setting is nighttime.

B. In both stories, George shows courage.

C. In both stories, Sam is afraid of an animal.

D. In both stories, Jeb faces dangerous weather.

Write

Describe how the challenges George faces in "Winter in the Rockies" are similar to and different from the challenges in "Summer on the Plains." Explain why the setting of each story is important. Use at least one example from each story in your response.

WRITING CHECKLIST

- ☐ I described the challenges in each story.
- ☐ I explained how the challenges were similar and different.
- ☐ I used complete sentences.
- ☐ I used correct spelling, punctuation, and capitalization.

Make Connections

Reread/Think

The texts in this unit tell how settlers traveled west and how their movement west changed not just their lives but those of others. In each section, describe a change and how it helped or hurt people. Include the title of the text that explains this effect.

Text details that tell how changes in travel helped people:

____

____

____

____

Text details that tell how changes in travel caused problems for people:

____

____

____

____

Talk

Imagine that you are a character in one of the stories. You can choose a character named in the story or create a new character. Talk about one change that has taken place and explain how it affects you. Use the sentence frames to get started.

A character I can imagine being is ___.

One change that would affect my character is ___.
The effect on my character would be ___.

Wild Weather

LESSON 15

Weather Watch

284

LESSON 16

Studying Extremes

300

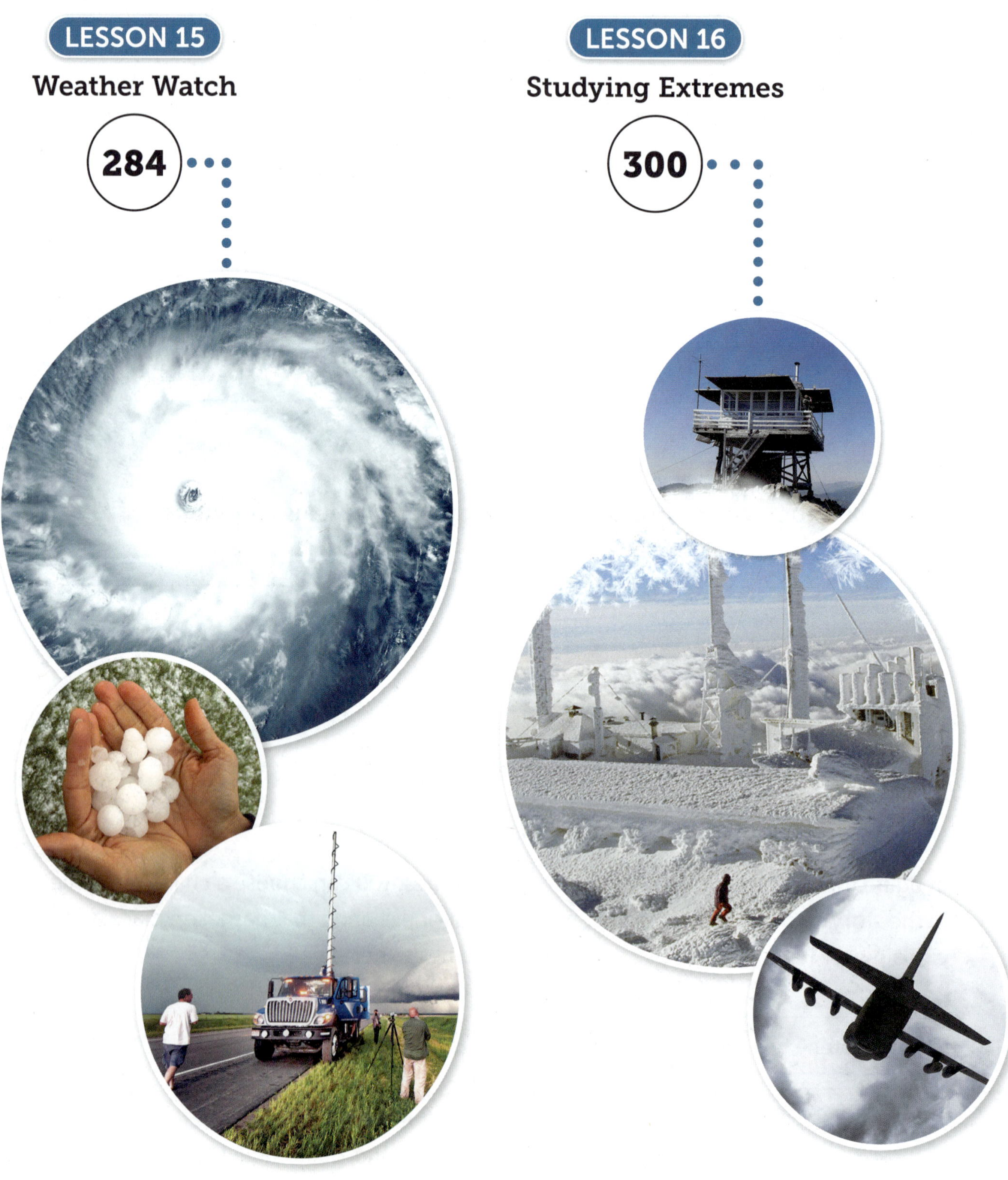

UNIT 5

SESSION 1 TALK ABOUT THE TOPIC

Weather Watch

FOCUS QUESTION

What makes some types of weather extreme?

NOTICE AND WONDER

Look at the three texts you will read in this lesson. What do you notice? What do you wonder? Discuss your ideas with a partner.

WHAT IS EXTREME WEATHER?

What do you think of when you hear the words *extreme weather*? Add a definition, an example, and a picture to the chart.

Definition	Example	Picture

Stormy Weather
by Ellen Bowcroft

Rocky Weather Ahead!
by Todd Tuell

Tornadoes
by Peter Murray

Stormy Weather

by Ellen Bowcroft

THUNDERSTORM FORMATION

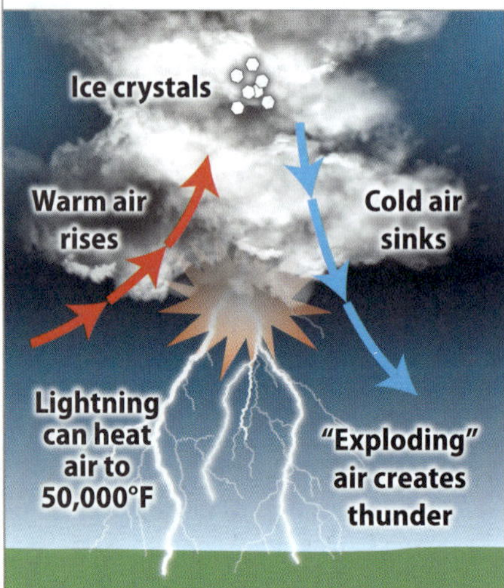

common = happening often

gusts = quick, strong rushes of wind

Boom! Whoosh! Roar! Whistle! Extreme weather is coming! Is it a thunderstorm, a blizzard, a tornado, or a hurricane? Here's how to find out.

Thunderstorms

1 Thunderstorms are a **common** form of extreme weather. They form when warm, moist air goes up into the sky and mixes with clouds. As winds become stronger, ice crystals in the clouds move around. This makes static electricity. You may already be familiar with static electricity. Have you ever walked across a rug in your socks and then felt a shock when you touched a doorknob? That's static electricity. Lightning is the same thing. When lightning travels toward the ground, it heats the air around it. This heat causes a lot of pressure to build up in the air very quickly. That air pressure explodes out like a popping balloon, making a loud noise we call thunder. *Boom!*

Blizzards

2 A blizzard is a very bad snowstorm that lasts three hours or more. In a blizzard, high winds blow constantly and there may be strong **gusts** that blow more than 35 miles per hour. So much snow whirls around that it might be impossible to see what's right in front of you. *Whoosh!*

Stop & Discuss

What makes thunderstorms and blizzards extreme?

Underline details that tell you how strong these storms are.

Tornadoes

3 Tornadoes, or twisters, can happen when warm, moist winds mix with cool, dry winds. They form over land and are shaped like a funnel, with a wide part on one end and a pointed tip on the other. Tornadoes spin around and around with winds that can blow up to 200 miles per hour. These storms sound like a train. *Roar!*

PARTS OF A TORNADO

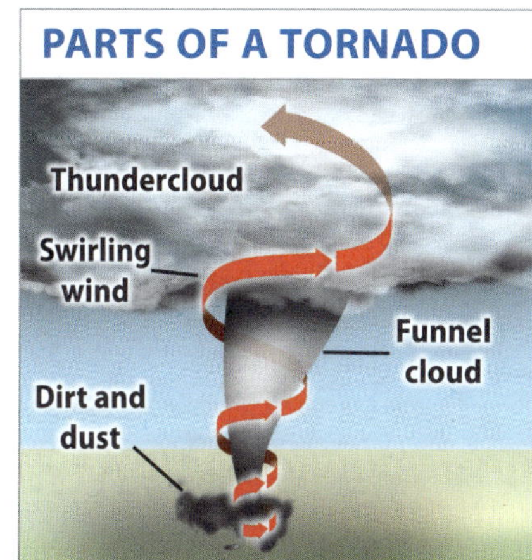

Hurricanes

4 Hurricanes are storms with strong winds and heavy rain. They form over warm ocean waters. Warm, moist air over the water rises, where it is replaced by cooler air. The cooler air warms and rises again. This cycle, or series of repeating actions, causes huge storm clouds to form that can be hundreds of miles across! In the northern part of the world, storms turn in a **counterclockwise** direction around an "eye" where the weather is perfectly calm. The strongest winds and heaviest rains are just outside of the eye. Not all hurricanes reach land. Many stay out at sea where their winds cause little damage. *Whistle!*

counterclockwise = the opposite direction of how clock hands move

5 What kind of extreme weather happens where you live?

STRUCTURE OF A HURRICANE

Stop & Discuss

What makes hurricanes and tornadoes extreme?

Underline details that tell you how strong these storms are.

Connect Words and Pictures

- **Images**, or pictures and drawings, can give you more information about ideas in a text. Some images include maps, diagrams, and photographs.
- Images may have **labels** and **captions**. These are words that tell more about the images.

Reread/Think

Reread "Stormy Weather." Answer the questions about extreme weather. Check the box that tells where you found the answer.

Question	Answer	Where I Found the Answer
How hot can lightning get?		☐ text ☐ image or labels
What part of a hurricane is calm?		☐ text ☐ image or labels
Where are the strongest winds and heaviest rains in a hurricane?		☐ text ☐ image or labels
What are the parts of a tornado?		☐ text ☐ image or labels
How fast do the winds in a tornado blow?		☐ text ☐ image or labels

Talk

Share your answers with a partner. Tell your partner where you found each answer. Then tell your partner how the information helps you know the type of weather is extreme.

To answer this question, I used information from ___.

This information helps me know ___ is/are extreme because ___.

Write

Write about one of the storms in "Stormy Weather." Explain why the storm is extreme. Include information that you learned from the text and the images.

Use helpful phrases such as these in your writing:

- The text states
- The words explain
- The image shows
- The diagram shows

WRITING CHECKLIST

- ☐ I wrote about what I learned from the text.
- ☐ I wrote about what I learned from the images.
- ☐ I used complete sentences.
- ☐ I used correct spelling, punctuation, and capitalization.

Rocky Weather Ahead!

by Todd Tuell

MAP OF THE ROCKY MOUNTAINS

severe = very bad

1 What do you know about the Rocky Mountains? You might know that the Rockies are very tall. You might also know that this mountain range runs through the western part of the United States. But did you know that the Rockies also have some of the most unpredictable weather in the United States? Though the area is known for its sunny days, the weather can turn **severe** in just minutes.

2 How can the weather change so quickly in the Rockies? It has to do with the slope and the height of the mountains. Wind has something to do with it, too. Wind blows up and down the mountains all the time. Up and down, up and down. Put these things together, and you get extreme weather.

Stop & Discuss

What causes the weather in the Rocky Mountains to change so suddenly?

Circle three words in paragraph 2 that explain what causes the sudden changes in the weather.

3 Hail is one type of extreme weather that happens in the Rockies. Hailstones are balls of frozen rain. How do they form? First, a strong wind pushes raindrops quickly up the mountain. Then, at the top, the raindrops freeze. The tiny frozen drops rise and fall in a circular motion, like they are being juggled. Each time they rise, more layers of very cold water freeze onto them. The balls of ice get bigger and heavier. Finally, they drop to the ground. Hailstones in the Rockies usually grow to the size of blueberries. However, some can be the size of golf balls, baseballs, and even grapefruits!

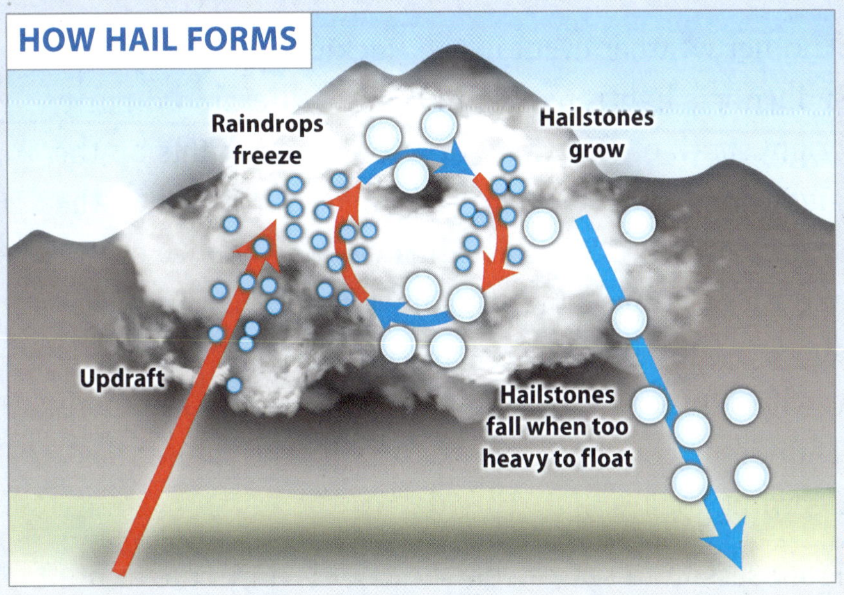

Stop & Discuss

How do hailstones get bigger and bigger?

Underline the sentence in paragraph 3 that explains this. Then explain it to your partner.

Hailstones get bigger when ___.

Visitors to the Rocky Mountains are given a diagram like this to help them understand the risks of lightning.

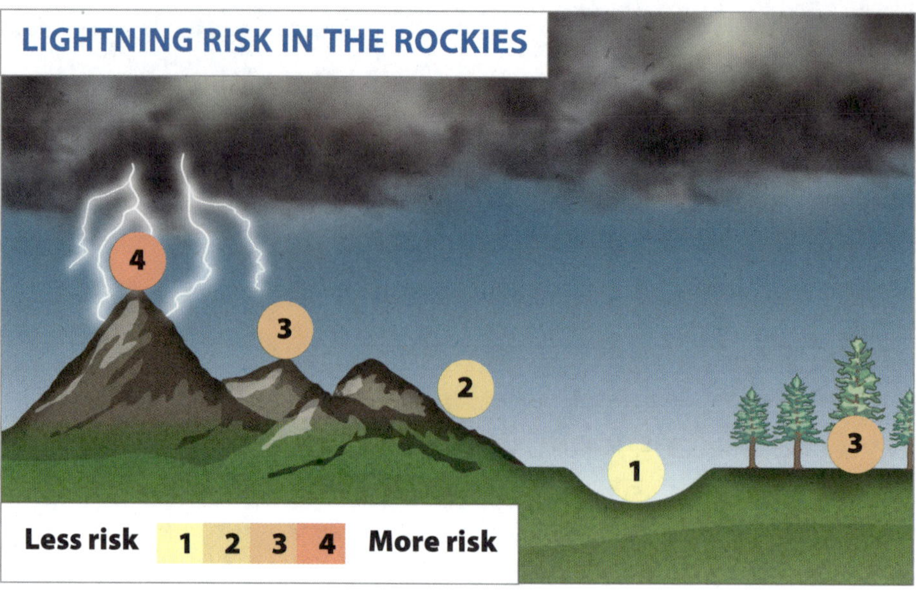

4 Another weather event in the Rockies that can happen suddenly is lightning. Lightning is that extraordinarily bright spark of electricity that sometimes lights up the night sky during a storm, and it's even hotter than the surface of the sun. It starts in a cloud, when ice crystals and water droplets bump against each other. In the clouds above mountains, ice crystals can form year-round. This is why lightning is so common in the Rocky Mountains. Thunder is common, too, because it's the sound that lightning makes.

5 From season to season, day to day, even minute to minute, it's hard to tell what weather in the Rockies will do next. It may be surprising and it may be severe at times. But the weather in the Rockies can be as beautiful as the mountains themselves.

Stop & Discuss

Why does lightning happen often in the Rocky Mountains?

Underline a sentence in paragraph 4 that explains why lightning forms there often.

Connect Words and Pictures

- You can combine the information in the words with the information from images to understand more about the topic of a text.
- The images in a text can help you understand more about what the words say.

Reread/Think

Reread "Rocky Weather Ahead!" Answer the questions below to show your understanding of weather in the Rockies. Check the box that tells where you found the answer. You can check more than one box.

Question	Answer	Where I Found the Answer
Where are the Rocky Mountains?		☐ text ☐ image, label, or caption
What causes raindrops to move up the mountainside?		☐ text ☐ image, label, or caption
Why do hailstones finally fall to the ground?		☐ text ☐ image, label, or caption
How big does hail usually get in the Rockies?		☐ text ☐ image, label, or caption
Where is the safest place to be in a lightning storm in the Rockies?		☐ text ☐ image, label, or caption

Talk

Choose one of the images from "Rocky Weather Ahead!" Discuss with a partner what the image shows. Then say how it helps you understand more about weather. Listen as your partner describes a different image.

This image shows ___.

It helps me understand ___.

Write

Choose hail or lightning from "Rocky Weather Ahead!" Use information from both the words and the images to describe how this type of weather happens. Then explain why it happens in the Rocky Mountains.

WRITING CHECKLIST

- ☐ I wrote about what I learned from the text.
- ☐ I wrote about what I learned from the images.
- ☐ I used complete sentences.
- ☐ I used correct spelling, punctuation, and capitalization.

TORNADOES

by Peter Murray

1 It is late afternoon on a hot summer day. The air is thick and moist. Tall, fluffy clouds appear in the sky. Then the wind begins to blow, getting stronger every minute. A scrap of paper sails through the air.

2 Over a few hours, the air cools and the sky turns yellow. Rain falls and lightning flashes. Seconds later, thunder booms. The bottom of the thundercloud **swells**, twists, and spins. Soon a cone-like shape drops from the cloud. This shape is called a funnel cloud.

swells = gets bigger

3 As the funnel cloud stretches downward, it sounds like rushing air. Then the tip of the cloud touches the ground. The noise, now more like a train, gets louder and louder. The funnel cloud has become a tornado.

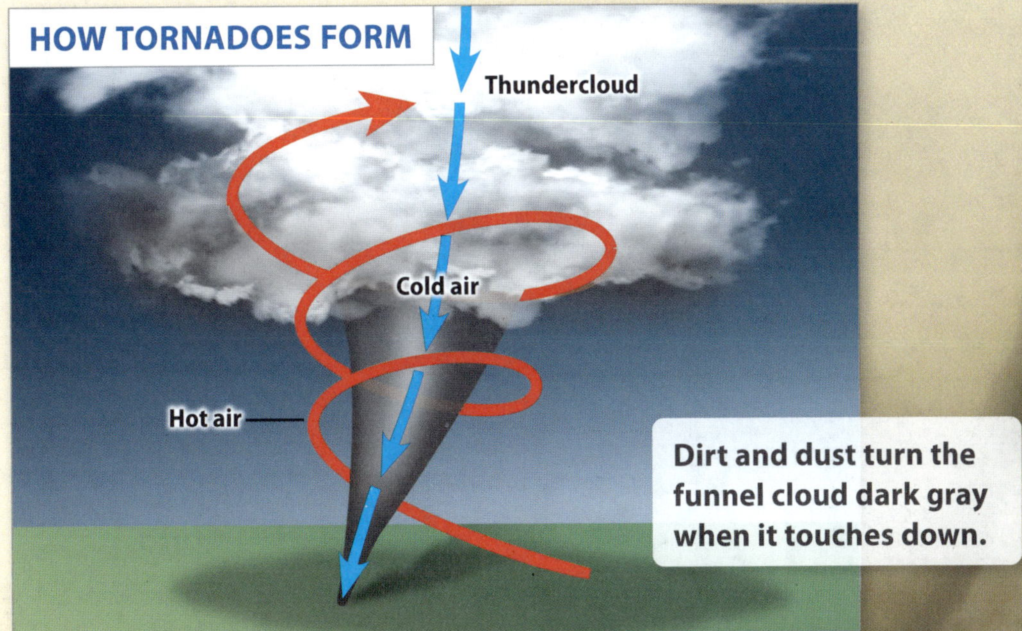

Dirt and dust turn the funnel cloud dark gray when it touches down.

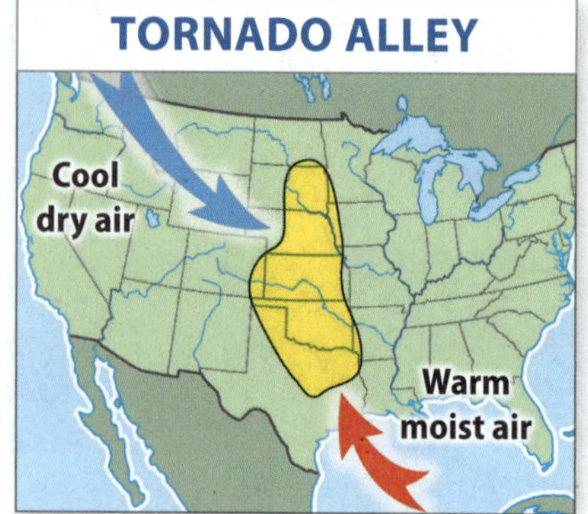

4 Hundreds of tornadoes like this touch down in "Tornado Alley" every year. This area is perfect for tornadoes because it is where warm ocean air from the Gulf of Mexico meets cool air from Canada. As this air comes together, it begins to swirl around itself, and this creates powerful winds.

5 As the air rises, it packs tightly together, or condenses. The winds and moist air keep moving, forming thunderclouds. Thunderclouds make tornadoes possible.

6 Most tornadoes touch down in open areas and last only a few minutes. But other tornadoes last for hours and travel quickly.

7 Large tornadoes can create very strong winds. And a tornado's swirling winds can create a powerful vacuum strong enough to suck up objects on the ground.

8 Scientists learn as much as they can about tornadoes. They study the winds and clouds of thunderstorms before tornadoes form. They also try to predict where each tornado will touch down. By studying tornadoes, scientists hope to keep people safe from these powerful forces of nature.

Weather scientists study tornadoes to better predict when they will happen.

Respond to Text

Reread/Think

1. What causes a funnel cloud to turn dark gray?
   - A. The air around it starts to cool.
   - B. Dirt and dust get pulled into it.
   - C. Lightning strikes the ground nearby.
   - D. Rain begins to fall from the thundercloud.

2. How does the air in a tornado move? Fill in the blanks using words from the bank.

ground	cold air	hot air	sky

The ____________ from the ____________ moves down while the ____________ from the ____________ moves up.

3. Where is Tornado Alley?
   - A. along the border of Canada
   - B. in the southern part of Canada
   - C. in the middle of the United States
   - D. along the coasts of the United States

4. What causes tornadoes to form in Tornado Alley? Fill in the blanks using words from the bank.

Canada	the Gulf of Mexico	moist	dry

The tornadoes in Tornado Alley form when warm, ____________ air from ____________ mixes with cool, ____________ air from ____________.

Reread/Think

5. Why does the author state that a "tornado's swirling winds can create a powerful vacuum"? (paragraph 7)

   A. A tornado blows objects around.

   B. A tornado pulls objects into itself.

   C. A tornado can help clean the air.

   D. A tornado makes strong winds.

6. Why do scientists try to predict where tornadoes will happen?

____

____

Write

Explain how tornadoes form and why they can be so damaging. Use information from the words and images in "Tornadoes."

____

____

____

____

____

____

____

____

____

____

____

WRITING CHECKLIST

- ☐ I wrote about how tornadoes form.
- ☐ I wrote about why tornadoes are damaging.
- ☐ I used information from words and images.
- ☐ I used correct punctuation, spelling, and capitalization.

Respond to the Focus Question

What makes some types of weather extreme?

Reread/Think

Choose one text from this lesson to reread.

TEXT: ______________________________

What is something you learned about extreme weather that interested you the most?

____

Talk

Share your detail with a partner. Tell why you found it the most interesting.

The detail that interested me most was ___. I chose this because ___.

As a group, discuss these questions. Take notes in the chart.

What makes some types of weather extreme? How are extreme weather events alike?

Type of Weather	What makes it extreme?

Write

What makes some types of weather extreme? Use details and examples from your discussion to support your response.

SESSION 1 TALK ABOUT THE TOPIC

Studying Extremes

FOCUS QUESTION

Why do people study extreme weather?

NOTICE AND WONDER

Look at the three texts you will read in this lesson. What do you notice? What do you wonder? Discuss your ideas with a partner.

WEATHER WORK

Think about one kind of extreme weather event, such as a hurricane, thunderstorm, or snowstorm. Circle two words you think can be used to tell about how people might study the weather you chose. Use the sentence frame to name the weather event and say what people might do to study it.

forecast	climb
measure	collect
fly	observe

While studying a ___,
people might ___ and ___.

At Home in the Sky
by Betsy Kepes

Weather Mountain
by Cheryl Bardoe

The Hurricane Hunter
by Helen Walz

AT HOME IN THE SKY

by Betsy Kepes

Storm's Coming

1 "Hurry!" my dad yells down to us. He's standing on the narrow porch that wraps around our lookout tower. We're spending the summer living in a small glass house perched on the **summit** of Coolwater Ridge in the Rocky Mountains of Idaho. Suddenly, the sky flings down hailstones. Mom and I race to the steep wooden steps of the lookout. Flashes of lightning brighten the sky, and thunder growls. Two hours ago the weather was clear, but now the wide sky is a strange purple-black.

summit = the highest point

Fire Spotted!

2 Inside the lookout, Mom grabs binoculars while I look out a window. "Downstrike!" I yell, and Mom looks where I am pointing. We see a bright line of flame. On a distant mountainside, lightning struck a tree, and now all the needles are burning. Mom jumps to the fire finder, and my dad calls the ranger station on the radio. He reports the fire's location and size. Soon, firefighters will arrive by airplane to put out the blaze.

What Is a Fire Finder?

A fire finder is a circular map the size of a large pizza. It is fastened to a metal ring and divided into 360 skinny sections. Lookouts use a tool attached to the map to determine which section the fire is in. They then report the information to firefighters.

Stop & Discuss

What do Mom and Dad do after the downstrike, and why?

Underline two sentences in paragraph 2 that support your response.

The Life of a Lookout

3 The United States Forest Service hires my parents and other lookouts to report fires. Our lookout is a one-room house with windows instead of walls. It is 12 feet (3.66 meters) square, about the size of six beds pushed together. All the inside furniture—bed, countertops, woodstove—is low so we can easily see out the windows.

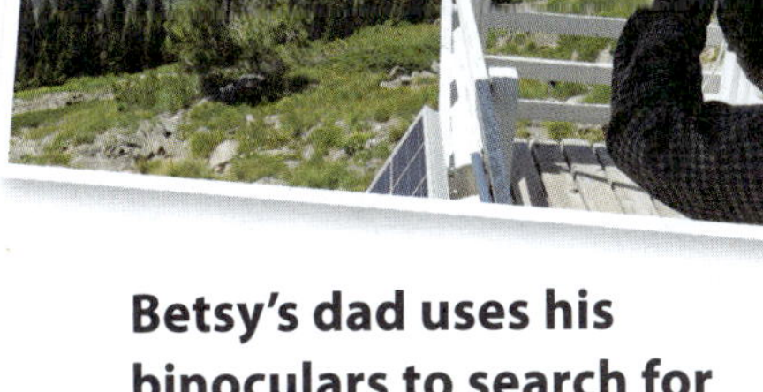

Betsy's dad uses his binoculars to search for forest fires.

4 Fires don't happen every day, though. When the weather is clear and quiet, we watch hawks soaring below our tower. We also wash the windows, chop firewood, and work on building our stone **outhouse**. We hike down a steep trail to get our water from an icy cold **spring**.

outhouse = a small outdoor bathroom

spring = a place where water rises from the ground

5 Usually, we are the only humans on the mountain, but sometimes tourists visit. They see that we don't have a TV or a computer. "Don't you get bored?" they ask me. I remember all the fires I've spotted. "Bored?" I say. "Never!"

Stop & Discuss

How are fire days different for the family than days with no fires to report?

Discuss with a partner the text details that help you describe each type of day.

I can tell that fire days are ___ because the text says ___.
I can tell that clear days are ___ because the text says ___.

Use Text Features

- **Text features** are special parts of a text that help you locate information or learn more about a topic. Examples of text features are titles, headings, and sidebars.
  - — A **title** is the name of the text.
  - — A **heading** is a title for a part of a text.
  - — A **sidebar** is a short text placed near the main text.

Reread/Think

Look for the text features in "At Home in the Sky." Use them to complete the chart.

Text Feature	Example from Text	What It Tells Me
Title	At Home in the Sky	
Second Heading		
Sidebar		
Third Heading		

Talk

Talk with a partner about the information you found by using text features. How did using text features make it easier to find information? How did using text features help you understand more about the topic?

The text feature ___ helped me understand the text by giving me clues about ___.

The text feature ___ helped me find information about ___.

Write

How does a fire finder help when the lookouts see a fire? In your response, explain which two text features helped you find the information.

WRITING CHECKLIST

- [ ] I explained how the fire finder is used.
- [ ] I explained which two text features helped me find this information in the text.
- [ ] I used complete sentences.
- [ ] I used correct spelling, punctuation, and capitalization.

Weather

by Cheryl Bardoe

1 It's hard to sleep at the top of Mount Washington in New Hampshire. It's too noisy. The howling winds sound like a freight train rushing past. It's also too cold. Buildings groan and pop as they freeze at night. Why would anyone want to sleep there? After all, many people say Mount Washington has the "worst weather in the world." But for some people, studying the "worst weather" is their job.

Working on Mount Washington

2 One weather observer we spoke to spends more than half the year living and working in the weather station at Mount Washington's peak. In January, temperatures average 5°F (–15°C) with **wind chills** much lower. The mountain is famous for its winds. January breezes blow more than 45 miles per hour (72 kilometers per hour) with gusts over 100 miles per hour (161 kilometers per hour)! The work done at the station helps scientists understand weather patterns, when the weather stays the same for days or weeks at a time. Also, the National Weather Service uses information from Mount Washington to make **forecasts** for the whole country.

wind chills = temperatures that show the effects of strong, cold wind

forecasts = scientists' descriptions of what they think will happen

Stop & Discuss

What is it like at the top of Mount Washington in January?

Use details from the text to support your answer.

Mountain

Walking in Wild Weather

current = the movement of water in a river or ocean

3 Getting around at the weather station is not easy. Walking into the wind, she says, is like walking across a river. "You lean into the **current**, and if it is steady, then you know what to expect." Gusting winds are a different story. "Gusts are like trying to walk into the ocean through breaking waves. Every time one hits, you might get knocked off your feet."

4 Getting lost in heavy snow or fog is also a real danger. When it's time to check the rainfall can in the thick mist of the fog, our weather observer moves with extra care. "There's a point when I can't see the can in front of me or the building behind me." She counts her steps there and back and tries not to let the wind blow her off her path.

A rainfall can measures how much rain has fallen.

Stop & Discuss

What extreme weather conditions are found at the weather station on Mount Washington?

Underline important words in paragraphs 3 and 4 that support your answer.

Snow and ice cover Mount Washington in winter.

withstand = to be strong enough not to be harmed by something

The Silly Side

What do weather observers do for fun? They play in the wind and do silly science experiments. For example, they freeze soap bubbles, like the one shown above. Sometimes they even use frozen tomatoes to hammer nails into wood!

Ice, Be Nice

5 Weather observers must also take care of the tools the scientists use for measuring weather. Most of the tools are designed to **withstand** fierce wind, ice, and cold. However, they can clog up with ice on stormy days. The observers have to climb up the weather tower and beat the ice off with a heavy metal tool. In strong winds, observers go out as a team. One person hacks away at the ice. The other person holds the worker's feet steady on the ladder.

6 Our observer is most nervous just before she heads outside. She checks her gear, the tools and clothing she needs for her work. Next, she practices what she must do in her mind. After she opens the door, she doesn't have time to be afraid. "Outside," she says, "you're completely focused on what you're doing."

7 But she loves the wild weather. And she loves her cold and windy job.

A weather observer hacks ice off of the weather tower with a big hammer.

Stop & Discuss

Which statement would the weather observer quoted in this article agree with?

- ☐ Working at a weather station can be dangerous and boring.
- ☐ Working at a weather station can be dangerous and exciting.

Use Text Features

- You have already learned about titles, headings, and sidebars. Other examples of text features are key words, visuals, and captions.
  - A **key word** is an important word from the text. Often, the meaning of a key word is also listed in the text.
  - A **visual** is a picture, such as an illustration or photo, that gives more information about the text.
  - A **caption** is a group of words or sentences that tell about an illustration or photo.

Reread/Think

Review the text features in "Weather Mountain." Use them to fill in the chart below.

Information You Are Looking For	Information You Found	Text Feature You Used
What is it like to walk in wild weather on Mount Washington?		
What do weather observers do when they are being silly?		
What does the weather station usually look like in winter?		
What is the meaning of the word *current*?		

Talk

Look at the chart and discuss how the text features helped you find information.

> One text feature that helped me understand the text is ___.

> The text feature helped me find important information in the text because ___.

Write

What is it like at the top of Mount Washington for the weather observer quoted in the article? Explain how two text features helped you find this information and understand more about the topic.

WRITING CHECKLIST

- ☐ I answered the question.
- ☐ I explained how I used text features to find this information in the text.
- ☐ I used complete sentences.
- ☐ I used correct spelling, punctuation, and capitalization.

THE HURRICANE HUNTER

by Helen Walz

Master Sergeant Karen Moore hunts a hurricane in a WC-130J Super Hercules aircraft.

Flying into the Storm

1 Out over the ocean, a hurricane is forming. But Karen Moore doesn't seek **shelter**. She gets into an airplane that flies right into the middle of the storm!

shelter = a safe place

2 Moore is a master sergeant in the United States Air Force Reserve. She is also a member of the Air Force's 53rd Weather Reconnaissance Squadron. This group is known as the Hurricane Hunters. They collect **data** about hurricanes. Then they share this information to help keep people safe.

data = information and facts

Saving Lives

3 "Every storm is different," says Moore. Sometimes the flight is "like a roller coaster ride." Other times it's too cloudy to see anything. The very center of a storm is often calm and surrounded by towering clouds.

Dropsondes hold measuring tools.

dissolve = to become part of a liquid

Storm Warning!

In 2017, Hurricane Maria ripped through Puerto Rico and other nearby islands. For weeks, the Hurricane Hunters flew all day and night, tracking the storm. Moore and the others in her squadron took turns so that a team was always in the air. They were able to warn people who live on islands so they could move away from the shore.

4 As the plane flies through a storm, Moore releases small tubes called dropsondes. Each one holds measuring tools. The tube is attached to a parachute. As dropsondes slowly fall, they measure wind speed, wind direction, air temperature, and more. When they hit the water, they **dissolve**. Moore and another member of her team work together to drop the dropsondes at just the right moment. If they drop them too early or too late, they won't get the information they need. Moore might also release similar measuring tools that float when they land in the ocean. These tools provide information about the ocean, such as the temperature.

5 Radio signals send data from the tools to meteorologists back on land. These weather scientists use the information to predict where the storm is going and how strong it will get. Then they can warn people who may be in danger. "The information we gather helps save lives," says Moore.

A Dream Come True

6 When Moore was a little girl, she would lie on a hill in her yard and wonder what was going on in the clouds. Now it's her job to find out. Moore says being a hurricane hunter "has been one of the most rewarding parts of my career. . . . It isn't a thing everyone gets to do." She hopes her story encourages others to get involved in this kind of work. "Don't let anything hold you back from doing what you want to do," she says.

Respond to Text

Reread/Think

Reread "Hurricane Hunters." Choose the best response to each question.

1. Use the headings in the text to help you find information and complete the chart using the phrases in the word bank.

Information in the Text

A. describes how storms are different

B. has advice from Moore to the reader

C. explains how Moore and her team gather information

D. tells about Moore as a child

Saving Lives	A Dream Come True

2. What information is found in the sidebar "Storm Warning!"?

A. The Hurricane Hunters are pilots in the U.S. Air Force.

B. The Hurricane Hunters learn information about oceans.

C. The Hurricane Hunters helped people in Puerto Rico.

D. The Hurricane Hunters first started flying in 2017.

3. Which would be the **best** heading for paragraph 2?

A. How Dangerous Are Hurricanes?

B. How to Collect Information

C. Tools for Watching Storms

D. Who Are the Hurricane Hunters?

Reread/Think

4. Read this sentence from paragraph 4.

> As the plane flies through a storm, Moore **releases** small tubes called dropsondes.

What is the meaning of the word *releases* as it is used in this sentence?

A. lets go

B. dries off

C. finds

D. builds

Write

What does a hurricane hunter do? In your response, explain how you used text features. Tell how they helped you find the information in the text and understand more about the topic.

WRITING CHECKLIST

- ☐ I answered the question.
- ☐ I explained which text features helped me find this information in the text.
- ☐ I used complete sentences.
- ☐ I used correct spelling, punctuation, and capitalization.

Respond to the Focus Question

Why do people study extreme weather?

Reread/Think

Choose one text from the lesson to reread.

TEXT: ____

Identify the weather event people study in the text you chose. Explain how and why they study it.

____

____

____

____

____

____

Talk

In a small group, choose one person to take notes. Share what you learned from the text you reread. Then imagine you could spend the day with one of the extreme weather watchers you read about. Who would you choose to spend time with, and why? What would you learn from the way this person studies weather?

I would spend the day with ___.

This person studies ___ because ___. I would learn about ___.

Write

Why is it important to study extreme weather? Use information from all three texts in your response.

SESSION 1 TALK ABOUT THE TOPIC

Weather Verses

FOCUS QUESTION

What is it like to experience severe weather?

NOTICE AND WONDER

Look at the poems you will read in this lesson. What do you notice? What do you wonder? Discuss your ideas with a partner.

WHAT IS POETRY?

Read the list of words. Circle words that you know the meaning of. Then talk with a partner to learn meanings of the words you don't know. Talk about how each word is connected to poetry.

rhyme	line	speaker
story	rhythm	stanza

Hurricane
by Dionne Brand

When Tornadoes Come Roaring In
by Alexandra Alessandri

Lightning
by Jennifer Jesseph

I Do Not Mind You, Winter Wind
by Jack Prelutsky

Crick! Crack!
by Eve Merriam

Hurricane

by Dionne Brand

clotheslines = ropes or wires on which washed clothes are hung to dry

blinds = window coverings

1 Shut the windows
Bolt the doors
Big rain coming
Climbing up the mountain

2 Neighbors whisper
Dark clouds gather
Big rain coming
Climbing up the mountain

3 Gather in the **clotheslines**
Pull down the **blinds**
Big wind rising
Coming up the mountain

Stop & Discuss

What is happening in the first three stanzas, or parts, of the poem?

Put a star (*) next to lines that describe what people are doing. Put a checkmark (✓) next to lines that describe the storm.

4 Branches falling
Raindrops flying
Treetops swaying
People running
Big wind blowing
Hurricane! on the mountain.

Stop & Discuss

How is stanza 4 different from stanzas 1–3?

Talk with your partner about the ways in which stanza 4 is different.

Stanza 4 is different because ___. I know because the text says ___.

Analyze a Poem

- Poets organize poems into stanzas.
- A **stanza** is a group of lines in a poem. Each stanza tells a part of the poem's story.

Reread/Think

Reread "Hurricane" and complete the chart. Use details from the poem to explain the actions of the people and the storm in each stanza.

Stanza	The Storm's Actions	The People's Actions
Stanza 1	Big rain is coming; the storm is coming.	People are getting ready for the storm by closing windows and doors.
Stanza 2		
Stanza 3		
Stanza 4		

Talk

Read the poem aloud to your partner. Listen as the poem is read to you. Talk about what happens in each stanza, using details from your chart. How does each stanza help build the story? How is stanza 4 different from the first three stanzas?

The idea in this stanza is ___.

It builds on the stanza before by ___.

The last stanza is different from the first three stanzas because ___.

Write

Explain how each stanza helps build the story in "Hurricane." Describe how stanza 4 is different from the first three stanzas. How does this help tell the story in the poem? Use text details to support your response.

WRITING CHECKLIST

- ☐ I described how each stanza helps build the story in the poem.
- ☐ I explained how the last stanza is different from the first three stanzas.
- ☐ I used complete sentences.
- ☐ I used correct spelling, punctuation, and capitalization.

SESSION 3 READ

When Tornadoes Come Roaring In

by Alexandra Alessandri

palm fronds = the leaves of palm trees

1 Storm clouds coat the sky
a greenish gray. Wind whooshes,
shaking **palm fronds** like pom poms.
Lightning zigzags. Thunder booms.
Hail plink, plank, plunks.

2 Then sirens wail, loud and strong:
"Tornado warning!" they cry.
Papa tugs me to a safe room
tucked away from windows.

3 Walls rattle. Ears pop.
The wind moans and groans
while we lie low and wait.
Its rumble builds into a roar, like a
Train chug-a-chugging toward us.

4 When it's over, silence stretches
until Mama says, "It's safe."
I follow them outside and watch as
sunshine chases storm clouds away.

Stop & Discuss

What words describe the way the storm looks? What words describe the way the storm sounds?

Talk about the words with a partner.

LIGHTNING

by Jennifer Jesseph

1 I see lightning,
and it's frightening
tearing up the summer skies.

2 Watch it flashing.
See it **slashing**.
Everything electrifies.

3 Hear it cracking.
Trees are **thwacking**.
I curl into a ball.

4 I cover my head,
and stay in bed
away from this big **squall**.

5 Now it's slowing.
The storm is going.
The lightning's not so bright.

6 It's getting dimmer,
just a glimmer
of flickering, flashing light.

slashing = cutting with a sharp movement

thwacking = hitting hard

squall = sudden wind, usually with rain or snow

Stop & Discuss

What does the speaker see and hear?

Put a checkmark (✓) next to the lines that describe what the speaker sees. Put a star (*) next to lines that describe the sounds.

Analyze a Poem

- Each stanza in a poem tells a part of the poem's story.
- Looking at how stanzas build a story or describe an experience helps you better understand a poem.

Reread/Think

Read "Lightning" aloud. Each stanza builds on the one before it. Think about what the speaker sees and hears in each stanza. Listen to how each stanza sounds. Fill out the chart to explain how each stanza helps build the poem's story.

Stanza	What Happens in "Lightning"?
1	The speaker sees lightning in "the summer skies." A storm is coming.
2	
3	
4	
5	
6	

Talk

Read the poem aloud. Then talk about what happens in each stanza, using details from your chart. How does each stanza help build the story? What do you learn in each stanza about what the speaker sees and hears?

Read the poem aloud once more. Which stanza is your favorite? What do you like about how the stanza sounds? How does that stanza help build the poem's story?

The poem tells the story of ___.

My favorite stanza, number ___, builds with the one before/after it by ___.

Write

How do the stanzas build on each other to tell a story in "Lightning"? Look at the describing words in each stanza. Listen to the way each stanza sounds when you read the poem aloud.

Write a paragraph about how each stanza helps tell the story. Use details from the poem in your response.

WRITING CHECKLIST

- ☐ I explained how the stanzas build on each other to tell the poem's story.
- ☐ I used complete sentences.
- ☐ I used correct spelling, punctuation, and capitalization.

I Do Not Mind You, Winter Wind

by Jack Prelutsky

1 I do not mind you, Winter Wind
when you come whirling by,
to tickle me with snowflakes
drifting softly from the sky.

2 I do not even mind you
when you nibble at my skin,
scrambling over all of me
attempting to get in.

attempting = trying

3 But when you bowl me over
and I land on my behind,
then I must tell you, Winter Wind,
I mind . . . I really mind!

Crick! Crack!

by Eve Merriam

1 *Crick! Crack!*
Wind at my back.

2 *Snit! Snat!*
Snatched off my hat.

3 *Whew! Whew!*
It blew and it blew.

4 Snapped at my ears,
Flapped at my shoes,

5 And now I've got only
One mitten to lose.

Respond to Text

Reread/Think

Reread "I Do Not Mind You, Winter Wind" and "Crick! Crack!" Choose the best response to each question.

1. Which stanza in "I Do Not Mind You, Winter Wind" talks about Winter Wind nibbling on the speaker's skin?

   A. stanza 1

   B. stanza 2

   C. stanza 3

   D. stanza 4

2. What does the word *scrambling* mean as it is used in stanza 2 of "I Do Not Mind You, Winter Wind"?

   A. stirring well

   B. making a mess

   C. moving quickly

   D. singing loudly

3. How is the last stanza of "I Do Not Mind You, Winter Wind" different from the other stanzas in that poem?

   A. The speaker tells what bothers him about the Winter Wind.

   B. The speaker gives details about the Winter Wind.

   C. The speaker describes what falling snow feels like on his skin.

   D. The speaker tells why he likes other seasons better.

Reread/Think

4. In the poem "Crick! Crack!," what snatches the speaker's hat?

A. her brother

B. the wind

C. a friend

D. the snow

5. Which part of "Crick! Crack!" tells about the speaker's shoes?

A. stanza 1

B. stanza 2

C. stanza 3

D. stanza 4

Write

Choose one of these poems: "I Do Not Mind You, Winter Wind" or "Crick! Crack!" Using details from the poem, describe what happens in each stanza of the poem.

WRITING CHECKLIST

- ☐ I explained how each stanza builds on the one before it.
- ☐ I used complete sentences.
- ☐ I used correct spelling, punctuation, and capitalization.

Respond to the Focus Question

What is it like to experience severe weather?

Reread/Think

Choose two poems from this lesson to reread. Write words and phrases from the poems that show what people see, hear, and feel as they experience severe weather. Circle the word or phrase that you think is the best description of severe weather.

Poem #1 Title:	**Poem #2 Title:**

Talk

Tell your partner about the words and phrases you wrote in your chart. Explain why you chose the one you circled. Then think of other kinds of weather you have experienced. Talk about the words and phrases you would use to describe them.

The word/phrase I chose is ___ because ___.

When the weather is ___, I see ___ and I hear ___.

WHAT WE LEARNED

Write other words and phrases that classmates share in response to this question:

What words best describe severe weather?

___

___

Write

Write a paragraph or a poem to describe what it is like to experience a kind of weather. Use details and examples from the poems in this lesson. Include details from your own experiences if you wish.

SESSION 1 MAKE CONNECTIONS

Weather All Around

TALK ABOUT WHAT YOU KNOW

Turn and talk with a partner about what you already know about extreme weather and the people who study it. Use the pictures and the sentence frames to help you.

One way to study extreme weather is ___.

One reason people study extreme weather is ___.

One type of extreme weather is ___. What happens during this kind of weather is ___.

LESSON 15
Weather Watch

LESSON 16
Studying Extremes

LESSON 17

Weather Verses

WEATHER ADDS UP

Think about what you have learned about different types of weather. Use the words in the word bank to complete each weather sentence.

tornado	blizzard	hurricane	hailstorm

lightning + ice crystals + strong winds = ____________________

cool, dry air + warm, moist air + funnel cloud = ____________________

snow + strong winds = ____________________

cool, dry air + warm, moist air + "eye" = ____________________

In the Clouds

by Roxanne Troup

1 Have you ever seen a thunderstorm up close—really close? Can you imagine meeting a thunderstorm in the clouds? One man did. And he lived to tell about it.

The Man Who Rode the Thunder

2 Lieutenant Colonel William Rankin is called “the man who rode the thunder.” He was an airplane pilot in the U.S. Marine Corps. On July 26, 1959, Rankin was flying over a thunderstorm in Norfolk, Virginia. Then something went terribly wrong with his **jet fighter**. Its single engine stopped, and warning lights flashed. He knew he needed to get out of the plane—fast. He pulled the eject lever. This made the top of his airplane rip away, and his seat shot into the sky.

jet fighter = fast airplane used by the military

Stop & Discuss

How did Rankin end up in the clouds, about to meet a thunderstorm?

Use details from the text and the images to explain what happened.

While flying ___, Rankin's plane ___.

So, first Rankin ___.

The next thing he did was ___.

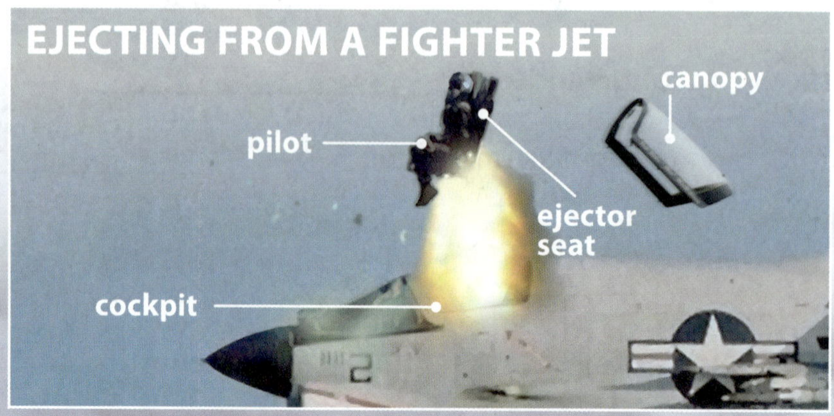

HAMMERED BY HAIL

Rankin felt like he had been "struck by little rocks." But they were not rocks. They were hailstones. Soon, the hail hit him with more force. "I felt as though I were being pounded by a symphony of hammers, drumming at every part of my body," he said.

3 Nearly nine miles up in the air, the temperature was –70°F (–57°C). It was so cold that Rankin's skin hurt. Ejecting at 500 miles per hour had sent Rankin "tumbling, spinning, and cartwheeling through space." He fell many miles, hurtling toward the earth at an incredible speed. As he fell into the thunderstorm, hailstones pounded his helmet like "it was raining baseballs."

4 Rankin reached for his parachute cord. But before he could pull it, his body jerked. The parachute had opened! "Overjoyed to be alive and going down safely," he said, "I thought the **ordeal** had ended. But it hadn't."

ordeal = a difficult event to live through

Stop & Discuss

How did Rankin's body move as he fell through the sky? What caused it to move that way?

Underline the details in paragraph 3 that describe his movements. Then explain what caused them.

Caught in the Currents

5 Rankin felt his body lift as he went through a dark cloud. Then fall. Then lift again. He was caught in the air currents. Then, C-R-A-A-A-C-K-K-K-K-K! Thunder exploded all around him. A blinding flash of light burned his eyes. Another boom shook his body and made his teeth vibrate. "I didn't hear the thunder," he later said. "I felt it."

6 Lightning slashed the sky all around Rankin. Sometimes it came very close. Rankin shut his eyes. But he could still see the lightning! "After each flash of lightning, everything turned completely black. . . . Even when I kept my eyes closed the lightning [was] blinding."

7 All the while, it rained. But instead of rain simply falling down on Rankin, it surrounded him. The parachuting pilot felt like he was in a swimming pool. He held his breath. He **gasped** for air. Again, Rankin felt his body lift. Then fall. Then lift again.

gasped = took quick, short breaths with difficulty

Stop & Discuss

What did Rankin see, hear, and feel in the thunderstorm?

Use details from paragraphs 5–7 to support your response.

Rankin felt his body ___. He also felt ___.

He saw ___. He heard the sound ___.

FROSTBITE

It's not surprising that Rankin got frostbite. Frostbite happens when skin is frozen by very cold air. The skin turns red, white, grayish-yellow, or other colors. It also hardens and may become numb, losing feeling. Most often, frostbite affects the nose, ears, cheeks, chin, fingers, or toes.

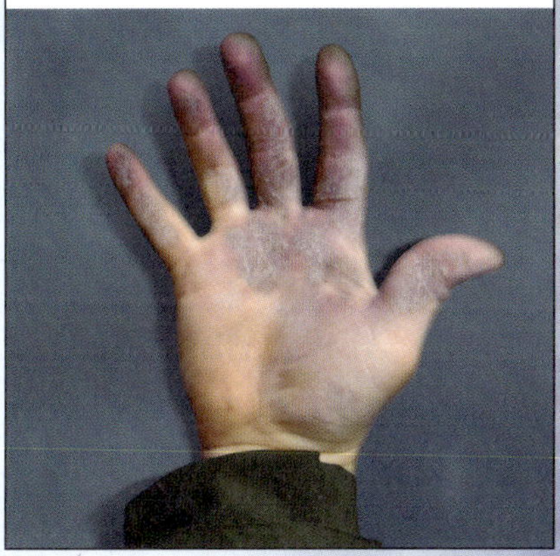

Back on the Ground

8 Rankin rose and fell in the clouds for more than half an hour. "I thought of myself as being on a strange Ferris wheel of nature," he said.

9 But eventually the storm blew itself out, and he slowly drifted toward earth. "It was an enormous **relief**, seeing a little bit of green . . . I forgot instantly about my aches and pains." Rankin prepared for a rough landing on the ground. But, thankfully, his parachute got caught in a tree. It slowed him down. Then he was on the ground. "I simply could not believe that I was on the earth—that I had survived."

10 Rankin untangled himself and got up. He stumbled to the road and found someone to drive him to town. His body was covered in bruises from the hail. At the hospital, he was treated for frostbite and other injuries. But he was alive. He had met a thunderstorm where it lived—in the clouds.

relief = a relaxed feeling that comes when something bad ends

Stop & Discuss

What caused Rankin's aches and pains? What made him forget about his pain?

Use details from the text and the illustrations to support your response.

Respond to Text

Reread/Think

Reread "In the Clouds." Choose the best response to each question.

1. Which part of the text tells how Rankin got to the hospital?

A. the section "The Man Who Rode the Thunder"

B. the section "Back on the Ground"

C. the sidebar "Frostbite"

D. the sidebar "Hammered by Hail"

2. Read this sentence from paragraph 9.

> But eventually the storm blew itself out, and he slowly **drifted** toward earth.

What is the meaning of *drifted* as it is used in this sentence?

A. rose

B. crashed

C. floated

D. dove

3. What does the diagram on page 334 help explain?

A. how Rankin felt in the storm

B. how fast Rankin was moving

C. how high Rankin flew in the air

D. how Rankin got out of the plane

4. Reread paragraph 7. Why did Rankin feel like he was in a swimming pool?

A. He was diving head first.

B. He was kicking his legs.

C. He was surrounded by water.

D. He was floating in the clouds.

5. Mark an X in the chart to show whether the detail is found in the section "The Man Who Rode the Thunder," "Caught in the Currents," or "Back on the Ground."

Detail	The Man Who Rode the Thunder	Caught in the Currents	Back on the Ground
There was a problem with Rankin's engine.			
Rankin's parachute was slowed down by a tree.			
Rankin felt his teeth vibrate when thunder exploded.			

Write

Look at the illustrations of William Rankin shown on pages 335 and 336. Which key events are illustrated in these pictures? For each picture, identify the paragraph that tells about the event the picture shows. Explain what you learned about the events by using both the text and the pictures. Use at least two details from the text to support your response.

WRITING CHECKLIST

- [ ] I explained how both pictures help readers better understand the text.
- [ ] I used two details from the text to support my response.
- [ ] I used complete sentences.
- [ ] I used correct spelling, punctuation, and capitalization.

Make Connections

Reread/Think

If you could study one kind of weather, what would it be? Write your choice on the line below.

MY WEATHER CHOICE: ______________________________

Choose one text that describes this kind of weather. Review that text to find interesting details about this kind of weather. Write down the interesting details. Then explain why you want to study the kind of weather you chose.

MY TEXT CHOICE: ______________________________

Details that I find interesting:

____

____

____

____

Why I want to study the weather I chose:

____

____

____

Talk

Meet as a group to talk about your choice and the details you find interesting. Use the sentence frames to get started.

I would like to study ___ because ___.

___ would like to study ___ because ___.

Artful Ideas

LESSON 18

Natural Creativity

344

LESSON 19

The Power of Art

362

UNIT 6

LESSON 20

Art in Action

Creative Solutions

SESSION 1 TALK ABOUT THE TOPIC

Natural Creativity

FOCUS QUESTION

How does nature give people ideas to make art?

NOTICE AND WONDER

Look at the texts you will read in this lesson. What do you notice? What do you wonder? Discuss your ideas with a partner.

WHAT IS ART?

What do you think of when you read the word *art*? Circle the words that make you think of art. Discuss why you circled some words and not others.

sculpture	trash	drawing
jewels	painting	feathers
chalk	plastic	glue

I circled the word ___ because I think art can be ___.

I did not circle the word ___ because I do not think art can be ___.

Big Bugs

by Jennifer Mattox

Searching for Trolls

by Gail Skroback Hennessey

Ocean Art

by Julie Reich

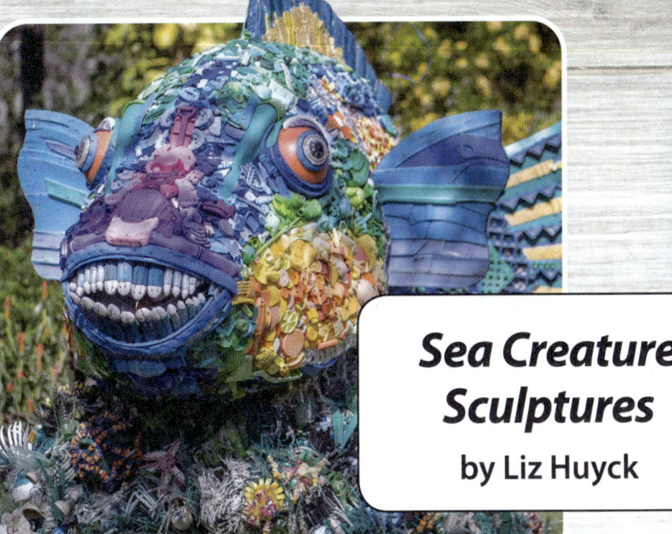

Sea Creature Sculptures

by Liz Huyck

SESSION 1 READ

Big Bugs

by Jennifer Mattox

1 Imagine walking through the park on a sunny day. You're looking at the plants and flowers when you notice two long antennae and a pair of enormous eyes. They're attached to a six-foot-long body with six legs! It's a giant beetle!

2 Before you scream and run away, look closer. That beetle isn't real. It's a wood sculpture. It was carved by artist David Rogers and is one of 14 bug sculptures on display in parks and gardens around the United States.

pollinate = help flowers make new flowers

3 Rogers's collection is called Big Bugs. It includes three monster ants. Each one stretches 25 feet (8 meters) long. That's as long as a school bus! There is also a praying mantis as tall as a two-story house. It stands nearly 18 feet (5 meters) tall on its skinny legs. Some of Rogers's other bugs are a grasshopper and a ladybug. Both of them are big enough to sit on.

4 Real bugs are tiny. So why did Rogers build his so large? Rogers hopes his jumbo sculptures will help people to stop and notice bugs. He believes that bugs are an important part of nature. They make the soil a better place for plants to grow, and they **pollinate** flowers. They eat other insects, and they are food for many creatures.

Stop & Discuss

Why does Rogers make large bug sculptures?

Include details from paragraph 4 that explain what Rogers thinks about bugs.

David Rogers thinks bugs are ___ because ___.

5 Making such enormous art is not easy. Some of the bugs took three months to build. Rogers began by carving pieces of wood into just the right shape and size. He used a mix of different woods to create each bug. He then connected the parts using metal rods. Finally, he gave them a coat of varnish for a smooth, shiny **finish**.

David Rogers works on a bug sculpture.

6 As a child, Rogers loved to make things. Using only sticks and string, he would build tiny villages small enough for an insect. One day, when he was older, he saw a bent tree that reminded him of the backbone of an animal. He added more branches to create a dinosaur. It was his first large sculpture.

finish = how the outside of an object is made to look

express = show what you think or feel

7 According to Rogers, materials can be found anywhere. He has also made sculptures by welding metal. By joining together old car parts, he made a housefly and a dragonfly.

8 Does this sound like fun to you? Good news—Rogers believes there's an artist in everyone. Of course, you might not start out by making a 25-foot (8-meter) ant. It took Rogers years to imagine and build his huge bugs. But as he says, "There's no right or wrong way to **express** yourself with art. Let your imagination run free."

Stop & Discuss

What materials does Rogers use to build his sculptures?

Underline details that tell you what materials he uses to make art these days.

This ant is as long as a school bus!

Analyze a Text

- When you read, pay attention to the important points. A **point** is an idea the author wants you to remember. An important point is a big idea in the text.
- Then look for key details. **Key details** are pieces of information that tell more about the important points.
- Thinking about important points and key details helps readers better understand the topic of the text.

Reread/Think

Reread "Big Bugs." Then read the important points in bold print in the chart. Look back at the text for key details that tell more about each important point.

<table>
<tr><th colspan="2">Big Bugs</th></tr>
<tr>
<td>David Rogers is an artist.
Key details about David Rogers's art:
• huge sculptures
• often made from wood
• sculptures of bugs
• placed outdoors in parks and gardens</td>
<td>Rogers wants people to notice bugs.
Key details about why Rogers wants people to notice bugs:
•
•
•</td>
</tr>
<tr>
<td>Sculptures can be made from materials you find.
Key details about materials artists can use:
•
•
•</td>
<td>Anyone can be an artist.
Key details about why Rogers thinks anyone can be an artist:
•
•</td>
</tr>
</table>

Talk

Discuss with a partner the key details you listed for each important point. Explain why you think each key detail is important.

One important point is ___.

A detail that supports the point is ___.

I did/did not include that detail because ___.

Write

Describe the bug sculptures that David Rogers makes and explain why he makes them. Include the important points and key details from your chart and partner talk.

WRITING CHECKLIST

- ☐ I included important points about the bug sculptures that David Rogers makes.
- ☐ I included key details that tell about the important points.
- ☐ I used complete sentences.
- ☐ I used correct spelling, punctuation, and capitalization.

SESSION 3 READ

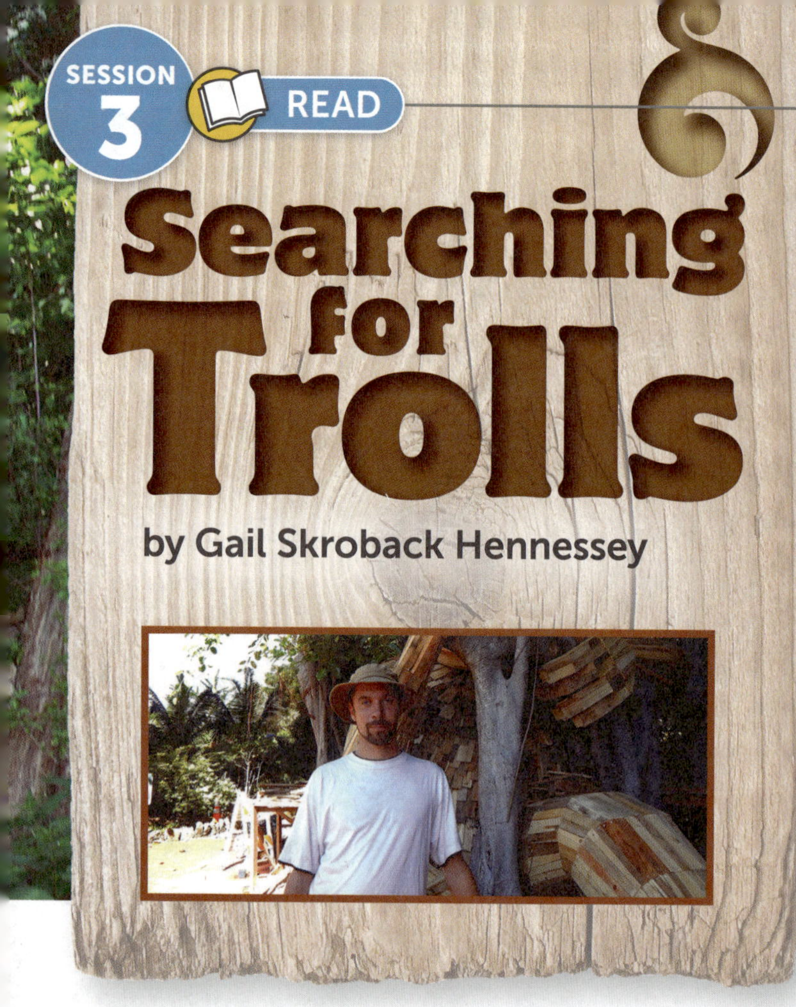

Searching for Trolls

by Gail Skroback Hennessey

1 Six trolls are hiding near the city of Copenhagen in Denmark. However, the artist who made them *wants* people to find them. Thomas Dambo created his extra-large wooden troll sculptures to get people out of the city and into nature. He calls his group of sculptures The Six Forgotten Giants.

2 Dambo started building things as a child. He used materials he found in the trash. As an adult, Dambo has continued to do this. Now he uses scrap wood and materials from old buildings to create his art.

3 Dambo chose to put his troll sculptures in quiet places in the woods and near lakes. He says he did this to "bring art out of the museum." He wants people to search for his trolls by leaving the usual roads and paths. A poem appears on a boulder next to each troll. The poems provide clues about where to find the other hidden giants. If people need help searching, they can use a map found online.

Stop & Discuss

Why does Dambo hide his sculptures in quiet places in the woods and near lakes?

Underline details in paragraphs 1 and 3 that explain what Dambo wants people to do.

Dambo hides his sculptures in nature because he wants people to ___.

4 Each of the different trolls has a name. Teddy Friendly **squats** on the shore of a lake. One of his arms stretches across a small stream so visitors can cross it easily. Oscar Under the Bridge is hidden under—you guessed it—a bridge! When people cross the bridge, they can see the long wooden fingers of one hand reaching up over the edge.

squats = bends one's knees and sits close to the ground

5 Little Tilde peeks out from between two trees. Animals and birds live in the 28 birdhouses Dambo built inside her. Hill Top Trine sits on a grassy hill. She rests her upturned hands on one knee. Children often climb into her **palms** for a better view.

palms = inside of the hands

6 Another troll is Sleeping Louis. He lies on his side, as if he's taking a nap. Visitors can crawl into his open mouth to escape the hot sun. Last, there is Thomas on the Mountain. He sits at the top of a hill with his long legs stretched out in front of him. Both he and his visitors enjoy the great view.

Stop & Discuss

How are Dambo's sculptures used by animals and people?

Use details from paragraphs 4–6 to support your answer.

The sculptures can be used by ___ for ___.

Two of Dambo's trolls

7 Copies of Dambo's trolls can be found in seven other countries, including the United States. All of them are made of recycled materials. Dambo invites everyone to reuse the things around them to create art. He wants people to "look at something and think not what it is but what it could become."

Stop & Discuss

Which statement would Dambo likely agree with?

- ☐ You should buy new materials to make art.
- ☐ You should use materials you find to make art.

Turn and talk with a partner about the statement you chose.

Dambo would agree that you should ___ because the text says ___.

Compare and Contrast Texts

- When you read texts on the same topic, you can compare and contrast their important points and key details to better understand the topic.
- When you **compare**, you look at how the texts are alike.
- When you **contrast**, you look at how the texts are different.

Reread/Think

Answer the questions in the chart with important points and key details about "Big Bugs" and "Searching for Trolls" to show how the artists are different.

Ways the Artists Are Different		
QUESTION	**BIG BUGS**	**SEARCHING FOR TROLLS**
What does their art show?		
Where is their art placed?		
What does the artist use to make their art?		
How does the artist want their art to affect people?		

Circle the phrase that shows how the artists are alike

- Both artists place their work **(inside / outside)**.
- Both artists use materials that are **(metal / reused or recycled)**.
- Both artists think **(anyone / a few people)** can be an artist.

Talk

Talk with a partner about your chart and the statements below it.

- How are the important points and key details in both texts the same?
- How are they different?

Use your chart and the words and phrases you circled to compare and contrast the information in the texts.

> Both texts tell about ___.

> One important difference is ___. In "Big Bugs," ___, but in "Searching for Trolls," ___.

Write

Write a paragraph that tells what you learned about art by comparing and contrasting "Big Bugs" and "Searching for Trolls." Tell how and why Rogers and Dambo make art. What is something both artists do? What is something only one artist does? In your response, include the similarities and differences you discussed with your partner.

WRITING CHECKLIST

- ☐ I included similarities between important points and key details in the two texts.
- ☐ I included differences between important points and key details in the two texts.
- ☐ I used complete sentences.
- ☐ I used correct spelling, punctuation, and capitalization.

____

____

____

____

____

____

____

____

____

____

____

OCEAN ART

by Julie Reich

Durán poses on a pile of sorted plastic trash.

1 Alejandro Durán was **horrified** when he first visited Sian Ka'an, Mexico. That day in 2010, the New York artist was expecting a beautiful, clean beach. Instead, the sand was littered with bottles and other plastic trash. The labels on the bottles were written in many languages. Durán realized the plastic had floated through the ocean from all over the world. Then it washed up onto the beach in Sian Ka'an.

2 The first thing Durán did was stuff the plastic into trash bags. But he didn't stop there. He used this plastic to start an art project that has continued for many years. It is called Washed Up: Transforming a Trashed Landscape. The project's two purposes are to clean up beaches and to let others know about plastic pollution.

3 Durán returns to Sian Ka'an every year. He gathers and washes plastic from the beach, and he sorts it by color. Then he transfigures it, changing the plastic into colorful art. He arranges the plastic pieces on or near the beach to look like rivers, **algae**, and other natural things.

horrified = very upset

algae = plant-like things that live in water

4 After Durán completes an artwork, he photographs it. Then he cleans up the plastic, saving it to use in other artworks. His photos appear in museums and other places worldwide. With his art, Durán hopes to send a message that there is too much plastic in nature.

5 Another part of Durán's work is leading community art projects. With Durán's help, groups of people collect plastic and use it for their own artworks. One group made a design that looks like ocean waves. Another group used blue and green plastic to form an image of planet Earth.

6 Cleaning beaches is one way to get rid of plastic in the environment. Reducing the use of plastic so there is less plastic waste is another solution. Even simple changes can help, like drinking from reusable water bottles. Durán says, "I see this project as a **plea** for help and a call to action." He hopes that people who see his art will do what they can to help.

plea = an act of asking for something

Two of Durán's art projects

Sea Creature Sculptures

by Liz Huyck

1 At the aquarium, people gather around a colorful fish sculpture. They take a closer look to see what it's made of. Are those bottle caps? A plastic shovel? A broken chair? Yes, the sculpture is made from plastic trash. And it all came from the ocean.

2 The beautiful rainbow fish was made by Angela Haseltine Pozzi. Haseltine Pozzi likes to go for walks on the beach near her home in Oregon. But she's bothered by all the plastic trash that washes **ashore**. So she turns it into art.

3 Haseltine Pozzi leads the Washed Ashore Project. The art project has two purposes: to clean up beaches and to teach people about the problem of ocean plastic. Project **volunteers** collect plastic from the beach. They wash it and sort it by color. Then Haseltine Pozzi and a team of other artists make large sculptures with the plastic. They have created about 70 sculptures of creatures such as fish, an octopus, and a polar bear. The sculptures travel to zoos and aquariums around the world.

Zooming in on Haseltine Pozzi's rainbow fish

ashore = onto the land

volunteers = helpers

The artist

A giant plastic jellyfish is taller than some trees.

4 The members of Washed Ashore have recycled more than 40,000 pounds (18,100 kilograms) of plastic from beaches in California and Oregon. The plastic comes from all over the world. It blows off streets and beaches into the ocean. Then, wind and ocean currents carry plastic trash back to a different shore, thousands of miles away. The trash in Haseltine Pozzi's sculptures includes water bottles, bottle caps, flip-flops, beach toys, and more.

5 The Washed Ashore sculptures show how beautiful sea creatures are. Haseltine Pozzi hopes her art will get people to think about how their everyday actions can harm ocean life. "Until we run out of plastic on the beach, we will keep doing our work," she says. "I believe that everybody working together makes big things happen."

Respond to Text

Reread/Think

Reread "Ocean Art" and "Sea Creature Sculptures." Choose the best response to each question.

1. Write a **D** to show if the detail tells about Alejandro Durán from "Ocean Art." Write an **H** if the detail describes Angela Haseltine Pozzi from "Sea Creature Sculptures."

______ Works with volunteers

______ Photographs finished artworks

______ Cleans beaches in Mexico

2. How are Alejandro Durán and Angela Haseltine Pozzi alike?

A. They both turn trash into beach toys.

B. They both show their art in aquariums.

C. They both want to do something about plastic trash.

D. They both make art in the shape of ocean animals.

3. Which sentence from "Sea Creature Sculptures" is similar to an idea found in "Ocean Art"?

A. "At the aquarium, people gather around a colorful fish sculpture." (paragraph 1)

B. "Haseltine Pozzi likes to go for walks on the beach near her home in Oregon." (paragraph 2)

C. "The plastic comes from all over the world." (paragraph 4)

D. "The Washed Ashore sculptures show how beautiful sea creatures are." (paragraph 5)

4. How is plastic trash able to travel thousands of miles?

A. Community artists carry it.

B. Ocean currents move it.

C. People litter with it.

D. Volunteers collect it.

Reread/Think

5. Read this sentence from paragraph 3 of "Ocean Art."

> Then he **transfigures** it, changing the plastic into colorful art.

What word helps you understand the meaning of *transfigures?*

A. changing

B. plastic

C. colorful

D. art

Write

What is one way Durán's Washed Up and Haseltine Pozzi's Washed Ashore Project are alike? What is one way they are different? Use details from both texts in your response.

WRITING CHECKLIST

- ☐ I explained how Durán's and Haseltine Pozzi's projects are alike and different.
- ☐ I used details from both texts.
- ☐ I used complete sentences.
- ☐ I used correct spelling, punctuation, and capitalization.

Respond to the Focus Question

How does nature give people ideas to make art?

Reread/Think

Choose one text from the lesson to review.

TEXT: ______________________________

What kind of art does the artist make?

____

Why does the artist make this kind of art?

____

____

Talk

Share what you learned about how nature gives people ideas for art. Discuss what you think about the artist's work. Use the sentence frames to begin.

Nature gives the artist the idea to make ___ because ___.

I think the artist's work is ___ because ___.

Then tell about something in nature that you think is important. What kind of art would you like to create to make people notice it? Use the sentence frames to discuss your ideas.

I think that one important thing in nature is ___.

I would like to create ___ to make people notice ___.

Write

Write about the artworks that one of the artists makes. Explain how nature gives the artist the idea to make the art. Then write about what art you would create to show why nature is important. If you wish, draw a picture of the artwork you would like to create.

SESSION 1 TALK ABOUT THE TOPIC

The Power of Art

FOCUS QUESTION

Why do people make art?

NOTICE AND WONDER

Look ahead at the play and the pictures in this lesson. What do you notice? What do you wonder? Discuss your ideas with a partner.

WORD SORT

Read the words about art. Sort the words into groups. Write the number on the line to show whether the word describes a type of art, a way to make art, or a tool for making art. You may use a word more than once.

1. drawing	3. scribble	5. paint	7. doodle	9. painting
2. pencil	4. mural	6. sketch	8. picture	

types of art ______

ways to make art ______

tools artists use ______

The words __ and __ are examples of __ because __.

Painting a Story

by Brooks Benjamin

A play

Painting a Story

by Brooks Benjamin

1 *Cast of Characters: Hasan, Mom, Dad, Nadia (a friend), Jacob Stevens (a local artist)*

Scene 1

2 (*The Yousef family's kitchen table. Hasan is drawing while Mom and Dad drink tea and talk.*)

3 **DAD:** The **discount** store opened down the street yesterday. (*sighing*) How is our bookstore going to **compete** with their lower book prices? I wish my parents weren't traveling now. I really could use their help.

4 **MOM:** The community has supported Yousef's Books and Bakery ever since your parents started the business. We'll be okay.

5 **DAD:** For how long, though?

6 (*Hasan sets his pencil down. He looks concerned.*)

discount = selling at lower prices

compete = do as well or better than others

Scene 2

7 (*School auditorium. There is a large screen. Students fill rows of chairs. Hasan and Nadia sit together. Hasan looks unhappy. He scribbles with frustration in his school notebook.*)

8 **NADIA:** What's wrong, Hasan? I thought you were excited about Jacob Stevens's visit since you want to be an artist, too.

9 **HASAN:** I *am* excited. But I can't stop thinking about my family's store. Dad says the new store may put our store out of business.

10 **NADIA:** (*looking shocked*) But everyone loves Yousef's! 

Stop & Discuss

What problem does the Yousef family have?

Underline three details that tell about the problem.

11 **JACOB STEVENS:** (*walks onto the stage*) Hi, everyone! I'm Jacob Stevens.

12 **HASAN:** (*pointing to the artist and whispering*) Hey, Nadia, I've seen him at our store!

13 **JACOB STEVENS:** When I was a kid, I drew on my bedroom walls a lot. My parents were *not* happy about it! But you know what? Now, drawing on walls is my job. You see, I'm a muralist. I use murals to tell stories. (*On the screen, he shows photos of murals.*) I work with communities, including this one, to tell stories that are important to them. These murals have gotten a lot of attention!

14 **HASAN:** (*eyes brightening*) That's it!

15 **NADIA:** *What's* it?

16 **HASAN:** I think I know how to save our store.

Stop & Discuss

Why does Hasan say "That's it!" in line 14?

Discuss your response with a partner. Include the text details you use to figure out the answer.

Hasan means ___. I know because the text says ___.

Analyze a Play

- A **drama**, also called a **play**, is a story that is performed by actors on a stage.
- Most plays are divided into parts called **scenes**.
- The events and actions in a play build from one scene to the next to tell the story.
- The beginning of a play often shows a problem. The scenes that follow build on that problem.
- Readers can better understand a play by thinking about what the characters say, do, think, and feel, and how the scenes build to tell the story.

Reread/Think

Reread Scenes 1 and 2 of "Painting a Story." In the chart, write the characters, the setting, and what happens. Remember to read all the text in the play to find the information you need.

Scene 1		
CHARACTERS	**SETTING**	**WHAT HAPPENS?**
Hasan Yousef, Mom, Dad	the Yousefs' kitchen table	A discount store has opened down the street. Hasan's father is worried that the community will stop supporting Yousef's Books and Bakery. Hasan is worried too.

Scene 2		
CHARACTERS	**SETTING**	**WHAT HAPPENS?**

Talk

Use the details in your chart to talk about what happens in each scene. How does Scene 2 build on what happens in Scene 1? Discuss with a partner.

> In Scene 1, the problem is ___.
> Then, in Scene 2, Hasan ___.

Write

How does what happens in Scene 2 build on the actions and events in Scene 1? Use text details in your response.

WRITING CHECKLIST

- ☐ I included details about the actions and events in Scenes 1 and 2.
- ☐ I explained how Scene 1 leads to Scene 2.
- ☐ I used complete sentences.
- ☐ I used correct spelling, punctuation, and capitalization.

Painting a Story

by Brooks Benjamin

Scene 3

1 *(The Yousef family's living room. Hasan holds his sketchbook for his parents to see.)*

2 **DAD:** You want to paint a *what*?

3 **HASAN:** A mural. Think of all the attention our store would get with a picture on the outside wall.

4 **DAD:** I know you love drawing, but I'm afraid all the doodles in the world couldn't help us now, Hasan. That new store has only been open one day, and we're already seeing fewer customers. I'm sorry, but a mural would just be a waste of time. (*He puts his head in his hands.*)

5 **HASAN:** (*flipping the pages of his sketchbook*) Our store is different. It has a story. We can show the whole history—how **Sitti** and **Jiddi** came to the United States, how they saved money to open their store.

Sitti = "grandmother" in Arabic

Jiddi = "grandfather" in Arabic

6 **DAD:** (*smiling*) Your grandmother wanted to wrap everyone in the smells and tastes of Syria. But your grandfather wanted a place that felt like the library where he'd worked in Damascus.

7 **MOM:** (*nodding*) So they compromised and opened Yousef's Books and Bakery.

8 **HASAN:** (*jumping in his seat*) Who *wouldn't* want to visit a bookstore filled with stories like ours? Don't you think Jiddi and Sitti would love it?

9 **MOM:** (*pats Hasan's arm*) Thank you for wanting to help, Hasan. Your drawings are wonderful, but a mural like that would require a professional.

10 **HASAN:** (*pauses, thinking*) Mom, you're a genius! 

Stop & Discuss

Why does Hasan think a mural could save the store?

Discuss with a partner why Yousef's is a good choice for a mural. Use details from the play in your response.

Yousef's is a good choice for a mural because ___.

Scene 4

11 (*Outside Yousef's Books and Bakery. Hasan, Nadia, Mom, and Dad watch Jacob Stevens* ***approaching****. Hasan holds his sketchbook.*)

approaching = coming nearer

12 **JACOB STEVENS:** Hello! Mr. and Mrs. Yousef, it's great to meet you. And you must be Hasan and Nadia. (*He shakes everyone's hands.*)

13 **MOM:** Hello, Mr. Stevens.

14 **HASAN:** Thanks for coming!

15 **JACOB STEVENS:** It's my pleasure. I'm eager to help with the mural. Hasan sent me his sketches. Your son is a talented artist.

16 **DAD:** (*smiling proudly*) Thank you. I just hope it's not too late to save our store.

17 **NADIA:** I am SO excited to be painting a real mural with a real artist!

18 **MOM:** We'll leave you to it. (*Mom and Dad go into the store.*)

Stop & Discuss

Why is Jacob Stevens at Yousef's Books and Bakery?

Discuss with a partner how you know.

shame = something to feel bad about

presentation = a talk in which someone shows or explains something

19 **JACOB STEVENS:** I'm looking forward to working with both of you, too. I haven't forgotten the time Yousef's Books and Bakery hosted one of my art shows. This place is important to more than just your family. It's a part of the community. It would be a real **shame** to give up without a fight, you know?

20 **NADIA:** Totally! How do we get started?

21 **JACOB STEVENS:** First, let's take another look at your drawings, Hasan. (*Pauses, flipping pages in the sketchbook. Hasan bounces on his toes, waiting.*) You really took my **presentation** to heart. There's a real story here. Tell me more about your grandparents while we get some supplies from my truck.

22 (*Hasan talks excitedly, while Jacob Stevens loads Nadia's arms with a tarp and hands her a can of paint. He pulls a long ladder from the back of the truck before the stage goes dark.*)

Stop & Discuss

Why does Jacob Stevens say to Hasan, "You really took my presentation to heart"?

Underline the text evidence that supports your response.

Jacob Stevens says this because he sees that ___.

Analyze a Play

- To understand how scenes in a play build on each other, first identify the problem. Scenes build on each other to show how characters try to solve the problem.
- Scenes also build on each other to show more about characters. Add the new information you learn about a character to what you already know.

Reread/Think

Reread Scenes 3 and 4 of "Painting a Story." In the chart, write the characters, the setting, what happens, and how the scene builds on the scenes before it. Remember to read all the text in the play to find the information you need.

Scene 3			
CHARACTERS	SETTING	WHAT HAPPENS?	HOW DOES THE SCENE BUILD?

Scene 4			
CHARACTERS	SETTING	WHAT HAPPENS?	HOW DOES THE SCENE BUILD?

Talk

Use the details in your chart to talk about what happens in each scene.

- How does Scene 4 build on what happens in Scene 3?
- What do we learn about the problem?
- What more do we learn about the solution Hasan wants to try and why he hopes it will work?
- How do these scenes build on Scene 1 and Scene 2?

In Scene 3, the problem is ___. Then, in Scene 4, ___.

These scenes build on Scenes 1 and 2 because we learn more about ___ and ___.

Write

Reread what you wrote about Scenes 1 and 2. Then write a summary of Scenes 1–4. Explain how each scene builds on the one before it. At the end of your summary, include a prediction about what might happen in Scene 5.

____

____

____

____

____

____

____

____

____

____

WRITING CHECKLIST

- ☐ I included details about the actions and events in Scenes 1–4.
- ☐ I explained how each scene builds on the one before it.
- ☐ I predicted how Scene 5 might build on Scenes 1–4.
- ☐ I used complete sentences.
- ☐ I used correct spelling, punctuation, and capitalization.

Painting a Story

by Brooks Benjamin

Scene 5

1 (*Outside Yousef's Books and Bakery. Nadia and Jacob Stevens are waiting by the mural. The mural includes four pictures of the Yousef family and how they came to own the store. A small crowd has gathered. Hasan leads Mom and Dad out of the store. They are covering their eyes.*)

habibi = "my dear" in Arabic

2 **HASAN:** Keep your eyes closed. Just a few more steps.

3 **MOM:** I can't wait to see it.

4 **DAD:** Neither can I.

5 **HASAN:** (*leading his parents through the crowd*) Well, you don't have to wait anymore. Open your eyes!

6 **MOM** and **DAD:** Oh!

7 **MOM:** ***Habibi***, it's beautiful!

8 (*Nadia, Jacob Stevens, and the crowd of people clap.*)

9 **HASAN:** (*pulling his parents toward the fourth picture*) I did this one. See. It's all of us. Mr. Stevens showed Nadia and me how to use the special brushes and which colors would be the brightest and last the longest.

10 **DAD:** I love it. And your grandparents will love it too. I will call them tonight and send photos. You have become a real artist, son. (*Hasan looks down at the ground, embarrassed by the praise.*)

11 **MOM:** Thank you, Mr. Stevens. And you too, Nadia.

especially = most of all

12 **DAD:** (*hugging Hasan*) And **especially** you.

13 (*The adults shake hands. Jacob Stevens gives Hasan and Nadia high fives. Everyone heads into the store. Hasan and Nadia are at the end of a long line of customers.*)

14 **NADIA:** Hasan, it seems to be working already! We could start our own mural business.

15 **HASAN:** Maybe one day. But for now, I just want to read a good book.

16 **NADIA:** Ooh! And have one of Sitti's famous treats!

Respond to Text

Reread/Think

Reread Scene 5 of "Painting a Story." Choose the best response to each question.

1. What is presented in line 1 of Scene 5?

A. the setting of the scene

B. the cast of characters

C. the stage directions

D. the character's words

2. When do Hasan's parents first see the mural?

A. Scene 5, lines 2 and 3

B. Scene 5, lines 3 and 4

C. Scene 5, lines 5 and 6

D. Scene 5, lines 7 and 8

3. What do the stage directions in line 12 show about Dad?

A. He cares for Hasan.

B. He is angry with Hasan.

C. He is looking for Hasan.

D. He wants Hasan's help.

4. Read the dialogue from the play.

> **NADIA:** Ooh! And have one of Sitti's **famous** treats!

What is the meaning of the word *famous*?

A. delicious

B. expensive

C. very large

D. well-known

Reread/Think

5. What do Hasan and Nadia do in Scene 5 to help the bookstore?

A. They draw pictures and put them on a website.

B. They show a mural they made of Hasan's family.

C. They take photos to send to Hasan's grandparents.

D. They write a letter and send it to an artist in the city.

Write

Describe what Nadia and Hasan do to help the bookstore. Explain how the events and actions in each scene build on the scene or scenes before it. Use words like *first, next,* and *then* in your response.

WRITING CHECKLIST

- ☐ I explained what happened in each scene.
- ☐ I explained how the events and actions in each scene build on the earlier parts of the play.
- ☐ I used words like *first, next,* and *then* to organize my response.
- ☐ I used correct spelling, punctuation, and capitalization.

Respond to the Focus Question

Why do people make art?

Reread/Think

Think about why Jacob Stevens, Hasan, and Nadia make art.

Talk

Share ideas about why people make art. What happens when Hasan, Nadia, and Jacob Stevens make art? How does making art make them feel? How does their art affect other people? Discuss your ideas with your group.

The character ___ makes art because ___.

Take notes on what your group learned about why people make art and how art affects people.

Notes

Write

Why do people make art? Use the examples of the characters in "Painting a Story" to support your response. Add examples from your own experiences as well.

SESSION 1 TALK ABOUT THE TOPIC

Art in Action

FOCUS QUESTION

How can people use art to show what they care about?

NOTICE AND WONDER

Look at the illustrations. They are all part of one story you will read. What do you notice? What do you wonder? Discuss your ideas with a partner.

WORDS CAN MAKE PICTURES

Sometimes authors use descriptive words to create an image in the reader's mind. Sometimes these words and phrases have other meanings, too. Pick one of these phrases and draw the image that comes to your mind. Then discuss what you think the author means by the phrase.

1. "my heart fluttered"
2. "rolled his eyes"
3. "my heart felt heavy"
4. "I felt very warm inside"

My drawing shows ___.

I think the phrase ___ means ___.

The Cherry Blossoms of High Street, Parts 1–3

by Nandini Bajpai

The Cherry Blossoms of High Street Part 1

by Nandini Bajpai

1 My older brother was waiting for me when I got off the bus, like he did every day after school. But on our chilly walk home, something was different. The cherry blossom trees along our street had bright yellow tape tied around them, the loose ends flapping in the wind.

2 "Samar ***Bhaiya***," I said to my brother, "what's the tape for?"

3 Samar made a whirring sound, like an electric saw. "The city marked the trees they're going to cut down," he said. "Then they're going to widen High Street."

4 My heart pounded. "What? That's horrible!"

5 "But look at the traffic, Jiya," he said, pointing at the long line of cars waiting at the stop light. "The bus takes forever. It'll be faster when the street has another lane."

6 "Couldn't they widen a different road?"

7 Samar shrugged. "It's not a big deal."

8 But it was a big deal. Even in the winter, the trees on High Street stood graceful and tall, holding up their bare branches like friends waving hello. When we moved to Michigan from India, I missed my friends. I also missed the *kachnar* trees near our old home in Delhi. They were covered in pink flowers every spring. My first spring in Michigan, seeing the pink cherry blossoms made me feel better. They were so much like the *kachnar* flowers.

Bhaiya = older brother

Stop & Discuss

Why is Jiya upset?

Discuss with a partner.

9 We walked up the stairs to our apartment. Inside, I dropped my backpack and took off my shoes.

10 “Mama,” I said, “Samar *Bhaiya* says the cherry blossom trees are going to be cut down!”

11 “I’m sorry, Jiya,” Mama said. She knew I loved the trees. “We got a **notice** about it, but I forgot to tell you.”

12 I looked out the window. The branches were making long, lacy shadows on the sidewalk.

13 “I wish I could see the cherry blossoms bloom one more time,” I said. *Wait—maybe I could!*

14 I pulled out my art supplies and cut a bunch of small, delicate flowers from pink construction paper. I punched a hole in each one and made a loop with string. Soon I’d created a huge heap of paper blossoms.

15 Samar poked his head into the room. He eyed the pink paper scraps and bits of string littering the floor.

16 “Mama’s not going to like this mess,” he said.

17 I gathered up a bunch of flowers in my arms. “I’ll clean it later. Help me take these outside.”

18 **Grumbling**, Samar helped me tie the flowers to the lower branches of the tree in front of our building. Soon the paper flowers danced in the breeze.

notice = a note that shares news

grumbling = complaining in a low voice

Stop & Discuss

How does Jiya get her wish to see the cherry blossom trees bloom one more time?

Talk to a partner about what Jiya does.

Jiya sees the cherry blossom trees bloom by ___.

Determine Point of View

- A **narrator** is the person who tells the story.
- A character's **point of view** tells what they think about the events of the story.
- Readers can tell a character's point of view by what they say or do.

Reread/Think

Reread Part 1 of "The Cherry Blossoms of High Street." Write down each character's point of view. Identify text details that show the characters' thoughts and actions and then write them in the chart.

What do the characters think about the plan for the cherry blossom trees?		
CHARACTER	**CHARACTER'S POINT OF VIEW**	**TEXT DETAILS**
Jiya	She thinks the trees are more important than a wider road.	• "'That's horrible!'" • "'Couldn't they widen a different road?'"
Samar		

Talk

Share with a partner the points of view you wrote in your chart for Jiya and Samar. Discuss the thoughts and actions from the text that show the characters' points of view. Then say whether you agree or disagree with the characters' points of view, and explain why.

Jiya/Samar thinks the plan to cut down the trees is ___.

I think this because ___.

I agree/disagree with Jiya/Samar because ___.

Write

Choose to write about either Jiya or Samar. Explain the character's point of view using text details that show their thoughts and actions. Then say whether you agree or disagree and explain why.

WRITING CHECKLIST

- ☐ I used text details to explain the character's point of view.
- ☐ I stated my point of view.
- ☐ I used complete sentences to explain my point of view.
- ☐ I used correct spelling, punctuation, and capitalization.

The Cherry Blossoms of High Street Part 2

by Nandini Bajpai

1 The next morning, some of my paper flowers had gotten wet, and some had blown away. I went to school with a lump in my throat. But that afternoon, when Samar and I were walking home from the bus stop, my heart fluttered when I spotted new decorations on High Street trees.

2 "Look, Samar *Bhaiya*!" I grinned wide and pointed to the flowers. "That means other people care about the trees just like I do!"

3 Samar just rolled his eyes.

4 The new decorations were different from mine. A few were made of cloth, and others were not even flowers. There were birds, squirrels, rainbows, and even a kite.

5 Under a tree in front of the High Street Artists building, a woman was standing at the top of a ladder. She was attaching flowers that spun like pinwheels.

6 "Hello!" I called up. "I like your flowers."

7 The woman **peered** down at me with a friendly smile. Samar tried to pull me along, but I shook him off. I told the woman that I had been the first one to add flowers to a marked tree.

8 "Thank you for doing that," she said. "I've done paintings of these trees in every season. I'll miss them." She nodded toward another woman and a little boy who were drawing chalk flowers on the sidewalk. "My sister and her son Finn will miss them, too."

peered = looked

Stop & Discuss

Why does Jiya's heart flutter when she sees the decorations?

Underline text details that support your answer.

9 "Are you an artist?" I asked.

10 "Yes. I'm Marta Garcia, and I have a **studio** in this building. Come visit with your family at the Art Walk this weekend. If the weather is OK, I'll be displaying some of my paintings on a table outside."

studio = a place where an artist works

11 Closer to home, a woman with a baby stroller was reaching up to a tree on her tiptoes. On the lower branches, she was hanging beautiful flowers knitted from the same pink yarn as the baby's sweater. And next door, a boy and his father, who we'd met many times, were looking up at a tree. The boy was holding a photograph of a Golden Retriever with a gray **muzzle**.

muzzle = the mouth and nose of a dog

12 "Shadow loved these trees," the boy told us. "It was so cool under them in the summer."

13 "I remember Shadow," Samar said. "He was very friendly."

14 The father lifted the boy up so he could tie the photograph onto a branch.

Stop & Discuss

How do other people show they care about the cherry blossom trees?

Underline examples in the text.

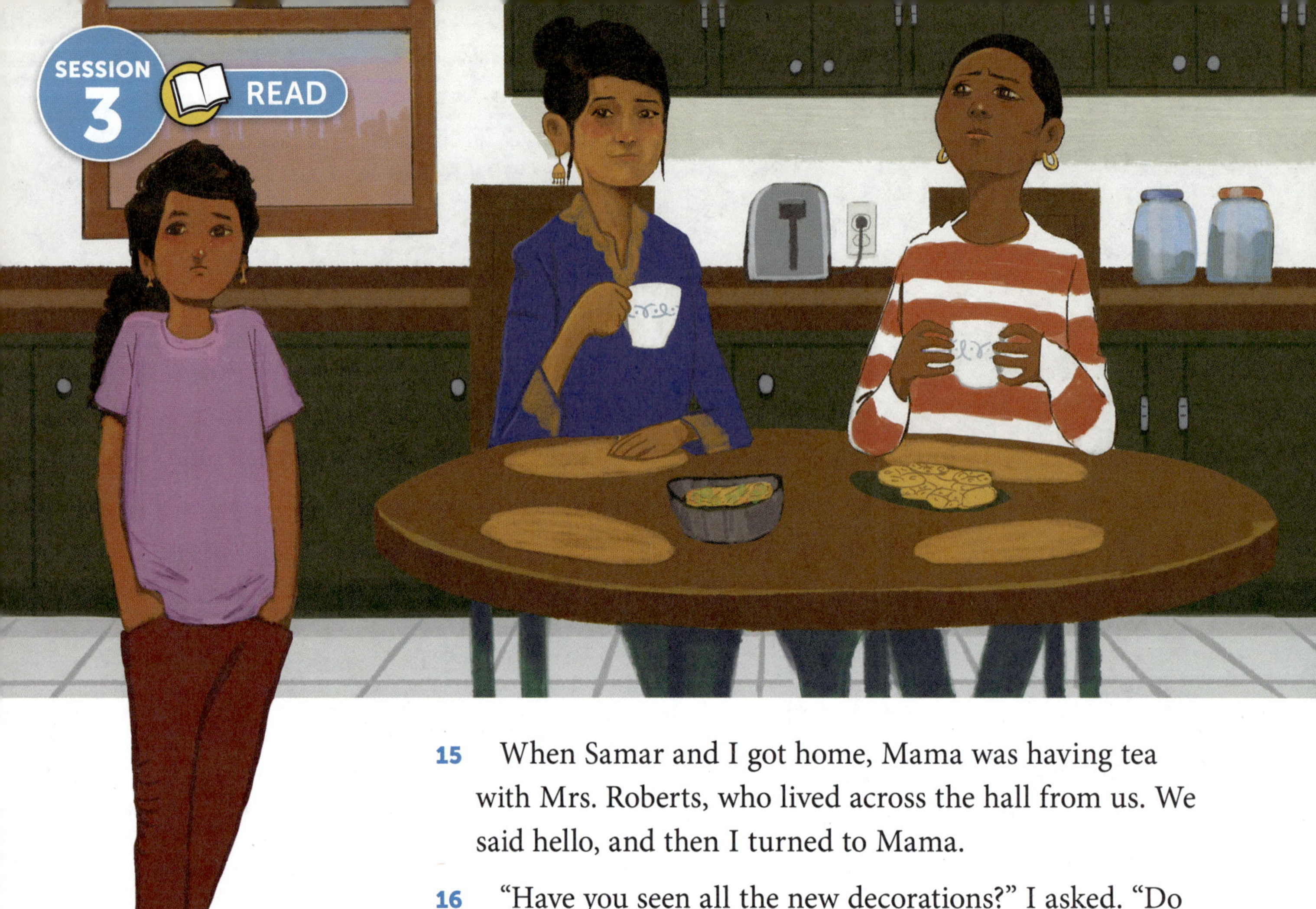

15 When Samar and I got home, Mama was having tea with Mrs. Roberts, who lived across the hall from us. We said hello, and then I turned to Mama.

16 "Have you seen all the new decorations?" I asked. "Do you think the city might decide to keep the trees?"

17 Before Mama could answer, Mrs. Roberts shook her head. "I hope not. We need a wider road."

18 I thought the trees were more important than the road, but Mama would tell me it was **impolite** to argue with an adult.

impolite = not good manners

19 Just then, we heard the rumble of trucks outside. Samar and I peeked out the window and spotted workers placing orange cones along the sidewalk.

20 "It looks like they're marking their work zone," he said.

21 I blinked back tears and stayed quiet, afraid I would start crying if I spoke. My heart felt heavy. I knew I had to do something more to help.

Stop & Discuss

What does Mrs. Roberts say about the trees and the plan for a new road?

Talk with a partner about what she says and how Jiya reacts.

Determine Point of View

- Each character has a point of view about the events in a story.
- Readers have their own point of view about events in a story. A reader's point of view is personal and may be different from those of the characters in a story. Notice what the narrator or a character says, thinks, and does. Then think about your own point of view. How is it the same or different?

Reread/Think

Reread Part 2 of "The Cherry Blossoms of High Street." Write down each character's point of view. Identify text details that show the characters' thoughts and actions and then write them in the chart.

What do the characters think about the decorations added to the cherry blossom trees?		
CHARACTER	**POINT OF VIEW**	**TEXT DETAILS**
Jiya	She is happy others care about the trees.	• "I grinned wide and pointed to the flowers." • "'That means other people care about the trees just like I do!'"
Samar		
Mrs. Roberts		

Talk

Look at the chart to discuss the points of view of Jiya, Samar, and Mrs. Roberts. Then decide your own point of view about the decorations added to the cherry blossom trees. Use details from the text to support your point of view.

__ point of view is __.

My point of view is __ because __.

Write

Choose to write about one character: Jiya, Samar, or Mrs. Roberts. Explain the character's point of view using text details that show their thoughts and actions. Then tell your own point of view and explain how it is the same or different.

WRITING CHECKLIST

- ☐ I stated a character's point of view.
- ☐ I used text details to explain the character's point of view.
- ☐ I stated my point of view.
- ☐ I used complete sentences to explain why I felt that way.
- ☐ I used correct spelling, punctuation, and capitalization.

The Cherry Blossoms of High Street Part 3

by Nandini Bajpai

1 By Friday, I had a plan. My parents and Ms. Garcia, the artist down the street, were going to help me make it work. At Saturday's Art Walk, I was going to set up a flower-making station at the end of her outdoor table. I hoped that adding even more flowers to the trees would make the city pay attention. Even Samar was going to help by taking photos of the decorated trees and posting them online. He still didn't really care about the trees, but he cared about me.

2 On Saturday morning, we bundled up in warm clothes and headed downtown. I sat at Ms. Garcia's table, and at first nobody noticed me. My father, who was standing nearby, suggested I make a sign.

3 "What a wonderful idea! Fiona and Finn can help," Ms. Garcia said as her sister arrived with Finn.

4 "What should we write?" I asked.

5 "Something that helps people understand how important the trees are," Fiona said.

6 After thinking for a moment, I wrote on bright pink paper in large letters: "Save the Trees!" Finn drew a tree and flowers next to the words.

7 Fiona was right. People started coming over and making flowers. I was surprised when Mrs. Roberts, our neighbor, tapped my shoulder.

8 "I've been thinking," she said with a grin. "We do need a wider road, but it would be a pity to lose the trees." She picked up a marker and a piece of paper.

mayor = the leader of a city

blurted = said suddenly

9 Samar dashed up to the table, nearly knocking it over in excitement.

10 "My pictures have gotten lots of attention," he said breathlessly. "Even the **mayor** has noticed, and now she's here! Look!"

11 The mayor was heading our way. Just in case I got to talk to someone important, I had practiced a speech about saving the trees. But when the mayor stood in front of me, I forgot everything I planned to say.

12 "Hello, Jiya," she said. "I've heard that you started this beautiful celebration for the trees."

13 "The trees make me happy," I **blurted** out. This was not the long speech I'd practiced, but it was true. "They make lots of people happy."

14 "So it seems," the mayor said. "Thank you for helping me see that."

15 "Can you please let the trees stay?" I asked in a tiny voice.

16 The mayor smiled. "I can't promise anything, but I will try. Maybe there are other solutions that will allow us to keep the trees."

17 I smiled back. Even though snow had started to fall, I felt very warm inside.

Respond to Text

Reread/Think

Reread Part 3 of "The Cherry Blossoms of High Street." Then choose the best response to each question.

1. How does Samar help Jiya?

A. He finds supplies to make signs.

B. He brings the mayor to their street.

C. He takes photos and posts them online.

D. He sets up a table for the flower-making station.

2. What does Jiya do that shows her point of view?

A. She gives a speech.

B. She makes a sign.

C. She takes pictures.

D. She writes a song.

3. What happens in the story that shows Jiya is nervous?

A. She writes on a piece of paper with a marker.

B. She forgets the speech she practiced.

C. She dresses in warm clothes.

D. She smiles at the mayor.

4. What does the mayor think at the end of the story?

A. There may be a way to save the trees.

B. It is still necessary to widen the street.

C. Everyone should put paper flowers on trees.

D. The city should have an Art Walk every month.

Reread/Think

5. What is the **best** meaning for the word *solutions* in paragraph 16?

A. problems

B. traffic

C. trees

D. answers

Write

What do the characters think about the cherry blossom trees of High Street being cut down? Describe the points of view of three characters. Use text details that show what the characters think, say, and do. Then explain your point of view about the trees being cut down.

WRITING CHECKLIST

- ☐ I described the points of view of three characters.
- ☐ I used details about what they say, do, and think to support my descriptions.
- ☐ I used complete sentences.
- ☐ I used correct spelling, punctuation, and capitalization.

Respond to the Focus Question

How can people use art to show what they care about?

Reread/Think

Think of two characters in the story who make art that shows what they care about. Describe the art they make in the story.

____

____

Talk

As a group, think about your friends, family, and what is happening in your community. Who or what do you care about? How could you use art to show that you care? What type of art would you make, and why? Take notes on what others say.

I would make art to show I care about ___.

The type of art I would make is ___. It shows that I care because ___.

Name:	Name:

Write

How is art a way for people to show what they care about? Use examples from all three parts of the text in your response.

SESSION 1 MAKE CONNECTIONS

Creative Solutions

TALK ABOUT WHAT YOU KNOW

Use the pictures to remember the texts that you read in this unit. Turn and talk with a partner about what you already know about art. Use the sentence frames to help you.

The ideas for making art can come from ___.

One reason people make art is ___. For example, ___.

LESSON 18

Natural Creativity

LESSON 19
The Power of Art

LESSON 20
Art in Action

A THOUSAND WORDS

Some people say, "A picture is worth a thousand words." Do you agree with this saying? Is art more powerful than words? Why or why not? Write down a few ideas and then discuss your thinking with a partner.

Friendship

by Louise Rozett

1 *Cast of Characters: Mr. Aron, Zack, Allie, Emiko, Ms. Ito*

SCENE 1

2 *Mr. Aron's third-grade classroom. Emiko and Allie sit next to each other. Their classmate, Zack, bursts into the room.*

3 **ZACK:** Sorry I'm late, Mr. A! (*Being silly, Zack does a little dance to his seat. His classmates chuckle.*)

4 **MR. ARON:** Thank you for joining us, Zachary. As you know, it's field-trip day! We're going to the museum to learn about **Kintsugi**. Who remembers what that is?

Kintsugi = a form of Japanese art

5 (*Emiko raises her hand and Mr. Aron calls on her.*)

6 **EMIKO:** Kintsugi is the Japanese art of mending broken **pottery** with glue and gold powder. I know about it because my grandparents have a bowl that's been fixed with Kintsugi. It's blue with a gold line like lightning.

pottery = objects made out of baked clay

7 **ALLIE:** (*proudly, to the class*) I got to use it when I went to Emiko's grandparents' house for dinner.

8 **MR. ARON:** Fantastic! All right, kids, let's line up.

9 (*Emiko and Allie gather their things.*)

10 **EMIKO:** I remember that day. You were worried you'd break the bowl again!

11 **ALLIE:** (*hiding her face in her hands*) It was so pretty, my hands were shaking and I spilled stew everywhere!

12 (*The girls laugh as Mr. Aron leads the class to the bus.*)

Stop & Discuss

How does the text show what kind of relationship Allie and Emiko have?

Talk about the details in Scene 1 that help you understand their friendship.

Is Golden

SCENE 2

13 *Outside the school. The class is **boarding** the bus. Allie sits, saving an open seat next to her for Emiko, but Zack sits in it instead.*

14 **ALLIE:** (*pointing at the seat*) Um, uh—

15 **ZACK:** My older brother did this trip last year. The museum's going to let us do a Kintsugi project and keep it!

16 (*Emiko gets on the bus and sees Zack in her seat. She looks at Allie with a questioning look on her face. Allie looks around, then points to an empty seat behind her.*)

17 **ALLIE:** (*to Emiko*) Sit there! I'll turn around so we can—

18 **EMIKO:** (***slumps** into the seat behind Allie*) Forget it.

19 **ZACK:** My brother's Kintsugi bowl has a zigzag and . . .

20 (*Zack keeps talking as the girls ride in silence.*) 

boarding = getting onto

slumps = sits heavily

Stop & Discuss

What happens on the bus? What problem does it cause?

Use details from Scene 2 to discuss with a partner.

On the bus, Allie ___, but Zack ___. This makes Emiko ___.

SCENE 3

21 *Inside the museum. Emiko and Allie don't say a word to each other as they follow their class through the museum. Then, suddenly, Emiko speaks.*

22 **EMIKO:** Why did you tell Zack he could sit with you?

23 **ALLIE:** I didn't! He just *sat*. I didn't want to be mean.

24 **EMIKO:** But you *were* mean. To *me*.

25 **MR. ARON:** Hurry, girls! Ms. Ito is waiting.

demonstrate = show how to do something

26 (*Emiko walks away from Allie as they enter the museum workshop. Ms. Ito begins to* ***demonstrate*** *Kintsugi.*)

27 **MS. ITO:** When a bowl cracks, some say it's broken or ruined. But Kintsugi artists mend the cracks with gold, making the pottery stronger and more beautiful. What else breaks besides bowls?

28 **ZACK:** Ooh! Ooh! Plates! Bones!

29 **MS. ITO:** Yes! Anyone else?

30 **EMIKO:** (*looking at Allie*) Friendship.

31 **MS. ITO:** True. And like a Kintsugi bowl, a friendship can become stronger and more beautiful after it is mended. Now, artists, let's see what you can do!

Stop & Discuss

How does Ms. Ito compare a friendship to a Kintsugi bowl?

Underline the sentence that supports your response.

32 (*Emiko goes to a worktable full of supplies. After a moment, Allie joins her, and they work without talking, dipping their brushes in the gold paint.*)

33 **EMIKO:** Maybe if we paint ourselves gold, everything will go back to normal.

34 **ALLIE:** (*grinning*) We could be real-life Kintsugi bowls.

35 (*The girls laugh together.*)

36 **ALLIE:** I'm sorry, Emiko. I didn't know what to say to Zack.

37 **EMIKO:** I'm sorry, too. I was upset because I thought you didn't want to sit with me.

38 **ALLIE:** I *always* want to sit with you!

39 **EMIKO:** Me too. If this ever happens again, let's talk about it right away.

40 **ALLIE:** Totally. I like that.

41 (*Allie holds up her bowl. The paint looks like a golden river flowing down the side of the bowl.*)

42 **ALLIE:** The fixed crack does make the bowl more beautiful!

43 (*Zack* ***approaches****, his hands covered in gold paint.*)

44 **ZACK:** Hey, can I borrow some paint? I used all of mine.

45 **ALLIE:** (*smiling*) Sure, Zack. Use all you want.

46 **EMIKO:** We're done fixing our cracks.

47 (*The girls* ***exchange*** *glances and smile.*) 

approaches = comes closer

exchange = trade

Stop & Discuss

What does Emiko mean when she says "We're done fixing our cracks" at the end of the scene?

Discuss two meanings for what she says.

One meaning of what Emiko says is that ___. The other meaning is that ___.

Respond to Text

Reread/Think

Reread "Friendship Is Golden." Choose the best response to each question.

1. What information is found in line 5?

A. the cast of characters

B. the setting of the scene

C. the directions to the actors

D. the words the actor speaks

2. What is the **best** summary of Scene 1?

A. Zack disturbs the class by arriving late.

B. Allie is surprised when Zack sits next to her.

C. Emiko talks about her grandparents' bowl in class.

D. Mr. Aron tells his class about an upcoming field trip.

3. **PART A**

How does Emiko feel in Scene 2?

A. upset that Allie did not save her a seat

B. excited to create a bowl at the museum

C. afraid to sit by herself behind Allie

D. mad that Zack is talking too loudly

PART B

Which line **best** supports the answer to Part A?

A. line 13

B. line 15

C. line 17

D. line 18

4. Read the sentence from line 27 of the play.

> But Kintsugi artists **mend** the cracks with gold, making the pottery stronger and more beautiful.

What is the meaning of the word *mend* as it is used in this sentence?

A. fix

B. paint

C. shape

D. cut

5. What do the stage directions in line 47 tell about Allie and Emiko?

A. They think Zack is being silly.

B. They have become friends again.

C. They are unhappy with each other.

D. They want to thank Ms. Ito for her lesson.

6. What lesson do Emiko and Allie learn?

A. Friendship can be repaired like cracks in a bowl.

B. Working carefully is the best way to finish a task.

C. Friends can be found in unexpected places.

D. It is best to listen to the advice of adults.

Write

Describe Emiko's point of view about how to communicate hurt feelings to a friend. Compare this to your point of view about the best way to tell a friend your feelings are hurt. Use at least two details from the play in your response.

WRITING CHECKLIST

- ☐ I described Emiko's point of view about hurt feelings.
- ☐ I used two details from the play.
- ☐ I compared my point of view to Emiko's point of view.
- ☐ I used complete sentences.
- ☐ I used correct spelling, punctuation, and capitalization.

Make Connections

Reread/Think

In this unit, you have learned about how artists share ideas and feelings with others through art. Often, artists hope their artworks will help people decide to take an action—to do something—to make the world a better place.

Look back at the texts in this unit. What piece of art in this unit gives you the strongest feeling of wanting to *do something* to make things better? Identify the text and describe the piece of art. Then explain why it makes you want to do something. What does it make you want to do?

TEXT: ______________________________

____

____

____

____

____

____

____

____

____

Talk

Meet with a group to discuss the artwork you chose and the action it brings to your mind. Explain what kind of action the artwork makes you want to take, and why. Use the sentence frames to get started.

The artwork that gives me the strongest feeling of wanting to do something is ___.

The artwork makes me want to take action and ___ because ___.

Unit Assessments

Read the folktale. Then answer the questions that follow.

The Lost Camel

A Folktale from India

1 There were once some **merchants** who traveled from place to place selling their goods. Late one evening, when they stopped to make camp for the night, they discovered that one of their beloved camels was missing.

2 At dawn the next morning, they set out to look for the camel. Along the way, they met a man walking along the path toward them. They stopped and asked him if he had seen a camel. The man told them he had not seen the camel, but he was sure he could tell them where the camel was. The merchants were confused by this. They began to question the man.

3 "Was the camel carrying a load?" they asked.

4 "Yes," the man answered. "He was carrying bags of wheat on his left side. He had a jar of honey on his right side. Furthermore, the camel is blind in one eye. And he has a missing tooth. But like I said, I haven't seen him. I can only tell you where you can find him."

merchants = people who buy and sell things

5 "But you have given a perfect description of our lost camel!" the surprised merchants exclaimed.

6 "You probably have hidden our camel. You plan to steal him!" another merchant added.

7 "I haven't seen him, and I'm not a thief!" the man answered sharply. "But I have lived in this land a long time. There are some things I know!"

8 "Then tell us. How do you know he was carrying wheat and honey?" the merchants asked **suspiciously**.

9 "I know he was carrying wheat because ants gathered around the grains that had fallen along the left side of the path. The bag was probably cut by some branches. I know he was carrying jars of honey because flies were swarming where the honey had dripped. The flies were on the right side."

10 "Fine. But how do you know he is blind in one eye?" one merchant asked.

11 "Because I noticed he had been **grazing** only on the right side of the path," the man answered.

12 "And how do you know the camel is missing a tooth?" another merchant asked.

13 "Because where he had chewed the grass, he left a clump in the middle of the bite. That told me he had a tooth missing."

14 "If the directions you give us are correct," the merchants said, "then we will reward you for the good news you have given us."

15 And so they got directions and went off to look for the camel. The merchants found the camel near where the man had said he saw the signs. They were very pleased to find their lost camel, and they greatly rewarded the man who had been so clever.

suspiciously = acting in a way that shows caution or doubt

grazing = chewing on grass

Respond to Text

Reread/Think

1. At the beginning of the story, what problem do the merchants have?
   A. They cannot find a place to camp.
   B. One of their camels is missing.
   C. They have to keep traveling.
   D. Nobody will buy their goods.

2. How does the man know the camel is blind in one eye?
   A. He knew the camel had wandered away from the other camels.
   B. He noticed that the camel grazed on only one side of the path.
   C. He saw the camel up close when he led it away from the camp.
   D. He asked the merchants what the missing camel looked like.

3. Why are the merchants confused by the man?
   A. The man says he has not seen the camel but knows where it is.
   B. The man asks the merchants what the camel was carrying.
   C. The man says he knows where the camel is but will not say where.
   D. The man tells the merchants he is also looking for the camel.

4. **PART A**

How do the merchants react at first when the man describes the missing camel?

A. They thank him and give him a large gift.

B. They think that he is making up a story.

C. They ask him to help them find their camel.

D. They believe that he stole their camel.

PART B

Which sentence from the text **best** supports the answer to Part A?

A. "'Was the camel carrying a load?'" (paragraph 3)

B. "'But you have given a perfect description of our lost camel!'" (paragraph 5)

C. "'You probably have hidden our camel.'" (paragraph 6)

D. "'How do you know he was carrying wheat and honey?'" (paragraph 8)

5. How does the man know the camel is missing a tooth?

A. He found the camel's missing tooth lying on the path.

B. He overheard the merchants talking about the camel.

C. He saw grains of wheat that were chewed by the camel.

D. He noticed the camel left behind a clump in a bite of grass.

6. Number the events from the story in the order in which they happen.

_______ The man explains how he knows about the camel without having seen it.

_______ The merchants notice a camel is missing.

_______ The merchants find their lost camel and reward the man.

_______ The merchants meet a man who describes the camel perfectly.

_______ The man gives the merchants directions for where to find their camel.

7. **PART A**

What do the merchants realize after they find their camel?

A. The man had been telling the truth.

B. The man had actually seen the camel pass by.

C. They could have found the camel on their own.

D. They should give the camel to the man as a reward.

PART B

Recount **two** details from the story that support the answer to Part A.

____

____

____

____

____

____

____

____

____

8. PART A

What causes the merchants to change their minds about the man they meet?

A. The man guesses correctly where the camel is.

B. They offer to reward him if he brings them the camel.

C. They find the camel where the man said it would be.

D. The man tells them he knows who took the camel.

PART B

Underline the sentence from paragraph 15 that **best** supports the answer to Part A.

> And so they got directions and went off to look for the camel. The merchants found the camel near where the man had said he saw the signs. They were very pleased to find their lost camel, and they greatly rewarded the man who had been so clever.

9. SHORT RESPONSE Reread this sentence from the text.

> "How do you know he was carrying wheat and honey?" the merchants asked **suspiciously**.

Why are the merchants *suspicious* of the man? Use **two** details from the text to support your response.

____

____

____

____

____

____

____

10. Read these sentences from the text.

> "I haven't seen him, and I'm not a thief!" the man answered sharply. "But I have lived in this land a long time. There are some things I know!"

What do these sentences tell readers about the man?

A. He wants to have his own camel.

B. He has learned a lot in his life.

C. He enjoys playing tricks on people he meets.

D. He actually does know where the camel is.

11. Read this sentence from paragraph 3.

> "Was the camel carrying a **load**?" they asked.

What is the meaning of *load* as it is used in this sentence?

A. a bundle

B. a merchant

C. a tooth

D. a reward

12. Read this sentence from paragraph 9.

> "I know he was carrying jars of honey because flies were **swarming** where the honey had dripped."

What is the meaning of *swarming* as it is used in this sentence?

A. stinging

B. eating

C. landing

D. flying

Write

EXTENDED RESPONSE What is the central message of the story? Use details from the story to support your response.

WRITING CHECKLIST

- [ ] I answered the question.
- [ ] I included details from the folktale to support my response.
- [ ] I used complete sentences.
- [ ] I used correct spelling, punctuation, and capitalization.

Read the science article. Then answer the questions that follow.

THE STRANGE POWER OF Volcanoes

by Magnus Krako

Photo taken during the Surtsey eruption in 1964

1 In 1963, a ship's captain sailing near Iceland saw smoke rising from the sea. He thought it was a ship on fire, but he found something much stranger. Hot melted rock, called lava, was shooting up to the water's surface from below. Ash made of bits of crushed rock also shot out. The captain was seeing an underwater volcano. The volcano erupted, or exploded, for more than three years. When it finally stopped, all that lava and ash had formed a new island in the ocean. The island was called Surtsey.

2 Volcanoes are found all over the world. They can be underwater like the one that formed Surtsey, or they can be on land. They can be found in deserts or jungles. Volcanoes can create new mountains. They can blow the tops off of old ones. They shape and reshape the land around us. They also give us a peek into what goes on below Earth's surface.

3 All volcanoes are mostly the same on the inside. A long skinny tube called a pipe forms the center of a volcano. The pipe starts in a pool of red-hot, liquid rock called a magma chamber. The pipe goes all the way up to the crater at the top of the volcano. This is where the volcano's vent is found. The vent is a crack in the Earth's surface. It lets smoke, ash, and lava out of the volcano.

4 To understand how a volcano erupts, think about a bottle of soda. When you shake soda in a closed bottle, bubbles form. The bubbles create a special kind of gas. Then, as more bubbles form, more gas forms. Inside the bottle, the gas and bubbles press harder and harder against the sides. This pressure builds and builds. Finally, when the lid is taken off, the soda sprays out.

5 This is how a volcano works. Hot, liquid rock makes different gases. The **pressure** from these gases builds up. After a while, the pressure gets too great. The gases push up the pipe and through the vent. They push other things out with it. Sometimes hot, liquid lava sprays out of the vent. Sometimes tiny bits of rock blast in a huge ash cloud. Not all volcanoes erupt in the same way. Some are quick and loud. Others move more slowly, with lava that flows like thick honey. No matter how a volcano erupts, it is an amazing thing to watch.

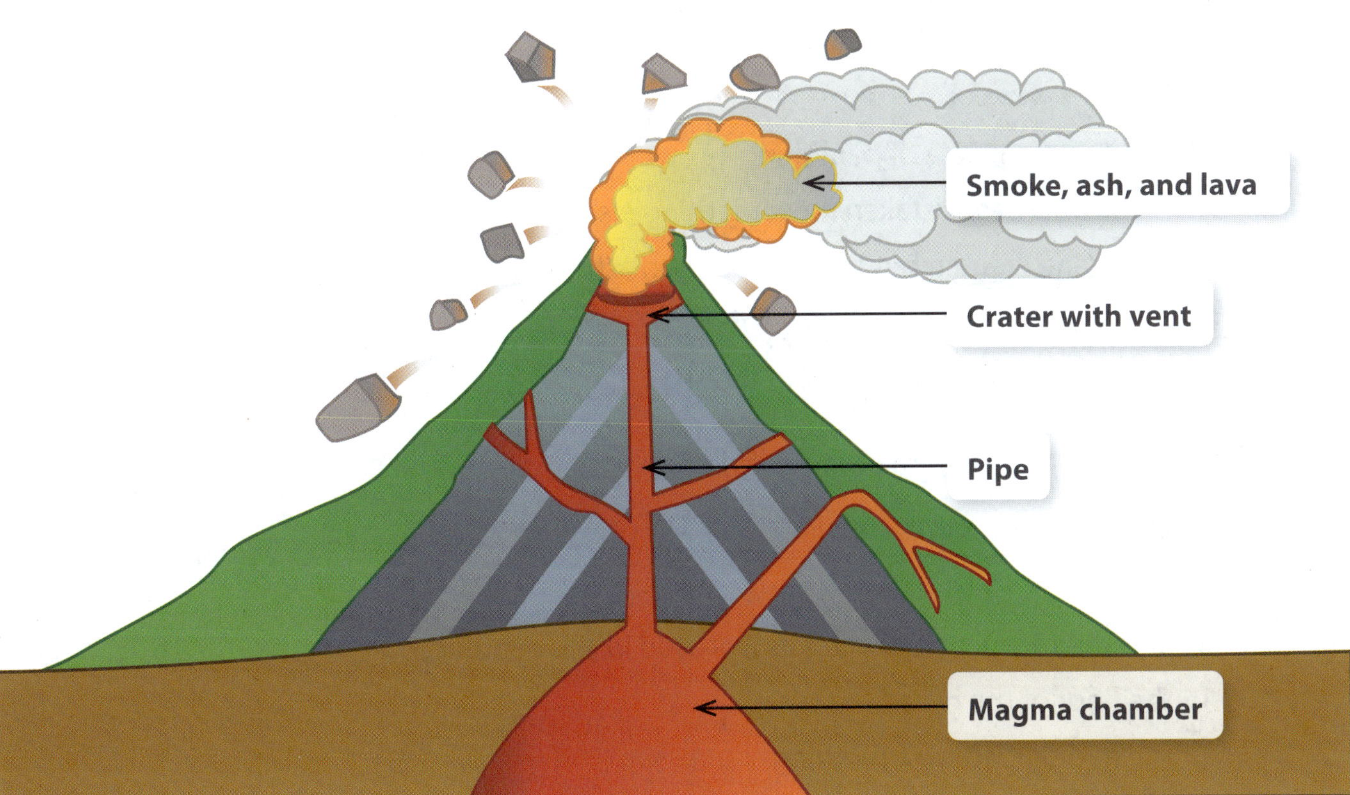

pressure = a force pressing against the surface of something

6 The ash from a volcanic eruption can change Earth's weather. In 1815, Mount Tambora in the Pacific Ocean erupted. It sent a huge ash cloud into the sky. The ash cloud stopped much of the sunlight from getting through. For more than a year, the weather everywhere on Earth was different. Summers were cold and cloudy. Snow fell and lakes froze, even in June!

7 Some people think volcanoes are scary—and they certainly can be. They are very powerful. Their red-hot lava can destroy anything in its path. Scientists study volcanoes safely to learn more about how Earth was formed and how it continues to change. This information is not only fascinating, but it is important as well. What scientists learn can help us know when a volcano will erupt, and it can also give us clues for what might happen in the future!

Respond to Text

Reread/Think

1. What is the main idea of paragraph 1?

A. A volcano was mistaken for something else.

B. A volcano created hot melted rock and ash.

C. A volcano erupted for three years.

D. A volcano formed an island in the sea.

2. Read this sentence from paragraph 1.

> Hot melted rock, called lava, was shooting up to the water's **surface** from below.

What is the meaning of *surface* as it is used in this sentence?

A. the floor of the ocean

B. the middle part of something

C. the ocean's waves

D. the top part of something

3. **SHORT RESPONSE** What details in paragraph 2 support the idea that volcanoes form all over the world? Use **two** details from the text in your response.

____

____

____

____

____

4. Read this sentence from paragraph 2.

> They also give us a **peek** into what goes on below Earth's surface.

What is the meaning of *peek* as it used in the sentence?

A. big hole

B. hot rock

C. quick look

D. small crack

5. Which statement about volcanoes is NOT true?

A. All volcanoes have a chamber filled with magma.

B. The eruption of a volcano always produces a gas cloud.

C. All volcanoes have a vent that lets smoke, ash, and lava out.

D. The gases in a volcano always cause pressure to build up.

6. According to the author, in what way is lava like honey (paragraph 5)?

   A. Lava can stick to things.

   B. Lava can take a while to form.

   C. Lava can have the same color.

   D. Lava can flow in the same way.

7. **PART A**

   According to paragraph 6, what effect can volcanoes have on the weather?

   A. They can make the oceans colder.

   B. They can make the winters hotter.

   C. They can make the summers colder.

   D. They can make the sunlight hotter.

   PART B

   Reread paragraph 6. Then underline **two** sentences that **best** support the answer to Part A.

   > The ash from a volcanic eruption can change Earth's weather. In 1815, Mount Tambora in the Pacific Ocean erupted. It sent a huge ash cloud into the sky. The ash cloud stopped much of the sunlight from getting through. For more than a year, the weather everywhere on Earth was different. Summers were cold and cloudy. Snow fell and lakes froze, even in June!

8. According to the author's point of view, what makes volcanoes mostly the same?

   A. the places where they form

   B. how they work on the inside

   C. their effect on the weather

   D. how they look on the outside

9. Choose **two** words from the word bank to complete the paragraph about how volcanoes work.

vent	magma	ash cloud

Hot, liquid rock in a ________________________ chamber makes different gases. The gases push up through a pipe in the volcano's center. The gases and lava come out of a ________________________ in the Earth's surface.

10. Why does the author compare an erupting volcano to a bottle of soda?

A. to show how liquids flow

B. to show how soda is made

C. to show how pressure builds

D. to show how lava is created

11. Which statement about volcanoes would the author **most likely** agree with?

A. Volcanoes are thrilling forces of nature.

B. Volcanoes are constantly changing.

C. Volcanoes are scary and unpredictable.

D. Volcanoes are quick and loud.

12. **PART A**

Which statement **best** describes the author's point of view about volcanoes?

A. They should be studied because they can help us learn about the world.

B. They are easy to understand because they are so similar to one another.

C. The most important thing about them is how fun it is to watch them erupt.

D. They are so dangerous that they should be avoided completely.

PART B

Which sentence from the passage **best** supports the answer to Part A?

A. "All volcanoes are mostly the same on the inside." (paragraph 3)

B. "No matter how a volcano erupts, it is an amazing thing to watch." (paragraph 5)

C. "Some people think volcanoes are scary—and they certainly can be." (paragraph 7)

D. "What scientists learn can help us know when a volcano might erupt, and it can also give us clues for what might happen in the future!" (paragraph 7)

Write

EXTENDED RESPONSE How and why does a volcano erupt? How can volcanic eruptions affect the Earth? Use at least **two** details from the text to explain the process.

WRITING CHECKLIST

- ☐ I explained how and why a volcano erupts.
- ☐ I explained how Earth is affected by volcanoes.
- ☐ I included details from the text.
- ☐ I used complete sentences.
- ☐ I used correct spelling, punctuation, and capitalization.

Read the story. Then answer the questions that follow.

Yosemite Morning

by Hilary Dumitrescu

1 It is quiet in the cabin when my brother and I wake up. We are at **Yosemite National Park** for a weekend adventure with Grandma and Grandpa. They are still sleeping, so we creep outside, as silent as mice, into the winter stillness.

2 Fresh snow has fallen overnight and blanketed the forest and rocks with a quilt of white. I take a deep breath. The mountain air feels icy. Suddenly, nearby, I hear a soft thump. I hear my brother squeal. When I turn around, he is standing there with his head covered in a thick crown of snow! He laughs and points up. The branches above him hold armfuls of snow, as if they are waiting to start a snowball fight with us.

3 We walk further along a path through the forest, our boots crunch-crunch-crunching in the snow. My brother walks ahead of me. At one point, his entire left leg is swallowed up by the snow. He's stuck! I run to help him, but I, too, sink completely. The snowbank is surprisingly deep. We are laughing, trying to free our legs from the snow's grip. I pull my foot out, finally, only to find that it's just my sock that has escaped! My boot is still buried. Our giggles echo throughout the forest, clear as bells.

Yosemite National Park = a large park known for its huge trees and cliffs

4 We finally free ourselves. I put my boot back on and we continue down the path. Tiny snowflakes swirl around us, dancing in the breeze. It feels like we are all alone, but there are signs of life everywhere. Rabbit tracks lead across a fallen log and disappear under a large bush. A woodpecker has hammered holes into the bark of an ancient tree. Half-chewed pinecones are scattered about, their seeds **devoured** by hungry chipmunks.

5 We come to a clearing. My brother holds up a hand, telling me to stop. In the distance we can see Half Dome, a huge, towering wall of rock. Visitors come from miles around to see this natural wonder. But that's not what my brother is pointing to. At the far edge of the clearing is a deer, standing perfectly still. The deer is watching us. We freeze. The deer freezes. Then, suddenly, something startles her. In a flash, she is gone.

6 We head back to the cabin, where Grandma and Grandpa have made breakfast. They give us each a warm plate of pancakes. We tell them about our early morning walk, as the kitchen wraps us in warmth. We have the whole day ahead of us. We wonder what other adventures await us in the forest.

devoured = eaten quickly

Respond to Text

Reread/Think

1. PART A

Read this sentence from paragraph 2.

> When I turn around, he is standing there with his head covered in a thick crown of snow!

What does this sentence show about the brother?

A. He has a hat shaped like a crown.

B. He is acting like a king.

C. He has a pile of snow on his head.

D. He is trying to be funny.

PART B

What detail from the text supports the response to Part A?

A. "my brother and I wake up" (paragraph 1)

B. "we creep outside" (paragraph 1)

C. "I take a deep breath" (paragraph 2)

D. "I hear a soft thump" (paragraph 2)

2. Read this sentence from paragraph 4.

Tiny snowflakes swirl around us, dancing in the breeze.

What does this sentence tell about the weather?

A. A lot of snow is falling on a sunny day.

B. There is a light wind, and a little snow is falling.

C. There is a heavy wind, and a lot of snow is falling.

D. A little snow is falling on a cloudy day.

3. Read this sentence from paragraph 5.

In a flash, she is gone.

What do the words *in a flash* tell about the deer?

A. The deer runs quickly.

B. The deer runs toward the sunlight.

C. The deer runs when lightning strikes.

D. The deer runs quietly.

4. Read this sentence from paragraph 6.

We tell them about our early morning walk, as the kitchen wraps us in warmth.

Use your own words to tell what the underlined words mean.

____

____

____

____

____

Read the article. Then answer the questions that follow.

The Buzz on Sniffer Bees

by Heather Roberson

1 Did you know that bees have a great sense of smell? You've seen the antennae, or feelers, on their heads. Those feelers have more than three thousand tiny smell **organs**. The organs help the bees identify more than 170 different odors. This is how they find food, water, and pollen.

2 Many animals have a better sense of smell than humans do. That's why people train dogs to sniff out scents. Bees have an even stronger sense of smell than dogs. So, scientists are looking for ways that trained bees can help people.

3 Scientists can teach bees to follow specific smells. First, the bees are given a smell to learn. Then they are sent toward the same smell in another area. When they find where the smell is coming from, they are rewarded with sugar water. Scientists repeat this process over and over. Finally, the bees connect the smell with a treat. Bees can be trained in about ten minutes.

organs = parts of the body that do certain jobs

4 Sniffer bees have been trained to find harmful materials. They can also sniff out health problems. They can smell a disease in someone's breath. They can uncover some kinds of cancer. They can spot a lung disease called tuberculosis (too ber kyoo LOW sis). They can also smell dangerous chemicals that cause explosions. In addition, they can find plant diseases and pests such as bedbugs. Sniffer bees make few mistakes.

5 One day, these tiny helpers may work in airports, farms, hospitals, and war zones. They will alert people to possible danger.

Respond to Text

Reread/Think

1. What is the main idea of this text?

A. Bees have a better sense of smell than dogs.

B. Bees can smell more than 170 different odors.

C. Bees like to drink sugar water.

D. Bees can be trained to help people.

2. **SHORT RESPONSE** What are antennae, and how are they used? Reread paragraph 1 for clues.

____

____

____

____

____

3. Read this sentence from paragraph 2.

> That's why people train dogs to sniff out **scents**.

What is the meaning of *scents* in this sentence?

A. water

B. odors

C. flowers

D. pollen

4. Scientists follow a series of steps to train the bees. What is the last step in the series?

A. Reward the bees with sugar water.

B. Send the bees to a different area.

C. Repeat the process over and over.

D. Give the bees a smell to learn.

5. PART A

What is the meaning of *specific* as it is used in paragraph 3?

A. strong

B. certain

C. pleasant

D. animal

PART B

Circle the underlined word or phrase that helps the reader understand the meaning of *specific*.

> Scientists can teach bees to follow **specific** smells. First, the bees are given a smell to learn. Then they are sent toward the same smell in another area.

6. In paragraph 4, the text states that bees can *uncover* some kinds of cancer. The prefix *un-* means "not" or "opposite." The root *cover* means "to hide." What does the word *uncover* mean?

A. to cure

B. to take off a blanket

C. to make known

D. to cause

7. Read this sentence from paragraph 5.

   They will **alert** people to possible danger.

   What is the meaning of *alert* in this sentence?

   A. to make a mistake

   B. to make a loud noise

   C. to give information

   D. to become scared

8. What would sniffer bees most likely be trained to find in a hospital?

   A. harmful materials

   B. dangerous chemicals

   C. health problems

   D. plant diseases

Write

EXTENDED RESPONSE What are sniffer bees, and how can they help people? Include at least two pieces of text evidence to support your response.

WRITING CHECKLIST

- ☐ I answered the question.
- ☐ I included at least two examples of text evidence to support my response.
- ☐ I used complete sentences.
- ☐ I used correct spelling, punctuation, and capitalization.

Read the article. Then answer the questions that follow.

A Plate of Pizza

by Karin Gaspartich

1 Two thousand years ago, Greeks baked flat, circular pieces of bread and used the bread like a plate. They would first eat the food on top of the bread. Then they would eat the bread "plate."

2 People started to put toppings on the flat bread before it went into the oven. This was an early form of today's pizza.

3 In Italy, hundreds of years later, people ate a form of pizza. Most people kept flour, water, oil, and spices in their homes. They could use these ingredients to make a simple form of pizza.

4 Pizza became popular among Italian workers who could only take short breaks for meals. These workers needed cheap food that could be eaten quickly. As a result, pizza sold by nearby **vendors** was perfect. It could even be eaten without plates and forks.

A Queen's Favorite Pizza

5 In 1889, the queen and king of Italy took a vacation in the seaside town of Naples. Queen Margherita saw people strolling outside eating pizza. She was curious about it, so she decided to try some pizza for herself.

vendors = people who sell things

6 Raffaele Esposito was a popular pizza maker in town. He was chosen to make a pizza for the queen. Esposito wanted her pizza to be extra special. So he made it using the colors of Italy's flag—red, white, and green. He used red tomatoes, white mozzarella cheese, and green **basil** leaves. The queen loved Esposito's pizza so much that she sent him a note of praise and thanks. Esposito named it Pizza Margherita in her honor. Soon, everyone in Italy wanted to try a piece.

7 Around that same time, workers began leaving Italy to live in America. Pizza bakers brought their recipes with them. An Italian man named Gennaro Lombardi opened the first **pizzeria** in New York City in 1895.

8 Pizza quickly became a favorite of American workers, too. It was tasty and easy to eat on the go. Before long, pizza was one of the most popular foods in the United States.

9 Maybe you could invent a pizza for someone. What would you put on top? What would you call it? Have fun . . . and finish your plate!

basil = a spice used in cooking

pizzeria = a pizza bakery

Respond to Text

Reread/Think

1. Number the sentences to show the correct sequence of events in the history of pizza.

_______ Italian workers ate pizza because it was fast and cheap.

_______ The Greeks baked flat, round pieces of bread that they used like plates.

_______ The first pizzeria opened in New York City.

2. Which phrase from paragraph 3 includes words that show sequence?

A. "hundreds of years later"

B. "a form of pizza"

C. "flour, water, oil, and spices"

D. "use these ingredients"

3. PART A

Read paragraph 4 from the text.

> Pizza also became popular among Italian workers who could only take short breaks for meals. These workers needed cheap food that could be eaten quickly. As a result, pizza sold by nearby vendors was perfect. It could even be eaten without plates and forks.

Which statement **best** describes how the sentences in the paragraph are connected?

A. They list the order in which events happened.

B. They describe the most important steps.

C. They describe a cause and its effect.

D. They compare two different events.

PART B

Underline two sentences that **best** support the answer to Part A.

4. Read paragraph 5 from the text.

> In 1889, the queen and king of Italy took a vacation in the seaside town of Naples. Queen Margherita saw people strolling outside eating pizza. She was curious about it, so she decided to try some pizza for herself.

Underline the sentence that shows a cause-effect relationship.

5. What did the queen's praise cause Esposito to do?

A. He renamed his restaurant after her.

B. He sent his recipe home with her.

C. He opened another restaurant.

D. He named a pizza after her.

6. How does paragraph 8 connect to paragraph 4?

A. by comparing the cost of pizza in America to pizza in Italy

B. by showing that workers outside of Italy also liked pizza

C. by comparing the way people in America and Italy ate pizza

D. by explaining that pizza is the most popular food in America

ASSESSMENT

Read the folktales. Then answer the questions that follow.

Anansi Tries to Steal All the Wisdom in the World

a folktale from West Africa

1 Anansi the spider was not very wise. He was a clever **trickster** who could fool almost anyone. But even Anansi knew he did not have much wisdom.

2 Then one day he had a thought. "If I can trick all the people in the village to give me their wisdom, I will become the wisest of all!"

3 So he went door to door, collecting the people's wisdom in a hollow **gourd**. "Please," Anansi said at each house, "tell me something you know and drop it in the gourd." The people were puzzled, but they each put a piece of wisdom in the gourd and wished him well.

4 Soon the gourd was overflowing with wisdom and could hold no more. Anansi needed a place to store it. He looked around and spotted a very tall tree.

5 "Ah," Anansi said, "I will hide my wisdom high up in this tree. Then I will never have to worry about someone stealing it!"

6 To keep it safe, Anansi tied the gourd to the front of his belly. Then he started climbing. But the gourd kept getting in his way. He could not climb high at all.

trickster = someone who plays tricks on others

gourd = a large fruit with a hard shell

7 Just then, Anansi's youngest son walked by. "What are you doing, Father?" asked the little spider.

8 "I am climbing this tree with my gourd full of wisdom," Anansi replied.

9 "But Father," said the son, "wouldn't it be easier if you tied the gourd onto your back?"

10 Anansi was quiet. Then he said, "Shouldn't you be going home?"

11 As soon as his son was gone, Anansi moved the gourd to his back. Then he continued up the tree with no problem. When he reached the top, he cried, "I collected so much wisdom. And yet, my baby son is still wiser than I am. Here! Take back your wisdom!"

12 Anansi lifted the gourd high over his head and emptied it into the wind. The wisdom blew far and wide across the land. And this is how wisdom came back to the world.

Anansi and the Lion

a folktale from West Africa

1 Anansi the spider caught some fish and cooked them. He put them in a sack to take into the forest, where he could eat them all by himself. "These will be very tasty," he chuckled.

2 Anansi hadn't gone far when he met Lion. Lion asked, "Well, brother Anansi, what have you got there?"

3 "Oh . . . just some old bones that I'm going to bury in the mountains."

4 Lion walked away, but then he started thinking. "I know that Anansi is a great trickster. He probably has something in that sack he doesn't want me to see. I will follow him to see what he's up to."

5 When Anansi got into the forest, he set his sack down. He took out one fish and ate it. He didn't think anyone else was around, so he took out another fish. But just then, Lion came up and said, "Well, brother Anansi, those don't look like bones to me."

6 "Oh! Brother Lion, I am so glad you have come. Never mind what I told you. I was only joking. Please join me."

7 So Lion sat down and began to eat with him. But before Anansi had eaten one fish, Lion had finished almost the whole sack. Anansi mumbled to himself, “Greedy fellow, eating up all my fish!”

8 “What did you say, Anansi?” said Lion.

9 Anansi was afraid of what Lion might do, so he replied, “I said you do not eat fast enough.” Anansi was quiet after that, but he still wanted to get back at Lion for eating most of his fish. He had an idea. “Which of us do you think is the stronger?” Anansi asked.

10 “Why, I am, of course,” Lion bragged. “You are only a tiny spider.”

11 Then Anansi said, “We will tie one another to that tree, and we shall see who is the stronger.”

12 They decided that Lion should tie Anansi first. Lion tied Anansi with fine string, and not very tight. Anansi twisted himself around two or three times, and soon he broke free.

13 Then it was Anansi’s turn to tie Lion. Lion said, “You must not tie me tight, for I did not tie you tight.”

14 And Anansi said, “Oh, no, to be sure, I will not!” But he tied Lion as tight as he could.

15 Lion tried and tried to get loose, but he couldn’t.

16 “That is what you get for eating my meal,” Anansi said. He took up his empty sack and left, leaving Lion tied to the tree.

Respond to Text

Reread/Think

1. In "Anansi Tries to Steal All the Wisdom in the World," why does Anansi go from door to door in his village?

A. He wants to collect hollow gourds.

B. He wants to find a good hiding place.

C. He wants to collect people's wisdom.

D. He wants to meet his neighbors.

2. Read this sentence from paragraph 4 of "Anansi Tries to Steal All the Wisdom in the World."

> Soon the gourd was **overflowing** with wisdom and could hold no more.

What is the meaning of *overflowing* in this sentence?

A. too light

B. too full

C. too wise

D. too small

3. **PART A**

Based on the illustration at the bottom of page 437, how does Anansi feel after his son speaks to him?

A. proud

B. excited

C. afraid

D. upset

PART B

Which line from the text **best** supports the answer to Part A?

A. "'What are you doing, Father?'" (paragraph 7)

B. "Then he continued up the tree with no problem." (paragraph 11)

C. "'Here! Take back your wisdom!'" (paragraph 11)

D. "The wisdom blew far and wide across the land." (paragraph 12)

4. In "Anansi and the Lion," what does the illustration on page 438 tell you about how Anansi is feeling?

A. Anansi is glad that Lion has joined him.

B. Anansi is upset that Lion is eating all the fish.

C. Anansi is hopeful that Lion will share with him.

D. Anansi is worried that Lion will get too full.

5. SHORT RESPONSE In the illustration on page 439, Lion is tied to a tree while Anansi walks away. How do the details in the illustration help you understand how both characters feel?

____

____

____

____

____

____

____

6. What is one way "Anansi Tries to Steal All the Wisdom in the World" is like "Anansi and the Lion"?

A. Wisdom is an important idea in both stories.

B. Fish are eaten by characters in both stories.

C. Anansi is happy at the end of both stories.

D. A tree is part of the setting in both stories.

7. What is one way Anansi's character is different in the two stories?

A. In one story, Anansi is upset at the end. In the other story, Anansi is smiling at the end.

B. In one story, Anansi lives in a village. In the other story, Anansi lives in a city.

C. In one story, Anansi is afraid to climb a tree. In the other story, Anansi lives in a tree.

D. In one story, Anansi buries wisdom. In the other story, Anansi buries bones.

Write

EXTENDED RESPONSE A trickster is a type of character who likes to play tricks on others. Compare and contrast how Anansi is a trickster in both stories. Use details from both stories to support your response.

WRITING CHECKLIST

- ☐ I compared and contrasted Anansi in both stories.
- ☐ I used details from both stories to support my response.
- ☐ I used complete sentences.
- ☐ I used correct spelling, punctuation, and capitalization.

Read the article. Then answer the questions that follow.

The Praying Mantid

by Sophie Burmeister

1 The praying mantid is a thin green or brown insect that looks like a small stick. It gets its name from the way its two front legs can bend. It looks as if it were praying. Most people call this insect a "praying mantis." But its real name is the "praying mantid."

Helpful Eaters

2 Praying mantids are carnivores, or meat eaters. They eat insects such as moths, grasshoppers, and flies. Some even eat birds, lizards, and frogs!

3 The eating **habits** of mantids are helpful to people. Farmers like mantids because they eat insects that could hurt their crops. Gardeners like mantids because they eat pesky insects that chew on fruit and flowers.

Mighty Hunters

4 Mantids may be tiny, but they are mighty. They are skillful hunters with an interesting way of catching their meals. Mantids camouflage themselves, or change their body color to match plants and trees nearby. This makes them hard to see against the background.

habits = usual ways of doing things

5 A mantid will sit for a long period of time and look like a twig or leaf. When its **prey** gets close enough, the mantid quickly catches and holds the prey with its front legs. These legs have sharp spines that keep the animal from escaping. Most mantids eat the head of the animal first.

Amazing Bodies

6 The mantid has three main body parts. The head is shaped like a triangle. It sits on a long, thin neck called a thorax. The thorax is connected to a long body, called an abdomen.

7 One of the most amazing features of a mantid is its eyes. There are five of them! A mantid has two large eyes, one on each side of the head. Three smaller eyes are set between the larger eyes. This gives the mantid excellent eyesight, which helps it catch prey. Mantids are also the only insects in the world that can turn their head completely from one side to the other. This makes it even easier for mantids to spot a tasty meal.

8 Mantids are very fast jumpers. They can make a complete leap in less than a second, before their **target** is aware of them. Right before a mantid leaps, it wiggles its body back and forth. It can twist and turn in different directions. When it finally leaps, its body spins as it shoots through the air.

9 People have been fascinated by mantids for thousands of years. There are even rock paintings of mantids made by ancient people. The mantid is an awesome insect!

prey = an animal that is hunted by another animal

target = something being aimed at

FAST FACTS

- North America has only 20 kinds of mantids, while Africa has 880 species.
- Mantids live mostly in warm or hot areas of the world.
- Most mantids are less than six inches long.

Respond to Text

Reread/Think

1. Look at the photograph at the top of page 444. Which detail from the text does the photograph **best** support?

   A. "It gets its name from the way its two front legs can bend." (paragraph 1)

   B. "The eating habits of mantids are helpful to people." (paragraph 3)

   C. "They are skillful hunters with an interesting way of catching their meals." (paragraph 4)

   D. "Most mantids eat the head of the animal first." (paragraph 5)

2. **PART A**

   Under which heading can the reader learn why farmers like mantids?

   A. Helpful Eaters

   B. Mighty Hunters

   C. Amazing Bodies

   D. Fast Facts

   PART B

   Write a sentence from the text that supports the answer to Part A.

   ____

   ____

   ____

3. What is the meaning of the word *pesky* as it is used in paragraph 3?

   A. colorful

   B. helpful

   C. interesting

   D. annoying

4. Look at the photograph at the bottom of page 444. Which detail from the text does the photograph **best** support?

   A. "Praying mantids are carnivores, or meat eaters." (paragraph 2)

   B. "This makes them hard to see against the background." (paragraph 4)

   C. "These legs have sharp spines that keep the animal from escaping." (paragraph 5)

   D. "The mantid has three main body parts." (paragraph 6)

5. Under which heading can the reader learn about a mantid's eyes?

   A. Helpful Eaters

   B. Mighty Hunters

   C. Amazing Bodies

   D. Fast Facts

6. **SHORT RESPONSE** How does the photograph at the top of page 445 help the reader understand paragraphs 6 and 7? Use **two** details to support your response.

7. What information is found in the sidebar called "Fast Facts"?

   A. what mantids eat

   B. how mantids sit

   C. where mantids live

   D. why mantids jump

8. What would be the **best** heading for paragraph 8?

A. Back and Forth

B. Fast Jumpers

C. Spinning Mantids

D. Twist and Turn

9. Use the word bank below to complete the sentences that follow.

leap	jumper	body	wiggles

A mantid ______________________ its body before it takes a ______________________. As the mantid flies through the air, its ______________________ spins.

10. What is the main idea of "The Praying Mantid"?

A. Praying mantids have amazing eyesight.

B. Praying mantids are often called praying mantises.

C. Praying mantids are interesting and unusual creatures.

D. Praying mantids have been around for thousands of years.

Read the poem. Then answer the questions that follow.

Squirrel

by Mary Ann Hoberman,
from *A Little Book of Little Beasts*

1 Grey squirrel
Small beast
Storing up a winter's feast,
Hides a hundred nuts at least.

2 **Nook and cranny** stocked with seed
Tucked away for winter's need.
Acorns stuck in hole and crack.
Will he ever get them back?

3 When the snow is piled up high
And the year is at December,
Can he really still remember
Where he hid them in September?

nook and cranny = small, hidden spaces

4 I have watched him from my window
And he always seems to know
Where the food he hid is waiting
Buried deep beneath the snow.

5 And I wonder
(Do you wonder?)
How he knows where he must go.

Respond to Text

Reread/Think

1. The sentences below describe how the events build in the poem. Write a number on each blank line to order the events in the poem from 1 to 4.

______ The speaker wonders if the squirrel will find the food later.

______ The squirrel hides food for winter.

______ The speaker watches the squirrel find its food.

______ Snow piles up and covers the squirrel's food.

2. What does the word *feast* mean in stanza 1 of the poem?

A. a special kind of nut

B. a big pile of snow

C. a secret hiding place

D. a large amount of food

Write

EXTENDED RESPONSE What questions does the speaker ask in stanzas 2 and 3? How does stanza 4 answer the questions? Use details from the poem to support your response.

WRITING CHECKLIST

- ☐ I answered both questions.
- ☐ I used details from the poem to answer the questions.
- ☐ I used complete sentences.
- ☐ I used correct spelling, punctuation, and capitalization.

Read the play. Then answer the questions that follow.

Campfire Songs

by Bernie Paw

1 **Cast of Characters:** Bear, Raccoon, Bobcat, a small group of humans

Scene 1

2 *A dark green forest. Bear, Raccoon, and Bobcat are walking through the forest looking for something to do. It is the end of the day.*

3 **BEAR:** Well, now that we've all had our dinner, what are we going to do for fun? (*He sighs and looks bored.*)

4 **RACCOON:** I've had all the nuts I need for a week. What else is there to do around here? (*He kicks a stone down the path.*)

5 **BOBCAT:** (*patting her stomach and yawning*) I'm full of meat! It sure is a boring night in the forest.

6 **RACCOON:** (*suddenly pointing with excitement*) Hey, what's happening over there in the field? Ah, some humans. They're sitting around a fire. It might be fun to watch them and see what they do. Humans can do some strange things!

7 **BOBCAT:** That's true! (*She laughs.*) Let's go see!

8 (*Bobcat, Bear, and Raccoon run off toward the field together.*)

Scene 2

9 (*A group of people can be seen around a* ***campfire****. Bear, Raccoon, and Bobcat are hiding behind some bushes, watching the people.*)

10 **BEAR:** (*scratching his head*) Well, look at that. The man is putting his fresh fish on the fire on some kind of shiny, thin piece of rock. Why would he want to burn perfectly fresh fish? (*He shakes his head.*) What a waste!

campfire = an outdoor fire for cooking or warmth

11 **RACCOON:** Yeah! (*He nods.*) And what are those weird, puffy little white blobs the girl just put on a stick? Why is she holding them over the fire? Is she going to burn them, too?

12 **BOBCAT:** (*laughing*) Good question! Silly humans. Why are they using other little sticks with rounded ends to scoop up their food? Why don't they just use their paws like us?

Scene 3

13 (*It is late at night. The animals are still watching the humans.*)

14 **BEAR:** Look at what the girl is holding. It has strings. Can you hear the sounds she makes when she touches the strings?

15 (*The people start to sing along with the guitar music.*)

16 **RACCOON:** Hmm. This is starting to sound kind of nice.

17 (*The animals lean on each other, eyes closed, and slowly sway back and forth. All three begin to yawn.*)

18 **BOBCAT:** (*sleepily*) Well, humans sure are strange, but they can make the sweetest sounds.

19 **BEAR:** (*almost asleep*) And here we thought there would be nothing interesting to do tonight.

20 (*One by one, Bear, Raccoon, and Bobcat curl up next to each other and fall asleep.*)

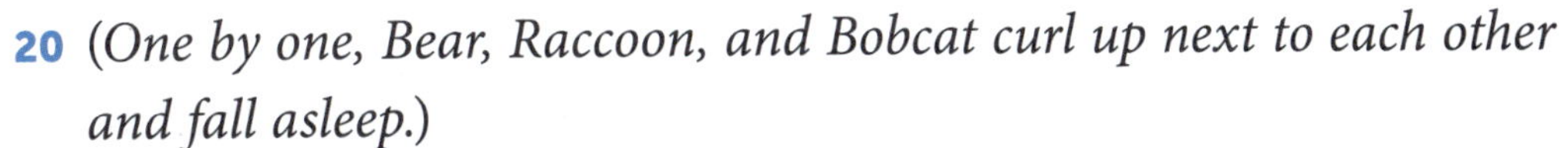

Respond to Text

Reread/Think

1. What is shown in line 2 of the play?

A. the cast of characters

B. the scene number

C. the characters' dialogue

D. the play's setting

2. In Scene 1, at what point does Raccoon first see the humans?

A. lines 1 and 2

B. line 4

C. line 6

D. lines 7 and 8

3. What do the animals decide to do after they see the humans?

A. run away from them

B. scare them

C. play music with them

D. watch them

4. In Scene 1, what is Raccoon's point of view about the humans?

A. He thinks they will harm the forest.

B. He thinks they might do something strange.

C. He thinks they might give the animals food.

D. He thinks they will run away from the animals.

5. PART A

What does line 10 tell readers about Bear's point of view?

A. He does not like that humans started a fire in the forest.

B. He does not understand that humans are cooking fish.

C. He is angry that humans have food and he does not.

D. He is itchy and scratches his head with his paw.

PART B

What detail **best** supports the correct response to Part A?

A. He shakes his head and asks a question.

B. He rubs his belly at the sight of the fish.

C. He wonders why his head is itching.

D. He asks the humans what they are doing.

6. What does line 12 tell readers about Bobcat's point of view?

A. She wants the humans to tell more funny jokes.

B. She hopes the humans share the puffy white blobs.

C. She thinks humans are strange for not having paws.

D. She thinks humans are silly for using tools to eat.

7. **PART A**

How does the animals' point of view about the humans change in Scene 3?

A. They find something about the humans that they like.

B. They decide that the humans are not worth watching.

C. They discover why the humans are sitting by the fire.

D. They come up with a plan to scare the humans.

PART B

Which line **best** supports the response to Part A?

A. line 13

B. line 14

C. line 18

D. line 20

8. What is the animals' point of view about the music?

A. They think it sounds nice.

B. They think it is too loud.

C. They find it confusing.

D. They find it exciting.

9. **SHORT RESPONSE** Describe what Bear, Raccoon, and Bobcat do in Scenes 1, 2, and 3. Use words like *first, next,* and *last* in your response.

ASSESSMENT

Read the articles. Then answer the questions that follow.

Signs in the Sky

by Michelle August

A halo around the moon can mean that rain is coming.

1 Today, every news channel has a weather person. They can **predict** the weather for days, or even weeks in advance. The science of predicting weather is called meteorology. It involves using special **devices** to track weather systems. However, long before people had this technology, they could predict the weather by observing the natural world.

2 For as long as people have grown their own food, they have wanted to predict the weather. Knowing the signs that told of coming rain or storms was important for survival. Over thousands of years, people learned to watch the sky for signs of coming weather. They even made up special sayings to remember the signs. Today, scientists have discovered something fascinating. Some of those old sayings were right!

predict = say that something will happen before it happens

devices = tools

3 ***Red sky in the morning, sailors take warning. Red sky at night, sailors' delight.*** This weather saying is at least half right. A red sunrise in the morning sometimes means that a storm is on the way. But if the sky is red at sunset, it usually means that a high-pressure system, or dry weather, is on the way. Today, weather satellites track the movement of storms. But it is still fun to remember the old saying!

4 ***Ring around the moon, rain's coming soon.*** Sometimes the moon looks like it has a ring around it. This happens when there are high clouds in the sky that contain water and ice. When the moonlight shines through the tiny pieces of ice, the light makes a circle around the moon. That same water and ice may soon fall as rain. So the old saying is true!

5 ***When clouds appear like rocks and towers, the earth's refreshed with frequent showers.*** This is another old rhyme that is true. Have you ever seen clouds that look thin and spread out? These are called cumulus clouds. They hardly ever carry rain. Other clouds are called cumulonimbus clouds. Strong winds cause these clouds to build up and grow tall, like towers. Heavy water in the clouds makes them look dark, like rocks. These clouds almost always bring storms.

6 Today, we have many kinds of technology to predict the weather. Weather satellites and weather **software** track storm patterns. But if all else fails, just look at the sky. The signs are out there!

software = computer programs

Storm clouds like these can bring wind and rain.

Mapping Sunshine and Rain

by Krista O'Connell

1 Weather is important to all of us. A farmer's field can be ruined if the weather is hot and dry. A picnic can be spoiled by rain. People like to know what the weather will be like tomorrow, three days from now, and even next week. This is now possible thanks to the science of meteorology.

The Weather Map

2 One of the tools used to predict the weather is a weather map. Meteorologists use special equipment to create these maps. The equipment is used to collect information about conditions in the sky.

3 A weather map might look complicated. But once you know what the shapes, **symbols**, and letters mean, you can make your own weather predictions. Look at the map on the next page as you read along.

What Weather Maps Can Tell Us

4 First, a weather map shows weather fronts. Two main types of fronts are warm fronts and cold fronts. Both form when cooler air and hotter air meet. The map shows the symbols for each type of front. Warm fronts often bring rain and clouds. Cold fronts bring clear skies and cooler weather.

5 Second, a weather map shows any weather systems in the area. These can be high pressure or low pressure systems. They are shown on the map by the letters H and L. Both types move from west to east.

symbols = shapes that stand for something

High pressure systems often result in nice, sunny weather. Low pressure systems are likely to cause rain.

6 Third, maps show what type of weather these fronts and systems will cause. For example, the map shows that the cold front near Denver is expected to bring snow. The cold front between Atlanta and Miami will likely bring rain and thunderstorms.

Signs in the Sky or Modern Maps?

7 It's true that looking into the sky can give some clues about what the weather will be in the near future. Most of us have seen dark clouds that fill the sky before a thunderstorm. The color of the sky and the look of the moon can provide other clues.

8 People no longer have to make a guess about the weather. There are now maps like the one below as well as other tools. These can help meteorologists make very exact weather **forecasts**. They can also help predict the weather before it ever arrives.

forecasts = guesses based on information

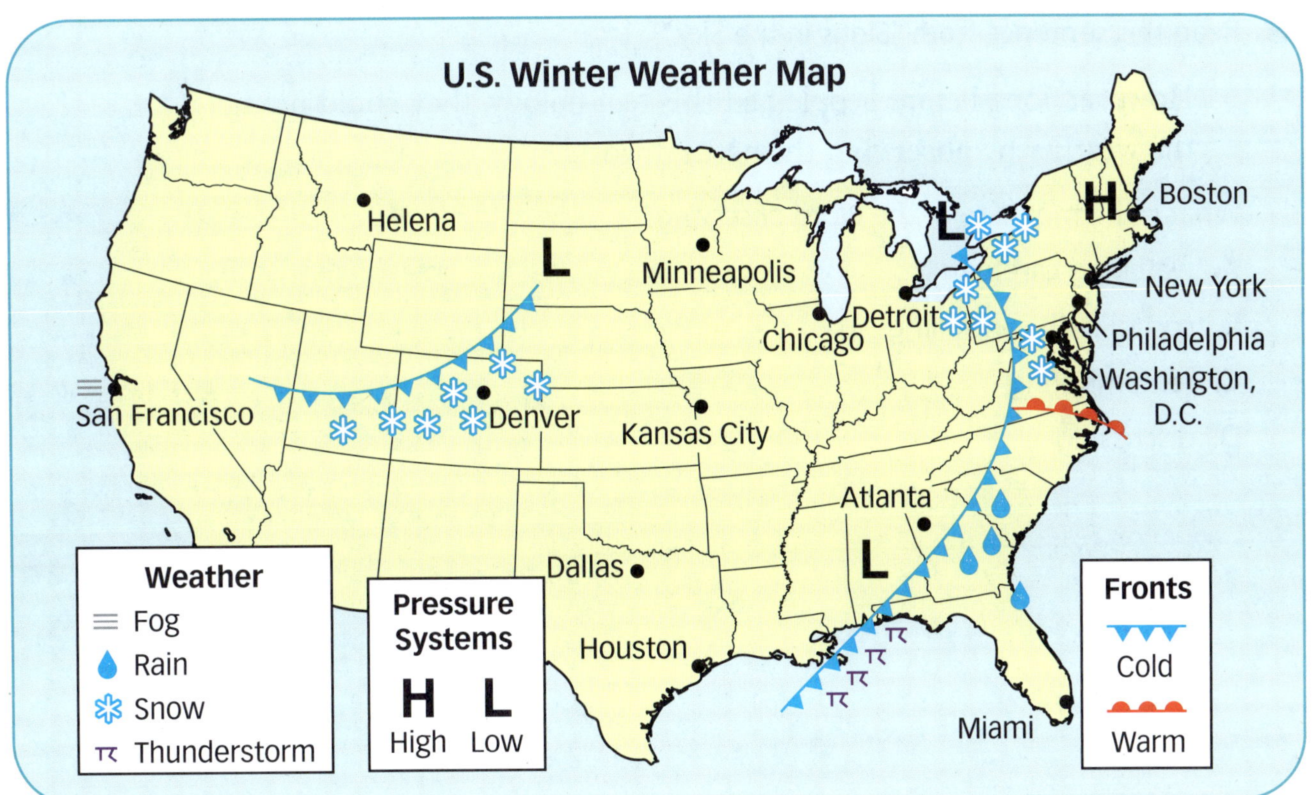

Respond to Text

Reread/Think

1. Mark an "**X**" to show if the detail tells about "Signs in the Sky" or "Mapping Sunshine and Rain."

	Signs in the Sky	Mapping Sunshine and Rain
The moon can sometimes look like it has a ring around it.		
In the past, people observed the natural world to predict the weather.		
Weather maps can show what weather is coming to an area.		

2. Read this sentence from "Signs in the Sky."

> However, long before people had this technology, they could predict the weather by **observing** the natural world.

What is the meaning of the word *observing*?

A. watching carefully

B. completely controlling

C. remembering

D. discussing

Write

EXTENDED RESPONSE Both "Signs in the Sky" and "Mapping Sunshine and Rain" are about predicting the weather. What are the different ways people have predicted the weather throughout history? Use details from both texts to support your response.

WRITING CHECKLIST

- ☐ I answered the question.
- ☐ I used details from both texts.
- ☐ I used complete sentences.
- ☐ I used correct spelling, punctuation, and capitalization.

Glossary of Terms

Academic Talk Words and Phrases

A

account a written or spoken retelling of an event or topic

act a main section, or part, of a play

actions things that a person or character does

alliteration repetition of initial consonant sounds to create a special effect

allusion an indirect mention or reference to something

analyze to closely and carefully examine a text or part of a text

B

bar graph a graph that uses two or more bars to show amounts or numbers that are being compared

base word a complete word that has no prefixes or suffixes added to it

C

caption a phrase or sentence next to a picture in a text that explains something about the picture

cast of characters a list of all the characters in a play, usually in order of appearance or importance

cause a reason, event, or action that makes something else happen

cause and effect a relationship between events in which one event—the cause—brings about, or causes, another event—the effect

cause-effect text structure a text organization that describes events, what made them happen, and how they affect other people and events

central message an important lesson about people or life that the author of a story wants to share

challenge a problem or difficulty that needs to be solved

chapter a section, or part, of a story or book

character a person, animal, or made-up creature in a story or play

character trait a quality or characteristic that a character in a story has, such as courage, pride, or honesty

chart an image that shows or organizes information so that it is easier to understand

chronological text structure a text organization in which events are described in the order in which they happen

chronology the order in which events happen

climax the most exciting or important part of a story, which usually comes near the end

compare to describe how two or more things are similar

compare-contrast text structure a text organization that describes the similarities and differences between two or more things

conflict a challenge that a character faces; a disagreement that people, characters, or organizations have with one another

context clues words, phrases, or sentences near an unknown word or phrase in a text that help you determine the meaning of the unknown word or phrase

contrast to describe how two or more things are different

D

describe to tell what something is like; to explain something

details facts, examples, or other pieces of information in a text

determine to find out or figure out something

diagram a drawing or picture that explains what something looks like or how it works

dialogue the words the characters say in a story or play

direct quotation the exact words that an author wrote or a speaker said; these words go inside quotation marks

drama a story that is performed on a stage by actors

E

effect something that happens as a result of something else

event something that happens in a story or in the natural world

Glossary of Terms (continued)

evidence facts, details, quotes, or other pieces of information used to support a point, idea, or reason

example something that shows what other things in a particular group are like

explain to describe or give details about something so it can be understood

F

figurative language a word or phrase that means something different from its regular or literal meaning and is used to make a comparison or create a certain feeling or mental image

first-person point of view when the narrator of a story is a character in the story who describes events using the pronouns *I*, *me*, or *we*; a first-person narrator can describe their own thoughts and feelings but not what other characters think or feel

firsthand account an informational text about an event written by a person who witnessed the event or took part in it

G

glossary a list at the back of a book of important words from the text and their meaning

H

heading a word or phrase at the beginning of a section of a text that tells what the section is about

historical fiction a story that takes place in the past

historical text an informational piece of writing that describes people, events, and ideas from the past

I

idea a thought, opinion, or belief that someone has about something

identify to be able to say who or what a person or thing is

illustration a picture in a text that gives more information about the text

image a drawing, photograph, map, or chart that shows information about something in a text

infer to reach a conclusion about a text based on text clues and background knowledge

inference a conclusion, or an idea you have about a text, based on details in the text and your own background knowledge

information facts and details about someone or something

integrate to put together or combine information on a topic from more than one text

interaction the way people or things act with or affect one another

K

key detail an important fact, example, or other piece of information in a text that helps explain the main idea

key word a word in bold print that calls attention to an important idea or piece of information in a text

L

label a word or phrase that gives more information about an image

lesson something learned in a text or story or through experience

literal having the usual or most basic meaning of a word's dictionary definition

M

main idea something important that an author wants readers to know about a topic

map a picture or drawing of an area that shows its cities, roads, rivers, mountains, and other features

metaphor a type of figurative language that compares two things without using the word *like* or *as*

mood the feeling a story creates in the reader; setting, word choice, and tone all contribute to mood

motivations the reasons why characters act, think, or feel the way they do

myth an ancient story told by a people or culture that explains their origin and history

Glossary of Terms (continued)

N

narrator the person or character who tells a story

nonliteral describing an unusual or unexpected meaning of a word or phrase

P

paragraph a group of sentences about a particular idea or topic

personification a type of figurative language that gives human qualities or characteristics to animals or objects

perspective (informational texts) what an author thinks or feels about a topic

perspective (literary texts) what a narrator or character thinks or feels about the events in a story

persuade to cause someone to do something or think a certain way about something by giving them good reasons for it

photo or photograph a picture made using a camera

phrase a short group of words that has meaning

play a story that is performed on stage by actors

plot the sequence of events in a story

poem a piece of writing in which the words are chosen for their beauty and sound; the words are often arranged in short lines

point an idea that an author wants readers to remember or believe is true

point of view (informational texts) what an author thinks or feels about a topic

point of view (literary texts) what a narrator or character thinks or feels about the events in a story

predict to say what you think will happen in the future

prefix a word part that comes at the beginning of a word and changes the word's meaning

problem a challenge that the main character or characters face

problem-solution text structure a text organization that describes one or more problems and solutions

Q

quote the exact words that an author wrote or a speaker said; these words go inside quotation marks

R

reason an explanation why an idea or point is correct or true

recount to retell events and details of a story or text in the order in which they happen using your own words

relationship the way in which two or more people, events, or things are connected

repetition the use of repeated words or sounds to show that something is important or to create a certain effect

research serious study of a topic, or the facts learned during that study

resolution the part of a story when the main conflict or problem is solved or when the main goal is reached; the resolution happens at the end of a story

respond to make a reply; to answer

result something that happens or exists because of something else that happened before

rhyme the repeated use of words that end in the same or similar sounds

rhythm the regular pattern of sounds in a poem or beats in a piece of music

rising action the part of a story when the main conflict or problem builds, creating excitement or suspense

S

scan to look quickly through a text to find a particular word or piece of information

scene a part of a play in which all the action takes place in the same setting; one or more scenes make up each act of a play

scientific text a piece of writing that gives information about a science topic or about how or why something happens in the natural world

secondhand account an informational text about a topic or event written by someone who did not experience it but instead found information and facts about it

Glossary of Terms (continued)

section a particular part of something, such as a paragraph or a chapter of a book

sensory details details that describe the way something looks, sounds, feels, smells, or tastes

sequence the order in which events or steps in a process happen

setting where and when a story or play takes place

sidebar a short text, often boxed, placed near the main text that gives more information about the topic

signal words words or phrases that show the connection between ideas or events

simile a type of figurative language that compares two things using the word *like* or *as*

skim to read through something quickly to find the main facts or ideas

solution the answer to a problem; the way the main characters resolve the conflict at the center of a story

source a text or image that gives information about a specific subject area or topic; a source may be printed or digital

stage directions instructions in a play that tell what actors should do, how actors should speak, and what should appear or happen on stage

stanza several lines of a poem that are grouped together to form one part of the poem

steps in a process a set of actions or directions to take in order to make or do something

story elements the major parts of a story, including the setting, characters, problem, solution, and theme

structure the particular way an author organizes a text, such as acts for a drama or stanzas for a poem

summarize to briefly retell in your own words the most important ideas, events, and details of a text

summary a short retelling of a text that includes the main idea and key details of a text, or the important events and details of a story

support to help explain or provide evidence for a main idea in a text

T

table of contents a list at the front of a book of the sections or chapters of the book in the order in which they appear

technical text a piece of writing that explains how to make or do something

text evidence a detail, fact, or example in a piece of writing that can be used to support an idea

text features special parts of a text that help you find certain information or learn more about a topic; titles, headings, sidebars, pictures, timelines, and glossaries are examples of text features

text structure the way an author organizes the ideas and information in a piece of writing; text structures include comparison, cause-effect, chronology, and problem-solution

theme an important message or lesson that an author wants to share about people or life

third-person point of view when the narrator of a story is not a character in the story and describes events using pronouns such as *he*, *she*, and *they*; a third-person narrator can describe what different characters think and feel

timeline a chart or image that shows the dates of important events in the order they happened, sometimes with additional details about the events

title the name of a text

tone the general feeling or attitude of a text or story

topic the general subject of a text

trait a quality or characteristic that a person or character in a story has, such as courage, pride, or honesty

V

visual an image or picture that appears with a text; visuals can include illustrations, photos, charts, diagrams, and timelines

visual elements features of an image that an artist can use to show meaning or feeling; shape and color are examples of visual elements

Credits

Text Credits

UNIT 1:

Pleasant DeSpain, "Ants Live Everywhere" from *Tales of Insects*. Copyright © 2002 by Pleasant DeSpain. Used by permission of August House.

Adapted from "Bear and Turtle Have a Race" (retold by) Pat Betteley, Cobblestone 2019 © by Cricket Media, Inc. Reproduced with permission

"Howling Up the Moon" by Diana C. Conway, Spider 2006 © by Cricket Media, Inc. Reproduced with permission

Stephen Krensky, "King of the Meadow" adapted from *Woodland Crossings*. Copyright © 1978 by Stephen Krensky. Used by permission of Atheneum Books for Young Readers, a division of Simon & Schuster.

Helena Ku Rhee, excerpt from *The Turtle Ship*. Illustrated by Collen King-Savage. Copyright © 2018 by Helena Ku Rhee. Used by permission of Lee & Low Books.

Adapted from "The Hermit's Secret" by Leslie Wyatt, Cricket 2020 © by Cricket Media, Inc. Reproduced with permission

Thelma Lynne Godin, excerpt from *The Hula-Hoopin' Queen*. Illustrated by Vanessa Brantley-Newton. Lee & Low, 2014.

UNIT 2:

Julie Murphy, excerpt from *Anglerfish*. Copyright © 2015 by Julie Murphy. Used by permission of Lee & Low Books.

Dan Risch, "Cloaked in Starlight," Copyright © by Highlights for Children, Inc., Columbus, OH. All rights reserved.

Adapted from "Slimy Snugglers" by Caryl Gobin Ulrich, *Ask* 2018 © by Cricket Media, Inc.. Reproduced with permission

Adapted from "Stay in Schools" by Kathy Kranking, *Ranger Rick*, September 2014. Used by permission of the National Wildlife Federation.

"Orcas on the Hunt" by Alicia Z. Klepeis. Copyright © 2018 by Lerner Publishing Group, Inc. Reproduced with the permission of Lerner Publications Company, a division of Lerner Publishing Group, Inc. All rights reserved.

UNIT 3:

Linda Sue Park, excerpt from *Prairie Lotus*. Copyright © 2020 by Linda Sue Park. Reproduced with permission by Clarion Books.

UNIT 5:

Peter Murray, excerpt from *Tornadoes*. Copyright © 2015 by Peter Murray. Reproduced with permission by The Child's World, Inc.

Adapted from "Wild, Wild Weather in the Wild, Wild West" by Todd Tuell, *Faces* 2011 © by Cricket Media, Inc. Reproduced with permission

"At Home in the Sky" by Betsy Kepes, *AppleSeeds* 2006 © by Cricket Media, Inc. Reproduced with permission

Adapted from "Weather Mountain" by Cheryl Bardoe, *Ask* 2014 © by Cricket Media, Inc. Reproduced with permission

Eve Merriam, "Crick! Crack!" from *Windy Day: Stories and Poems*. Copyright © 1988 by Eve Merriam. Reproduced with permission by J.B. Lippincott Junior Books.

Dione Brand, "Hurricane" from *A Caribbean Dozen: Poems From Caribbean Poets*. Copyright © 1994 by Candlewick Press. Reproduced with permission by Candlewick Press.

Jack Prelutsky, "I Do Not Mind You Winter Wind" from *Windy Day: Stories and Poems*. Copyright © 1988 by Jack Prelutsky.. Reproduced with permission by J.B. Lippincott Junior Books.

"Lightning" by Jennifer Jesseph, *AppleSeeds* 2007 © by Cricket Media, Inc. Reproduced with permissionAdapted from "In the Clouds" by Roxanne Troup, *Cricket* 2019 © by Cricket Media, Inc. Reproduced with permission

UNIT 6:

Jennifer Mattox, "Big Bugs," Copyright © by Highlights for Children, Inc., Columbus, OH. All rights reserved.

Adapted from "Trolling for Trolls" by Gail Skroback Hennessey, *Faces* 2020 © by Cricket Media, Inc. Reproduced with permission

Adapted from "Washed Ashore" by Liz Huyck, *Ask* 2019 © by Cricket Media, Inc. Reproduced with permission

UNIT ASSESSMENTS:

"Patriot Pizza," by Karin Gaspartich. From Highlights, January 2007. Copyright © Highlights for Children, Inc., Columbus, Ohio. All rights reserved.

Mary Ann Hoberman, "Squirrel" from A Little Book of Beasts. Copyright © 1973 by Mary Ann Hoberman. Used by permission of the Gina Maccoby Literary Agency.

Illustration Credits

pp. cvr (c), 5 (r), 221 (tl, cl, bc), 256-260, 262-264, 265, 267-286, 273 (br): Sibu Puthenveettil

pp. 2 (bl), 8 (cr), 27 (c), 32-34, 74 (tr): Helena Ku Rhee, excerpt from *The Turtle Ship*. Illustrated by Collen King-Savage. Lee & Low, 2018

pp. 2 (tl), 9 (tr), 76-79: Setor Fiadzigbey

pp. 2 (br), 9 (tl, cl, bl), 42-44, 48-50, 53-54, 75 (l): Raúl Colón

pp. 2 (tr), 9 (cr, bc, br), 58-61, 64-66, 69-70, 75 (r): Thelma Lynne Godin, excerpt from *The Hula-Hoopin' Queen*. Illustrated by Vanessa Brantley-Newton. Lee & Low, 2014.

pp. 5 (c), 220 (tl, cl), 223 (t, c), 224-225, 272 (t, bl), 228-229 (bg), 230: Serena Malyon

pp. 6 (bl), 283 (bc, br), 317 (bl, br), 327-328, 333 (cr, b): Brave Union

pp. 7 (tl), 342 (tr), 362, 364-365, 368-370, 373-374, 395 (l): Rama Duwaji

pp. 7 (bl), 343 (tl, cl, b), 378-381, 384-386, 389-390, 395 (r): Sibu Puthenveetil

pp. 8 (tl), 11 (t), 12-13, 74 (tl): Jensine Eckwall

pp. 8 (cl), 11 (c), 16-18, 74 (bl): Kim Ekdahl

pp. 8 (bl), 11(b), 21-22, 74 (bc): Nabila Adani

pp. 8 (tr), 27 (t), 28-29, 74 (tc): Stephanie Fizer-Coleman

pp. 8 (br), 27 (b), 37-38, 74 (br): Isabel Muñoz

pp. 161 (tl), 194-197, 200-202, 205-206, 211 (r): Teresa Martinez

pp. 220 (bl, br), 223 (bl, br) 233-236, 272 (bc, br): Maya McKibbin

pp. 221 (tr), 274-277: Charles Chaisson

pp. 283 (cl), 316 (cl), 322-323, 333 (cl): Guy Sheild

pp. 283 (bl), 316 (cr), 324, 333 (cr): Antonio Javier Caparo

pp. 283 (tl), 318-319, 333 (t): Alleanna Harris

pp. 283 (tr), 334-337: Dave Seeley

pp. 286-287, 290-292, 295-296: Joe Lemmonier

pp. 396-399, 434 (r): Yuta Onoda

pp. 406-406: Prem Sai G S

p. 415: QBS Learning

pp. 436-439: Anastasia Magloire Williams

pp. 454-455: QBS Learning

p. 463: Mary Jo Heil

Photography Credits

p. cvr (kids): fstop123/E+/Getty Images

p. cvr (underwater): Irina Markova/Shutterstock

p. cvr (train): Arcansel/Shutterstock

pp. cvr (turtle), 3 (br), 85 (br), 135 (b), 146 (b), 151 (br): Westend61 - Gerald Nowak/Brand X Pictures/Getty Images

pp. cvr (watercolor), 4 (watercolor): Andreykuzmin/Dreamstime.com

pp. cvr (keyboard), 4 (keyboard), 174 (keyboard): Yuriy Kirsanov/Dreamstime.com

pp. cvr (composition book), 4 (composition book) 174 (composition book): HardtIllustrations/Dreamstime.com

pp. cvr (girls), 4 (girls), 174 (girls): Monkey Business Images/Dreamstime.com

pp. cvr (hurricane), 6 (br), 282 (tl), 285 (t), 287 (b), 332 (tl): NASA

pp. cvr (reef), 84 (cl), 87 (b), 97, 150 (bl): Csaba Tökölyi/Moment/Getty Images

pp. cvr (manatees), 85 (tc), 137 (inset), 135 (t), 151 (tr): imageBROKER/Alamy Stock Photo

pp. cvr (bus), 168 (bus): Jiawangkun/Dreamstime.com

pp. cvr (train), 168 (train): Philip Scalia/Alamy Stock Photo

pp. cvr (subway station), 168 (subway station): Leungphotography/Dreamstime.com

pp. cvr (books), 174 (books): New Africa/Shutterstock

pp. cvr (ant), 7 (br), 342 (tl), 345 (t), 346, 347 (b), 394 (t): David Rogers

pp. cvr (mantis face), 445 (t): Paul Looyen/Shutterstock

pp. cvr (bee), 426 (b): Apinan/Shutterstock

pp. 2-3 (bg), 136-137 (bg): Lisa Strachan/Shutterstock

pp. 3 (tr), 84 (tl), 87 (t), 89 (t), 150 (tl): wildestanimal/Moment/Getty Images

pp. 3 (tl), 84 (tr), 103 (t), 104-105, 150 (tr): superjoseph/iStock/Getty Images

pp. 3 (bl), 84 (cr), 103 (c), 110, 150 (cr): BluePlanetArchive/Doug Perrine

pp. 4 (t), 160 (tl), 163 (tl), 165 (tl, tr), 210 (tl): PG Arphexad/Alamy Stock Photo

pp. 4 (br), 160 (cl), 163 (c), 168 (main street), 169 (bus sign, Tate, town hall, town sign, traffic signal, van), 170 (bus sign), 210 (cl): Patrick Dodson

pp. 4 (t), 160, 163-165, 210: Parkpoom4/Dreamstime.com

pp. 4 (musical notes), 174 (musical notes): abstract/Shutterstock

pp. 4 (bass), 174 (bass): Kaycco/Dreamstime.com

pp. 4 (trumpet), 174 (trumpet): Richard Cote/Dreamstime.com

pp. 4 (globe), 174 (globe): Abdulgamid Buraganov/Dreamstime.com

pp. 4 (maracas), 174 (maracas): Phana Sitti/Dreamstime.com

pp. 4 (pencil), 174 (pencil): anigoweb/Shutterstock

pp. 5 (l), 220 (br), 241 (b), 251 (train), 273 (bl): Apic/Hulton Archive/Getty Images

pp. 5 (smoke), 220 (br), 241 (b), 251 (smoke), 273 (bl): Nils Z/Shutterstock

pp. 6 (lightning), 285 (c), 292 (b): Robert Glusic/Photodisc/Getty Images

pp. 6 (tl), 301 (b), 311: U.S. Air Force photo by Tech. Sgt. Michael Farrar

pp. 6 (tr), 312 (dropsonde): Science History Images/Alamy

pp. 26-27: Rawin Tanpin/Dreamstime.com

pp. 84 (bl), 87 (c), 94, 150 (cl): NOAA Office of Exploration and Research

pp. 84 (br), 103 (b), 113 (t), 150 (br): Georgette Douwma/Stockbyte/Getty Images

pp. 85 (tl), 119 (t), 120-121 (t), 151 (tl): Ron Sanford/Corbis Documentary/Getty Images

pp. 85 (cl), 119 (c), 126, 151 (cl): ullstein bild/Getty Images

pp. 85 (bl), 119 (b), 130: Flip Nicklin/Minden Pictures

pp. 85 (cc), 135 (cc), 140, 151 (cr): SellOnlineMarketing/iStock /Getty Images Plus

pp. 85 (tr), 155 (inset): Sirachai Arunrugstichai/Myanmar Ocean Project

pp. 86-87 (bg): Rich Carey/Shutterstock

pp. 87 (c), 92-94 (bg), 150 (bl): inusuke/ iStoc/Getty Images Plus

pp. 88-89 (bg): PhotoGoricki/iStock/Getty Images Plus

p. 88 (inset): Jay Fleming/Corbis Documentary/Getty Images

p. 89 (b): Solvin Zankl/NPL/Minden Pictures

pp. 92 (inset), 93 (t,b): Solvin Zankl/Alamy Stock Photo

p. 98: cinoby/E+/Getty Images

pp. 102 103 (bg), 108-110 (bg), 113-114 (bg): Rich Carey/Shutterstock

p. 108: BluePlanetArchive/Doug Perrine

p. 113 (b): Georgette Douwma/Stockbyte/Getty Images

p. 114: imageBROKER/Alamy Stock Photo

pp. 118-119: Vlad61/Shutterstock

p. 121 (b): Nature Picture Library/Alamy Stock Photo

p. 124: Cultura Creative RF/Alamy Stock Photo

p. 125: WaterFrame/Alamy Stock Photo

pp. 129, 151 (bl): Martin Strmiska/Alamy Stock Photo

pp. 134-135 (bg): Joshua Fuller/Unsplash

p. 136 (inset): ©Shane Gross /iLCP

p. 141 (l): Paul S. Wolf/Shutterstock

p. 141 (r): Tory Kallman/Shutterstock

p. 142: Ocean Alliance

p. 145 (t): Ralph Pace/Minden Pictures

p. 146 (t): Texas Sea Grant via CC BY 2.0

pp. 152-153 (bg): Images & Stories/Alamy Stock Photo

p. 153 (inset): Leo Francini/Alamy Stock Photo

pp. 154-155 (bg): Images & Stories/Alamy Stock Photo

pp. 160 (cl), 163 (c), 169 (ticket), 210 (cl): Dukesn/Shutterstock

pp. 160 (bl), 163 (b), 173 (Gabriela), 210 (bl): Courtesy of Kiernan Photography

pp. 160 (bl), 163 (b), 173 (flower), 210 (bl): Chatree988/Dreamstime.com

pp. 160 (bl), 163 (b), 173 (palm tree illo), 210 (bl): Antikva/Shutterstock

pp. 160 (bl), 163 (b), 173 (watercolor), 210 (bl): LightField Studios/Shutterstock

pp. 160 (cl), 169 (microphone), 210 (cl): Eakrin Rasadonyindee/Dreamstime.com

pp. 160 (br), 179 (b), 189, 210 (br): Andrea Cipriani Mecchi

pp. 160 (tr), 181 (l), 211 (l): Kathryn Scott/Denver Post/Getty Images

pp. 160 (cr), 184 (l), 185, 186 (puppets), 179 (c), 210 (tr): Division of Cultural and Community Life, National Museum of American History, Smithsonian Institution

pp. 161 (r), 212-215: RHAA Landscape Architects and Planning

pp. 162-163: Felix Mizioznikov/Shutterstock

p. 164: Sarayut Thaneerat/EyeEm/Getty Images

p. 168 (trees): Alpegore/Dreamstime.com

p. 173 (hurricane): Harvepino/Shutterstock

p. 173 (bird): Artem Pechenkin/Unsplash

p. 173 (palm tree photo): Aidan Formigoni/Unsplash

p. 173 (sky): Mike C. S./Unsplash

pp. 173-174 (watercolor): Balasoiu Claudia/Dreamstime.com

pp. 173-174 (watercolor): tekhyart/Shutterstock

p. 174 (lockers): Joseph Morelli/Dreamstime.com

p. 174 (flag): Paulus Rusyanto/Dreamstime.com

p. 174 (paint): Agave Studio/Shutterstock

pp. 178-179 (bg): Lasse Kristensen/Dreamstime.com

p. 180: Courtesy of Lilian Negron

p. 181 (r): Linda Williams/Dreamstime.com

p. 184 (b): Richard Thomas/Dreamstime.com

p. 186 (book): Courtesy of the Pura Belpré Papers at the Center for Puerto Rican Studies Library & Archives. Hunter College, City University of New York

p. 190 (Marley only): Andrea Cipriani Mecchi

pp. 220 (tr), 241 (t), 242-243, 273 (tl): GraphicaArtis/Getty Images

pp. 220 (cr), 241 (c), 247, 273 (cl): Bettmann/Getty Images

pp. 222-223 (bg): Courtesy National Archives, photo no. 286053

p. 229 (inset): fourmonths/Shutterstock

pp. 240-241 (bg): Jason Rambo/Alamy

pp. 241 (cl), 246: The Picture Art Collection/Alamy

p. 248 (compass rose): Hey Darlin/iStock.com

p. 248 (map): Krasovski Dmitri/Shutterstock

p. 252 (l): The Denver Public Library, Western History Collection, Z-5816

p. 252 (r): Union Train Depot in Cheyenne, NEG 4661. J.E. Stimson Collection, Wyoming State Archives

pp. 282 (cl), 291 (tr), 332 (cl): milehightraveler/iStock/Getty Images Plus

pp. 282 (bl), 296 (b), 332 (bl): Jim Reed Photography/Science Source

pp. 282 (tr), 301 (t), 302-303 (t), 332 (tr): AP Photo/Ted S. Warren

pp. 282 (cr), 301 (c), 306-307 (b), 332 (cr): Christopher J. Morris/Stone/Getty Images

pp. 282 (br), 312 (sky), 332 (br): sebastian-julian/E+/Getty Images

pp. 282 (br), 312 (plane), 332 (br): U.S Air Force

pp. 284-287 (bg): Harshit Sharma/Unsplash

pp. 285 (b), 295 (bg): Warren Faidley/The Image Bank/Getty Images

pp. 290-291 (b): Pierre Steenberg/Alamy

p. 291 (cr): Warren Faidley/The Image Bank/Getty Images

pp. 300-301 (bg): Cultura Motion/Shutterstock

p. 302 (l): Charles White

p. 303 (r): AP Photo/Ted S. Warren

pp. 306-308 (t): Sergei Dvornikov/Shutterstock

p. 307 (c): Helen H. Richardson/The Denver Post via Getty Images

p. 308 (c): Pixabay

p. 308 (b): Portland Press Herald/Contributor/Getty Images

pp. 316-317 (bg): SEAN GLADWELL/Moment/Getty Images

pp. 342 (bc), 345 (bl), 355 (cr, b), 356 (tr, b), 394 (cr): Alejandro Duran

pp. 342 (bl), 345 (br), 357, 394 (b): Damon Higgins/The Palm Beach Post/ZUMA Wire/Alamy Stock Photo

pp. 342 (cl), 350 (r), 394 (cl): ©Osvaldo de la Fuente

p. 345 (bg): Manun Ngueampha/Shutterstock

pp. 345 (c), 352: Guillaume Baviere

p. 347 (t): MediaNews Group/Boulder Daily Camera/Getty Images

p. 350 (tl): Carabiner/Dreamstime.com

p. 350 (b): LATIF KASSIDI/EFE/Newscom

p. 351: Flemming Foged Photography

p. 355 (tl): Michal Nyvlt/Dreamstime.com

p. 355 (tr): Teacher Photo/Shutterstock

p. 355 (cl): Oleksandr Shyripa/Dreamstime.com

p. 356 (tl): Uzenix/Dreamstime.com

p. 356 (c): Anton Starikov/Dreamstime.com

p. 357 (b): The Washington Post/Getty Images

p. 358: Damon Higgins/The Palm Beach Post/ZUMA Wire/Alamy Stock Photo

p. 414: FLPA/Alamy Stock Photo

p. 423 (b): Michael Warwick/Shutterstock

p. 423 (t): Mariemily Photos/Shutterstock

p. 422: Creative Travel Projects/Shutterstock

p. 426 (t): Razvan Cornel Constantin/Dreamstime.com

p. 432 (r): George Rinhart/Corbis Historical/Getty Images

p. 432 (l): Daboost/Dreamstime.com

p. 433: Stockcreations/Dreamstime.com

p. 444 (t): Kristina Postnikova/Shutterstock

p. 444 (b): Robert Byron/Dreamstime.com

p. 445 (b): NDanko/Shutterstock

p. 450: Jungle Bandana/Shutterstock

p. 451: Ed8563/Dreamstime.com

p. 460, 461: swa182/Shutterstock

p. 464: Kim Steele/Photodisc/Getty Images